THE Weekend Woodworker's PROJECT COLLECTION

40 Projects for the Time-Challenged Craftsman

FROM THE EDITORS OF POPULAR WOODWORKING

POPULAR WOODWORKING BOOKS
CINCINNATI, OHIO
www.popularwoodworking.com

Read This Important Safety Notice

To prevent accidents, keep safety in mind while you work. Use the safety guards installed on power equipment; they are for your protection.

When working on power equipment, keep fingers away from saw blades, wear safety goggles to prevent injuries from flying wood chips and sawdust, wear hearing protection and consider installing a dust vacuum to reduce the amount of airborne sawdust in your woodshop.

Don't wear loose clothing, such as neckties or shirts with loose sleeves, or jewelry, such as rings, necklaces or bracelets, when working on power equipment. Tie back long hair to prevent it from getting caught in your equipment.

People who are sensitive to certain chemicals should check the chemical content of any product before using it.

Due to the variability of local conditions, construction materials, skill levels, etc., neither the author nor Popular Woodworking Books assumes any responsibility for any accidents, injuries, damages or other losses incurred resulting from the material presented in this book.

The authors and editors who compiled this book have tried to make the contents as accurate and correct as possible. Plans, illustrations, photographs and text have been carefully checked. All instructions, plans and projects should be carefully read, studied and understood before beginning construction.

Prices listed for supplies and equipment were current at the time of publication and are subject to change.

Metric Conversion Chart

TO CONVERT	TO	MULTIPLY BY
Inches	Centimeters	2.54
Centimeters	Inches	0.4
Feet	Centimeters	30.5
Centimeters	Feet	0.03
Yards	Meters	0.9
Meters	Yards	1.1

Distributed in Canada by Fraser Direct
100 Armstrong Avenue
Georgetown, Ontario L7G 5S4
Canada

Distributed in the U.K. and Europe by David & Charles
Brunel House
Newton Abbot
Devon TQ12 4PU
England
Tel: (+44) 1626 323200
Fax: (+44) 1626 323319
E-mail: postmaster@davidandcharles.co.uk

Distributed in Australia by Capricorn Link
P.O. Box 704
Windsor, NSW 2756
Australia

Visit our Web site at www.popularwoodworking.com.

Other fine Popular Woodworking Books are available from your local bookstore or direct from the publisher.

14   13   12   11   10   5   4   3   2   1

Library of Congress Cataloging-in-Publication Data

The weekend woodworking projects collection / from the editors of Popular woodworking. -- 1st ed.
    p. cm.
  Includes index.
  ISBN 978-1-4403-0888-8 (pbk. : alk. paper)
  1. Woodwork--Patterns. I. Popular woodworking.
  TT180.W3467 2010
  684'.08--dc22

                            2010015396

ACQUISITIONS EDITOR: David Thiel
SENIOR EDITOR: Jim Stack
DESIGNER: Brian Roeth
PRODUCTION COORDINATOR: Mark Griffin
PHOTOGRAPHERS: Staff of Popular Woodworking
ILLUSTRATORS: Staff of Popular Woodworking

About the Authors

STEVE SHANESY, publisher of *Popular Woodworking Magazine*, is a native of Troy, Ohio, and has more than 20 years experience in cabinet shops. Steve graduated from Ohio University with a BS in journalism and from Los Angeles Trade Technical College with a certificate in cabinetmaking and millwork. He worked as foreman at AE Furniture Manufacturing in Los Angeles —the city's premier commercial and residential furniture maker.

CHRISTOPHER SCHWARZ, executive editor for *Popular Woodworking Magazine*, is a long-time amateur woodworker and professional journalist. He built his first workbench at age 8 and spent weekends helping his father build two houses on the family's farm outside Hackett, Ark. — using mostly hand tools. He has journalism degrees from Northwestern University and The Ohio State University and worked as a magazine and newspaper journalist before joining *Popular Woodworking* in 1996. Despite his early experience on the farm, Chris remains a hand-tool enthusiast.

ROBERT W. LANG, senior editor for *Popular Woodworking Magazine*, grew up in northeastern Ohio and has been a professional woodworker since the early 1970s. He learned woodworking repairing wooden boats on Lake Erie and in a large commercial shop in Cleveland. Along the way he studied industrial design at The Ohio State University. His experience includes building custom furniture and cabinets as well as managing and engineering large architectural millwork projects. He is the author of several "Shop Drawings" books about furniture and interiors of the Arts & Crafts Movement of the early 1900s.

GLEN HUEY, senior editor for *Popular Woodworking Magazine*, is a long-time professional woodworker, author, DVD host and woodworking teacher. Glen joined the staff of *Popular Woodworking* in 2006.

DAVID THIEL has been a woodworker (both professionally and for fun) for more that 30 years. He spent 10 years as a senior editor for *Popular Woodworking Magazine* and is now the executive editor for *Popular Woodworking* books. David also appeared as the host of DIY Network's Tools & Techniques series for more than 100 episodes.

JIM STACK, senior editor for *Popular Woodworking* books, is a flat-lander who grew up in south central Nebraska. He graduated from the Berklee College of Music in Boston with a Bachelor's degree in music composition. After moving to Cincinnati, he worked in local cabinet- and furniture-making shops for almost 20 years. He now builds guitars and other contraptions as the mood strikes him. Jim joined F+W Media in 1999.

CHRIS GLEASON is an author for *Popular Woodworking* books. His latest book is titled, *Kitchen Makeovers for any Budget*.

DANNY PROULX wrote several bestselling books for *Popular Woodworking* books. He passed away in 2004.

THANE LORBACH was a contributor to the book, *Building Furniture for Country Living*, published by *Popular Woodworking* books.

ROBERT BELKE is the author of several woodworking books, including *Classic Country Furniture*, published by *Popular Woodworking* books.

JOHN MCGUANE is coauthor of *The Essential Pine Book*, published by *Popular Woodworking* books. He has been a woodworker since 1971.

TABLE OF CONTENTS

SECTION ONE: **ACCESSORIES**

SECTION TWO: **BOOKCASES & SHELVING**

SECTION THREE: **MIRRORS**

SECTION FOUR: **STORAGE**

INTRODUCTION

The Weekend Woodworker's Project Collection is in your hands, so you open it to the table of contents. There you see 40 projects to choose from. As you peruse the list, your senses start to tingle because you've just found the perfect project!

You've worked hard all week and you want to relax, unwind and forget about it. Your woodworking shop is calling your name, your tools have been idle all week and they are rarin' to go.

As you descend the stairs into your basement shop or take the walk to your garage workshop, you're thinking about that new project. You've chosen one that will give you a mental challenge and put your woodworking skills to good use.

The plans for your project are clearly drawn and easy to read. The cutting and supplies lists have helped determine what you needed to pickup from your local home center or lumberyard.

As you review the step-by-step photos (with captions that explain what is being shown), you know how to start your project. You're in the zone now, so you let the sawdust start to fly.

Woodworkers are the sort of people who like to make things with their hands and minds. It's the sort of activity that takes you to another place — away from the hustle and flow of the workplace, shopping malls and television.

Your family knows that this is the thing that keeps you sane and they like it when they hear the tools running, the hammer and chisel cutting the perfect mortise and the hand plane singing. The question they might have is: what is he/she building this time?

Is it a clock for the mantel or a hanging clock? Is it a mirror for the bedroom? Could it possibly be that cool-looking cutting board(s) that you saw in the book? There are so many projects you saw as you thumbed through the book: trivets, a Franklin chair that folds into a step ladder, a set of Barrister bookcases that would look great in the den, traditional hanging shelves, a game box, a spice cabinet (perfect for the kitchen) and a jewelry armoire that's beautiful all by itself.

The family room could use a media storage rack, the bedroom needs a quilt rack, a new mailbox would be nice, a couple of clever-looking boxes would be fun. One of the boxes is for storing silverware, which would sure be handy for the dining room. The rec room has space for a modest-sized wine rack and a pretty wooden basket to hold some cut flowers is made-to-order for the coffee table.

There are other projects that would make great gifts; like a knockdown bookcase, a pendulum wall clock, a spiral-staircase table, a cute little step stool, an oval box similar to a Shaker box, a wastebasket or a three-tier keepsake chest.

Woodworkers everywhere will enjoy making any of these projects. The woodworking skills needed range from basic to advanced, so there is indeed something for everyone.

The Weekend Woodworker's Projects Collection, from the editors and contributing editors of *Popular Woodworking Magazine* and *Popular Woodworking* books, is a must-have compilation of woodworking projects that will keep you busy for many weekends, well into the future.

Two Cutting Boards

BY KEN BURTON

Cutting boards might not be the most glamorous of woodworking projects, but they are not without merit. They don't use up a lot of material, and so are nice to give away as casual gifts or even as seasonal promotions for your valued customers. They are a great way to use up scraps that are too small to use, but are too big to throw away. (Don't laugh — you know exactly what I'm talking about.) And if you sell your work at craft fairs, you can usually keep the price point down to where it is manageable for most people.

Design-wise, almost anything goes. A cutting board's function is pretty much built right in, so your primary concerns are aesthetic ones. You can easily cut and sand a pretty piece of wood and call it a cutting board, or glue several contrasting pieces together for a more striking effect (Goodness knows I've made more than my share of cutting boards this way.) If you're looking to make something a little more unusual, try one of the cutting boards shown here.

The shape of the first cutting board is what I've come to call a "squircle" or square circle. It starts out as three separate pieces of wood edge glued together. The squircular cutting boards in the photo are made from oak and walnut with a 3/16-inch strip of cherry glued in between. (The cherry strip doesn't show much in the photos, but it should provide a nice contrast in between the oak and the walnut as it darkens over time. The circular cutting board is made from cherry and hickory and is glued up a few pieces at a time. I usually try to use 5/4 or even 6/4 stock for cutting boards as I like the look and feel of the extra thickness. I also think thicker cutting boards are less likely to warp.

SQUARE/CIRCLE CUTTING BOARD ■ INCHES (MILLIMETERS)

REFERENCE	QUANTITY	PART	STOCK	THICKNESS	(mm)	WIDTH	(mm)	LENGTH	(mm)	COMMENTS
A	1	side 1	hardwood	1 1/8	(29)	5 3/4	(146)	35	(889)	
B	1	case bottom	hardwood	1 1/8	(29)	20 3/4	(527)	35	(946)	contrasting color to side 1
C	1	back brace	hardwood	3/16	(5)	1 1/8	(29)	35	(945)	contrasting color to both sides 1 and 2

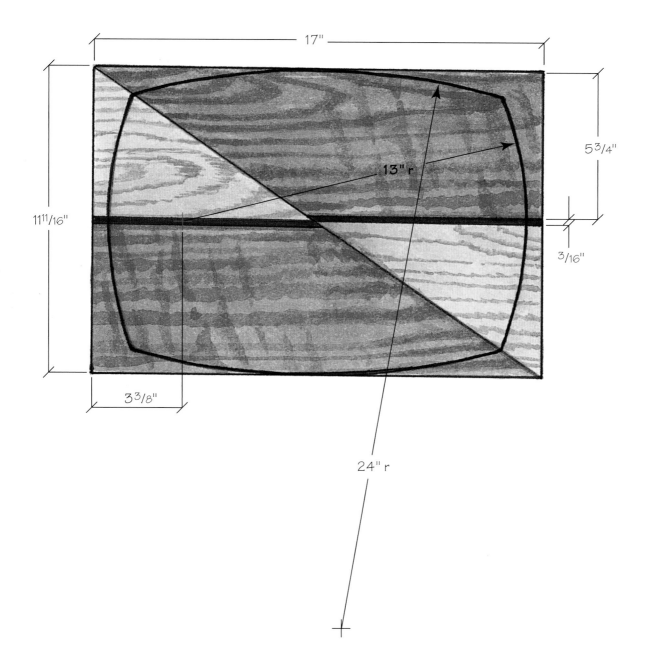

1 Crosscut the initial glue-up
Start by edge-gluing the three pieces of wood. In order to achieve the look here, you actually need enough material to make two cutting boards — they'll end up as color opposites of one another. Cut the glued up plank into two pieces, each 17"-long (after cutting the dadoes for the bottom and shelf.)

2 Trace the blank to make a cradle
Place one of the blanks on a piece of MDF or plywood with two of the blank's opposing corners aligned with one edge of the sheet. Trace the corner of the blank. Cut along these lines to make a cradle for both cutting and gluing the pieces. To make the cuts, measure the angles with a T-bevel. Pivot the miter gauge to the appropriate setting and guide the piece through the cuts on the table saw. Don't worry about over-cutting the corner by a little to make sure the cuts meet. Go ahead and make a second cradle while you're at it.

3 Cut the diagonal
Hold the blank in the cradle and adjust the rip fence so the blade starts cutting right through the blank's corner. Guide the cradle along the fence to make the diagonal cut. Cut both blanks in this manner.

4 Glue up
Run the cradle pieces through the saw, cutting the corners back ½-inch or so. This will keep the corners from running into each other during glue-up. Take the matching pieces from the two blanks and glue them together along the diagonal. The cradles serve to keep the clamp pressure perpendicular to the glue line. Be careful to align the pieces just right. You have two options here: You can align the tips of the triangles, or you can align the narrow strip on each piece so it looks continuous.

5 Lay out the arcs

When the glue dries, unclamp the pieces and scrape away any squeeze-out. Draw center lines both along the length of the piece and across its width. Lay out the arcs; for the side arcs, the center is actually off the piece itself. To lay these out, draw a line on your bench and align the cutting board with its center line right on top of the bench line. Swing the arc with a set of trammel points or with a pencil tied to a string.

6 Screw the carrier in place

Draw a center line along the length of a scrap of plywood. Align the center line on the cutting board with the center line on the plywood and some double-sided tape in between. Flip the sandwich over and screw the plywood to the cutting board. Note: I thought this would be a simple matter of driving the screws into the waste area. This worked great for the first cut, but the waste was gone when I went to set up the second cut. I ended up driving the screws through the plywood into the cutting board along the center line. I tried to space them an equal distance in from either edge. Afterwards I plugged the holes with a contrasting wood.

7 Cut the side arcs

Measure 24" from the arc drawn on the cutting board and drill a ¼" hole through the plywood on its center line. Adjust the center pin on the circle-cutting sled so it is centered 24" from the blade. Place the plywood on the pin and cut the arc. Note: To cut an arc on the table saw, hold the workpiece in one position and slide the sled through the cut. Then reposition the workpiece slightly and make a second cut and so on, gradually creating the arc. Repeat the process to cut the second side.

8 Cut the end arcs

Drill ¼" holes for the end arcs. Adjust the circle-cutting sled to cut a 13" radius arc. Cut the end arcs the same way you cut the side arcs.

9 Cut the profile

Chamfer the edges of the cutting board with a V-cutter in a moulding head. To accommodate the curves, make two curved fences radii that match that of the two arcs. Unfortunately you'll need to cut these fences with something other than the table saw — a band saw or saber saw will work, or use a coping saw and make the cut by hand. Smooth away any lumps with sandpaper. Make the fences from ¾" plywood or MDF, and screw them to second pieces of scrap. Lay out the curves by tracing the arcs. To use a curved fence, clamp it to the regular rip fence. Adjust the fence until the tip of the cutter comes up about ¹⁄₁₆" behind the fence's curved face. Play with the height of the cutter to get the profile you're after. Make the cut by pushing the piece along the curve.

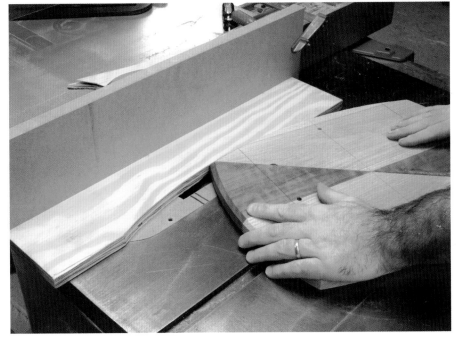

10 Cut the sides

To help eliminate tear-out, make the cuts across the ends first, then switch fences and cut along the sides. After cutting the chamfers, sand the cutting board and finish it. Once the finish cures thoroughly (usually after a week or so) all the solvents will have evaporated leaving behind a food-safe finish. You can also use mineral oil.

Which Glue to Use?

When choosing a glue to use for a cutting board, you need to consider that the board will be frequently immersed in water. That said, I have a cutting board I made almost twenty years ago that has stood up to years of hot dish water and even the occasional ride through the dish washer, and it was put together with regular yellow glue. However, to be on the safe side, these days I use glue that is designed for water resistance. Most frequently I use outdoor yellow glue. I have also had luck with polyurethane glue and plastic resin glue.

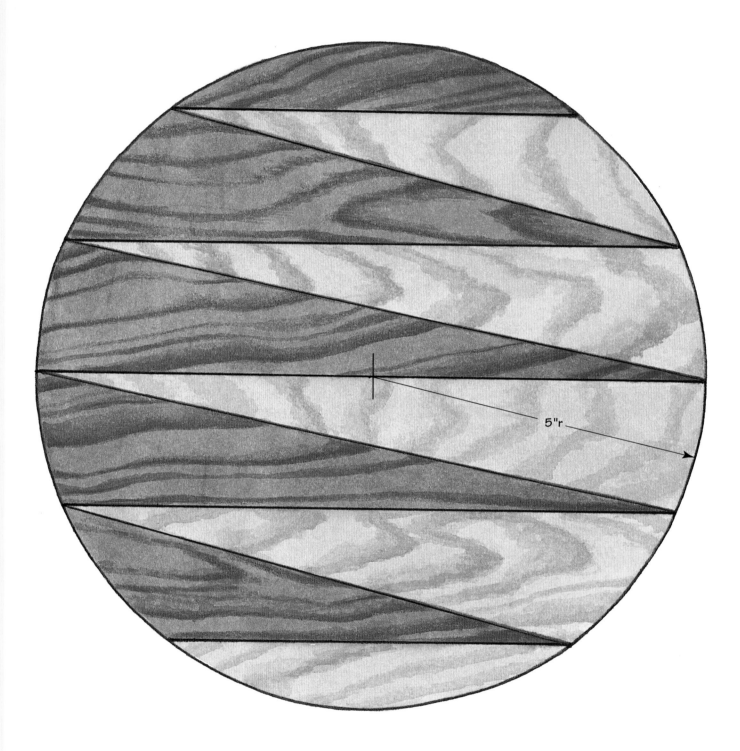

5"r

CIRCLE CUTTING BOARD ■ INCHES (MILLIMETERS)

REFERENCE	QUANTITY	PART	STOCK	THICKNESS	(mm)	WIDTH	(mm)	LENGTH	(mm)	COMMENTS
A	2	center pieces	hardwood	1¼	(32)	2⅛	(54)	22	(559)	one of each species
B	4	outer pieces	hardwood	1¼	(32)	2	(51)	10⅝	(207)	two of each species
C	2	outside pieces	hardwood	1¼	(32)	1⅛	(28)	9⅝	(244)	one of each species

1 Cut the blanks to length

Cut two pieces of contrasting species of wood and edge-glue the pieces together.
When the glue dries, crosscut the blank into two pieces.

2 Taper the first piece
Lay out a taper cut on one of the pieces. Position the piece on a carrier board with the taper layout aligned with the edge of the board. Screw fences to the carrier to hold the piece in position. Adjust the rip fence so that the blade runs along the edge of the carrier. Hold the piece in place and guide the carrier along the fence to make the cut. Cut the second piece with the same setup. This time however, cut the taper on the second species. Mark the tapered sides.

3 Rip the second side parallel to the first
Set the rip fence to make a 2"-wide cut. Cut the pieces, running the marked sides against the fence.

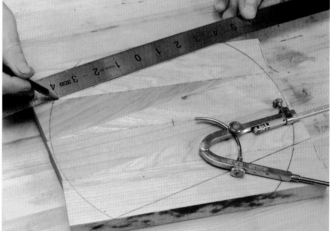

4 Glue-Up
Glue the two pieces together along the marked sides, carefully aligning the ends. While you are gluing, also glue two additional 2"-wide pieces to the outside of the assembly. Remember to alternate the two species.

5 Lay out the next tapered cut
Measure along the center glue line to find the center of the blank. Lay out a 10"-diameter circle from this point. Lay out tapers across the outer pieces. One end of the taper should occur where the circle intersects with the outer edge of the piece and the other end should occur where the circle intersects the inner (glued) edge.

Protecting Your Bench

When I do a glue up on my bench, I try to remember to protect the bench top with some newspaper or waxed paper. This helps keep the mess to a minimum, plus it prevents the piece from actually sticking right to the bench.

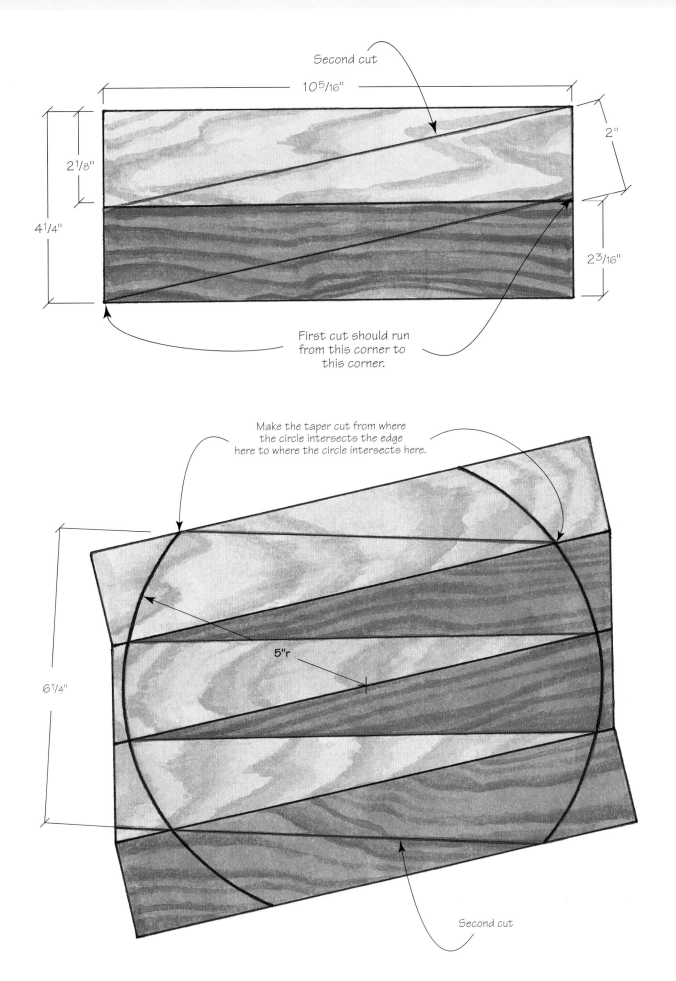

Second cut

10⁵/₁₆"

2"

2¹/₈"

4¹/₄"

2³/₁₆"

First cut should run
from this corner to
this corner.

Make the taper cut from where
the circle intersects the edge
here to where the circle intersects here.

5"r

6¹/₄"

Second cut

6 Cut the new taper
Place the blank on a carrier board with this new taper layout aligned with the edge of the carrier. Screw fences to the carrier to hold the piece in position. Adjust the rip fence so the blade runs right along the edge of the carrier. Hold the piece in place and guide the carrier along the fence to make the cut as you did in step two.

7 Rip the second side
Set the rip fence to cut the second side. It should be a 6¼"-wide cut, but cut to your layout line rather than arbitrarily setting the saw for 6¼". Glue a second set of pieces to the outside edge of the blank. Continue the circle layout and taper these two pieces. Add two final pieces to the outside edges. These two pieces have to be only 1⅛" wide.

8 Cut the blank round
Drill a ¼" hole at the center of the circle. Set up the circle-cutting sled to cut a 5"-radius (10"-diameter) circle. Place the cutting board on the pin and make repeated cuts to make the cutting board round. Sand away any facets that are left when you are through cutting.

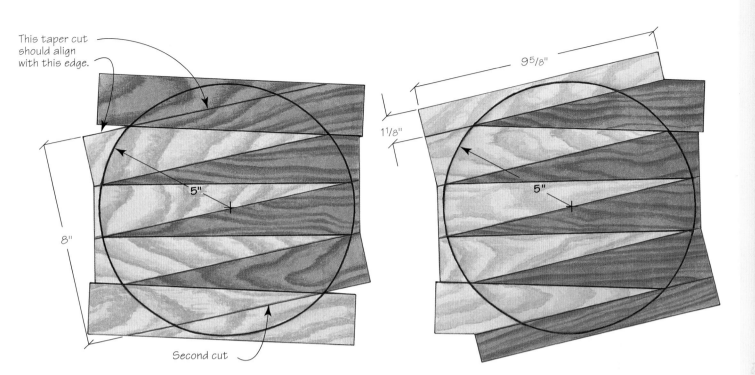

This taper cut should align with this edge.

Second cut

5"

8"

9⁵/₈"

1¹/₈"

5"

9 **Preparing to cut the profile**

The top edge of the cutting board is chamfered, while the bottom edge is coved. Set up a moulding head with the appropriate cutter and make a concave fence with a 10"-diameter curve. Lower the moulding head beneath the surface of the table. Position the fence so that the center part of the curve is over the center of the cutter and clamp it in place. Turn on the saw and slowly raise the moulding head to expose as much of the cutter as you need. To get the cut started, hold the piece against the corner of the fence and slowly pivot it into the cut.

10 **Cutting the profile**

Once the cutting board is against the fence, slowly rotate it counterclockwise to make the cut. After you make a complete revolution, carefully pivot the piece out of the cut. Repeat the process to cut the profile on the other side, changing the cutter if you desire. Sand and finish the cutting board. As with the squircle cutting board, I usually use an oil-varnish blend as a finish. Once the finish thoroughly dries the solvents evaporate, leaving a food-safe coating.

Three Trivets

BY KEN BURTON

If you're looking for a quick project with a little pizzazz, consider building a trivet. The ones you find here definitely fall under the category of "scrap box projects" because they use a minimal amount of material — the kind of pieces you're likely to find in your scrap box. They make nice presents or, if you sell your work, excellent "entry-level" products you can offer at a modest price point.

If you want to share your love of woodworking with a youngster, these are great projects to build together (you cut, they can help sand, glue and clamp). In fact, my mother still has the trivet I made with help from my father — I was probably seven or eight years old at the time. I seem to recall having grand plans for making a zillion of them and selling them door-to-door, but that's another story.

Design-wise, the sky is the limit. You can follow the plans shown here or take the basic idea and put your own slant on it. Of the three designs in the photo, the circular one and the rectangular one are simple to make and follow essentially the same process. The diamond design is a little more involved, but the general idea is similar to the other two. The basic plan calls for two runners dadoed into a series of cross pieces. If you keep this plan in mind, there is no end to the possibilities.

The one problem I've come across when making a batch of trivets occurs during finishing. Each has a lot of nooks and crannies to deal with, so applying finish can be a tedious job. Spraying is one option. Or, if you prefer a wiped on finish, consider pouring the finish into a shallow tray and dipping the pieces. Then set up a rack so the excess can drain back into the tray. That's how I finished these trivets.

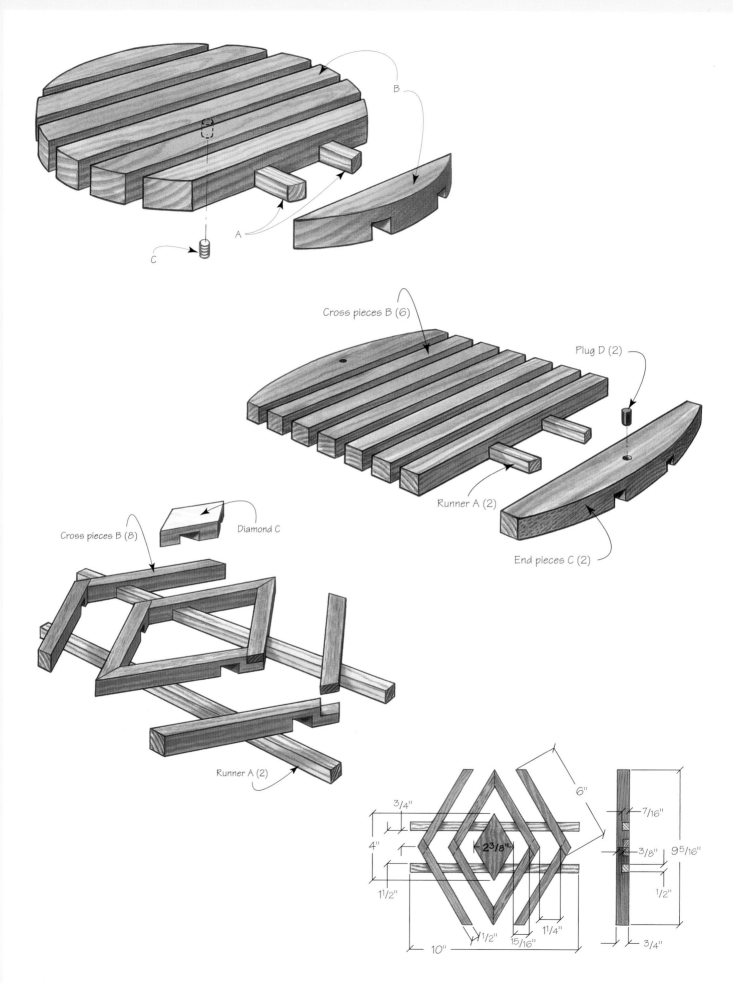

B

A

C

Cross pieces B (6)

Plug D (2)

Runner A (2)

End pieces C (2)

Cross pieces B (8)

Diamond C

Runner A (2)

3/4"

4"

1 1/2"

6"

2 3/8"

1/2"

15/16"

1 1/4"

10"

7/16"

3/8"

9 5/16"

1/2"

3/4"

ROUND TRIVET ■ INCHES (MILLIMETERS)

REFERENCE	QUANTITY	PART	STOCK	THICKNESS	(mm)	WIDTH	(mm)	LENGTH	(mm)	COMMENTS
A	2	runners	hardwood	$1/2$	(13)	$1/2$	(13)	$9 1/2$	(241)	
B	7	cross pieces	hardwood	$7/8$	(22)	$7/8$	(22)	9	(229)	contrasting color to side 1
C	1	plug	hardwood	$1/4$D	(6)					

RECTANGULAR TRIVET ■ INCHES (MILLIMETERS)

REFERENCE	QUANTITY	PART	STOCK	THICKNESS	(mm)	WIDTH	(mm)	LENGTH	(mm)	COMMENTS
A	2	runners	hardwood	$1/2$	(13)	$1/2$	(13)	$12 1/4$	(311)	
B	6	cross pieces	hardwood	$7/8$	(22)	$7/8$	(22)	9	(229)	
C	2	end pieces	hardwood	$7/8$	(22)	$1 1/2$	(38)	9	(229)	
D	2	plugs	hardwood	$1/4$D	(6)					

DIAMOND TRIVET ■ INCHES (MILLIMETERS)

REFERENCE	QUANTITY	PART	STOCK	THICKNESS	(mm)	WIDTH	(mm)	LENGTH	(mm)	COMMENTS
A	2	runners	hardwood	$7/16$	(11)	$1/2$	(13)	10	(254)	
B	8	cross pieces	hardwood	$3/4$	(19)	$1/2$	(13)	6	(152)	
C	1	diamond	hardwood	$3/4$	(19)	$2 3/8$	(60)	4	(102)	

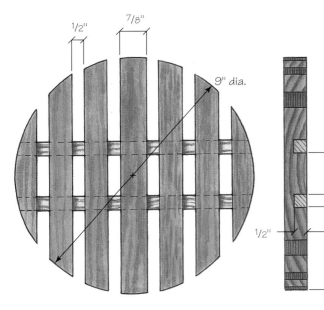

Top View   Side View

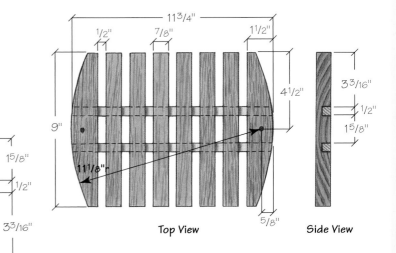

Top View   Side View

Round and Rectangular

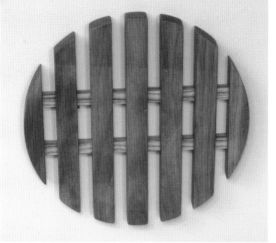

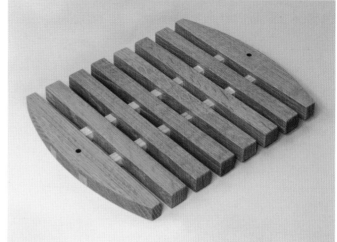

1 Rip the runners

Rip the runners to the listed thickness and width. Be sure to use a push stick to keep your fingers away from the blade. Note: The piece in the photo is a scrap leftover from another project that happened to have a bullnose profile cut on one edge. There is no need for you to duplicate this.

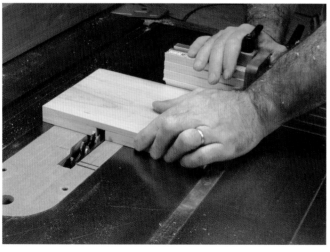

2 Cut the dado

For the cross pieces, cut a piece to the listed thickness and length but leave it wide enough to make some, if not all, the pieces you need. Set up a ½"-wide dado blade and adjust its height to ½". Cut two dadoes across the piece, using the miter gauge to guide the piece through the cut. Set up a stop to control the location of the dadoes.

3 Rip the pieces to width

Rip cross pieces to width. Again, use a push stick to keep your fingers at a safe distance.

4 Put the cross pieces on the runners
Apply glue to the inside of the dado cuts. Put the cross pieces on the runners, using scraps of runner as spacers. Clamp the pieces together, using two extra runners under the clamp blocks to focus the pressure where it needs to go.

5 Measure to set up the jig
Cut the curves on the trivets with the aid of a circle-cutting jig. To set the jig for the proper radius, place it on the saw and measure out from the blade. Mark the jig, then loosen the pin and move it to align with the mark. For most cuts, the exact setting isn't critical — as long as you're within ⅛" or so, everything will be fine.

6 Cut the rectangular trivet
Drill two ¼" holes, one in each of the wide end pieces. I drilled the holes in the top side, but they could easily go in the bottom. Make the holes about ⅜" deep. Set up the jig to cut an 11⅛" radius. Place the trivet blank on the pin and cut the curve on one end by making a series of cuts, pivoting the piece slightly after each. Keep a tight grip on the piece to prevent it from spinning. Repeat the process with the second end. Plug the holes with contrasting hardwood.

7 Cut the round trivet
With the round trivet, drill the ¼" pivot hole in the center of the middle cross piece. Set up the circle-cutting jig for a 4½"-radius circle. Place the trivet blank on the pin. Achieve a round shape by making a series of cuts, turning the blank slightly after each. Again, keep a firm grip on the piece to prevent it from spinning under pressure from the blade. Sand and finish as desired.

Diamond

1 Cut the cross pieces at an angle
Cut the runners and cross pieces to the sizes listed in the materials list. Cut the ends of the cross pieces at a 60° angle. Guide the pieces through the cut with a miter gauge, using a stop to control their length.

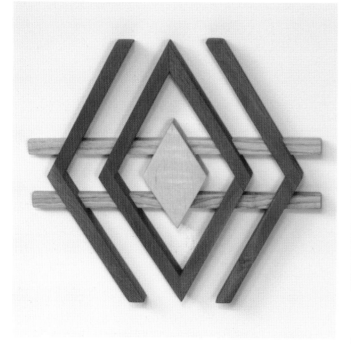

2 Cut the notches
Keep the miter gauge set at 60°. Set up a ½"-wide dado blade and set its depth for half the thickness of your stock. Clamp a sacrificial fence that extends past the blade to your miter gauge. This provides extra support for the pieces as well as helping to prevent tear-out. Cut a ½"-wide notch on one end of each cross piece, using a stop to maintain consistency.

3 Clamp the pieces
Apply glue to the mating surfaces and clamp pairs of the cross pieces together. When the glue dries, sand everything flush.

5 Cut the cradle

Extend one of the layout lines all the way across the face of the cradle board. Draw square lines down the edges of the cradle from either end of the extended layout line. Place the cradle on a carrier board with the extended layout line aligned with the edge of the carrier. Adjust the rip fence so the saw cuts along the edge of the carrier. Screw fences to the carrier to hold the cradle in position. Add a toggle clamp to the carrier to help hold the piece in position. Clamp the cradle in place and guide the carrier along the rip fence to make the cut. Stop cutting at the intersection (but don't worry if you overcut the corner a little.) Carefully back the carrier out of the cut. Turn the piece over to make the second cut. Repeat the process to make a second cradle.

4 Mark a cradle

Cut two pieces of ¾" plywood or MDF to serve as cradle boards. Hold one of the V-shaped pieces on top of the cradle with the V's outside corners aligned with the long edge of the cradle. Trace the V with a pencil.

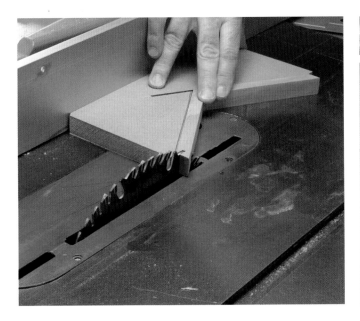

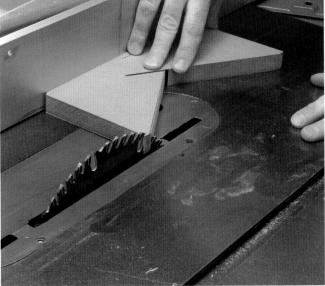

6 Miter a V

Adjust the rip fence so the saw cuts right along the edge of one of the cradle boards. Hold one of the Vs in the cradle and push the cradle along the fence to miter both ends. Repeat the process with a second V.

7 Cut the ears off the cradle

While it was easier to make the layout with the V-shaped piece at the edge of the cradle, you'll need to cut the corners off the cradle so they won't interfere with subsequent operations. Set the rip fence to cut about ¼" off the cradle boards. Note: Both cradle boards in the photo are missing their outside corners. This is not important at all — I just used some scrap.

Getting Things to Line Up

Why bother to use multiple stops to cut the dadoes? It's tempting to make a single setup and simply reverse the pieces in the cradle to make the cuts. However, if any of the angles are off, the dadoes won't line up and assembly will be a real headache. If you invest a little time in the initial setup, glue-up will be much less stressful.

8 Glue the mitered surfaces
Apply glue to the mitered surfaces of the two Vs you cut. Clamp the pieces together, using the cradles to help distribute the pressure. Note: Be gentle with the clamp pressure — you can easily break the pieces or, if you really crank down on the clamps, pop the corner joint.

9 Cut the diamond
Cut the blank for the diamond to the size listed in the materials list. Lay out the diamond and place it on a carrier board with one of the layout lines aligned with the edge of the carrier. Screw fences to the carrier to hold the piece in position and add a toggle clamp for support. Set the rip fence so the saw will cut along the edge of the carrier. Guide the carrier along the fence to make the cut.

10 Cut the second side of the diamond
Turn the blank over and clamp it to the carrier to make the second cut.

11 Make the third cut
Reposition the fences on the carrier board to set up for the third and fourth cuts. Make the third cut, then turn the piece over and do the fourth.

12 Cut the dadoes
Set up a ½"-wide dado blade and set its height to ½". Screw an extension fence that extends past the blade to your miter gauge. Hold one of the cradles against the fence and position stops on either side of the blade to control the location of the dadoes. Stack one of the separate Vs and the diamond in the cradle and cut the two dadoes — the first with the cradle against one stop, the second with the cradle against the second stop.

13 Cut the diamond frame and the second V
Using the same cradle and stops, load the diamond frame and the second V in the cradle, and make the dadoes. Push the pieces through the cut slowly to minimize tear-out. Glue the various cross pieces and the diamond to the runners, taking care to get the spacing right. Finish the trivet with your favorite wood finish.

Franklin Chair

BY JOHN MCGUANE

Legend has it that the design for this ingenious piece of furniture, also known as a ladder chair or library chair, was invented by Benjamin Franklin. This attractive, useful chair easily converts into a ladder, enabling you to reach the top shelves of bookcases and cabinets without having to pull your stepladder out of storage.

This project is made of yellow pine purchased at a local home-improvement center. I used yellow pine because of its strength and stability. Although I finished my Franklin chair with shellac, it can be painted to fit any room or decor.

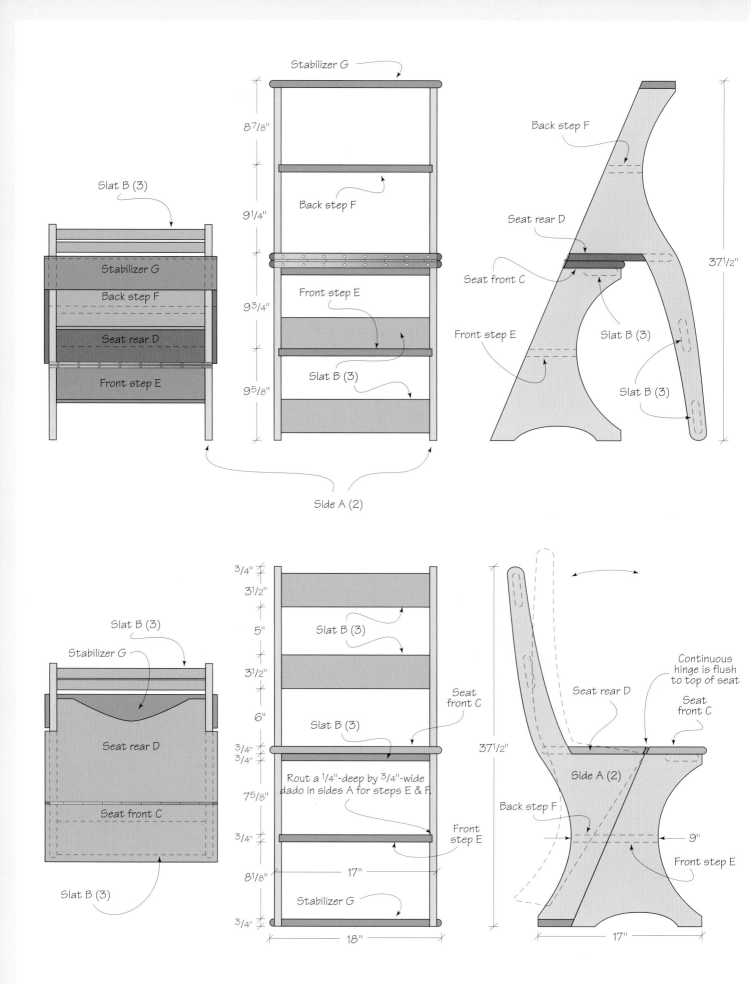

Stabilizer G

Slat B (3)

Stabilizer G
Back step F
Seat rear D
Front step E

8 7/8"

9 1/4"

9 3/4"

9 5/8"

Back step F

Front step E

Slat B (3)

Side A (2)

Back step F

Seat rear D

Seat front C

Front step E

Slat B (3)

Slat B (3)

37 1/2"

Slat B (3)

Stabilizer G

Seat rear D

Seat front C

Slat B (3)

3/4"
3 1/2"
5"
3 1/2"
6"
3/4"
3/4"
7 5/8"
3/4"
8 1/8"
3/4"

Slat B (3)

Slat B (3)

Rout a 1/4"-deep by 3/4"-wide
dado in sides A for steps E & F.

Stabilizer G

17"

18"

Seat
front C

Front
step E

Continuous
hinge is flush
to top of seat

Seat rear D

Seat
front C

Side A (2)

Back step F

Front step E

37 1/2"

9"

17"

REFERENCE	QUANTITY	PART	STOCK	THICKNESS	(mm)	WIDTH	(mm)	LENGTH	(mm)	COMMENTS
A	2	sides	yellow pine	¾	(19)	20¼	(514)	37½	(953)	
B	3	rails	yellow pine	¾	(19)	3½	(89)	15½	(394)	
C	1	seat front	yellow pine	¾	(19)	18	(457)	6⁵⁄₁₆	(160)	23° bevel on hinge edge
D	1	seat rear	yellow pine	¾	(19)	18	(457)	10⁷⁄₈	(276)	23° bevel on hinge edge
E	1	front step	yellow pine	¾	(19)	5⅛	(130)	16	(406)	23° bevel on one long edge
F	1	back step	yellow pine	¾	(19)	4¼	(108)	16	(406)	23° bevel on one long edge
G	1	top stabilizer	yellow pine	¾	(19)	3¾	(95)	17½	(445)	

Supplies

1	17¾"(451mm) brass-plated continuous hinge
28	⅜"-diameter x ¼"-long (10mm x 6mm) maple plugs
28	No. 10 x 2" (51mm) steel screws
10-20	No. 20 biscuits
	wood glue

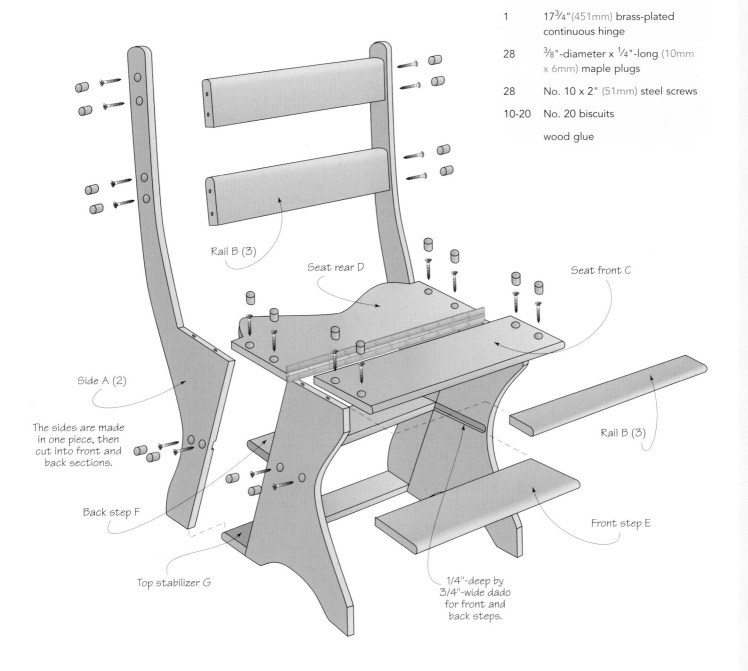

Rail B (3)

Seat rear D

Seat front C

Side A (2)

The sides are made in one piece, then cut into front and back sections.

Back step F

Top stabilizer G

Rail B (3)

Front step E

1/4"-deep by 3/4"-wide dado for front and back steps.

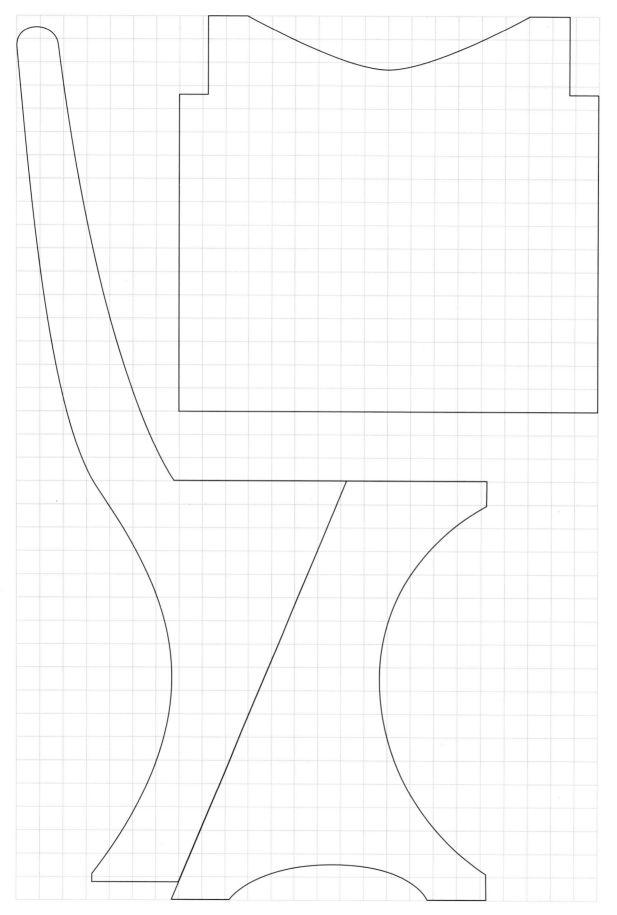

Each square represents 1".

1 The yellow pine for this project was purchased from a local home-improvement center. Yellow pine is strong and stable when properly seasoned. It's an excellent material for projects that require strength and rigidity.

Tip

Chairs and ladders need to support a wide range of loads. Think carefully when you build anything that could cause an injury if a failure in design or workmanship should occur. Pay special attention to your load-supporting joints. I reinforced all the joints of this project with 2" steel screws. The screw heads are countersunk and plugged. The screws make assembly much easier, as clamping is not required.

2 Use your compound miter saw to cut the boards to the proper lengths. Then cut the slots for the biscuits. Be sure the location of the biscuits won't be on the cutting line of the side pattern.

This folding ladder was the model for the Franklin chair.

3 Use battens to help keep the glued-up sides flat.

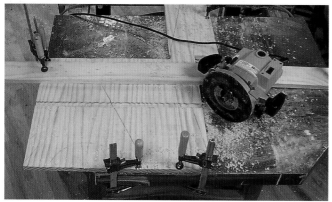

4 Glue the final wing piece on the long, back edges of the sides. Then, using a straightedge and a router, cut a ¼"-deep by ¾"-wide dado in the sides for the front and back steps. Be sure to make right and left sides.

5 Draw the pattern on the side blanks (see pattern illustration on page 34). Then, using a jigsaw, separate the front and back parts of the sides.

6 The side pattern is one idea of how the chair could look. Feel free to change the pattern to suit your tastes.

7 The jigsaw is a good tool for cutting the sides. You could also use a band saw.

8 Finish cutting the back part of the sides.

9 Use your own sense of design when laying out the curves on your chair. Just be careful not to compromise strength by removing too much material. You can use a bucket or other round object to help lay out the curves.

10 Cut the steps and slats to size and check the fit of all the parts. Sand them before final assembly.

12 After cutting the seat to shape, separate the front and back parts. Then attach the continuous hinge to the parts. The bevels on the hinged-edges of the seat should match the angle of the front and back parts of the chair sides. Finally, attach the seat to the chair, using glue and screws. Plug all the screws holes on the chair and sand them flush.

13 Finish the chair how you like. I used three coats of amber shellac.

Mantel Clock

BY DAVID THIEL

BY COMBINING SOME CLASSIC ARTS-AND-CRAFTS ELEMENTS, AND STORE-BOUGHT WORKS, A NEW CLASSIC IS BORN.

You might not be ready to build your own sideboard, but you can start your Arts and Crafts collection with this simple clock. The only tough part of the project is finding a great piece of quarter-sawn white oak (1" × 6" × 96").

First Things First

Cut the pieces according to the Schedule of Materials. Resaw and book match the front for an impressive appearance. Taper the front to an 8" width at the top. Then, crosscut a 4° angle on the top and bottom edges of both sides, parallel to one another.

Cut the Front

Cut the dial hole and pendulum slots in the front (see page 93 for pattern). Use a chamfer bit to cut the angle profile in the dial hole.

Cut the Top and Bottom

To cut the top and bottom chamfer details (including the ⅛" bead), use your table saw. Start by making a ⅛"-deep cut 1" in on the ends and front edges. Cut the bevel by running the pieces on edge (use a zero-clearance throat plate) with the blade set to 23°. Set the blade height to intersect with the bead cut and set the fence to leave the ³⁄₁₆" flat shown in the diagram. To inset the front ¼" back from the sides, lay it on a ¼" piece of Masonite as a spacer; glue the two sides to the face.

MANTEL CLOCK ■ INCHES (MILLIMETERS)

REFERENCE	QUANTITY	PART	STOCK	THICKNESS	(mm)	WIDTH	(mm)	LENGTH	(mm)
A	1	front	white oak	1/2	(13)	9	(229)	14	(356)
B	1	bottom	white oak	3/4	(19)	5	(127)	12	(305)
C	1	top	white oak	3/4	(19)	5	(127)	10	(254)
D	2	sides	white oak	1/2	(13)	3¹⁵/₁₆	(100)	14¹/₈	(359)
E	1	back	oak plywood	1/4	(6)	9⁷/₈	(251)	14⁹/₁₆	(370)
F	1	dial support	pine	3/4	(19)	5¹/₂	(140)	6	(152)
G	4	fake tenons	white oak	1/4	(6)	1/2	(13)	1¹/₂	(38)
H	8	fake pins	white oak	1/8	(3)	1/4	(6)	1/4	(6)

Supplies

1 - Dial face
Clock Prints
www.clockprints.com
Paper face: AC8 PWW Clock

1 - Clock Movement
Rockler
800-279-4441 or www.rockler.com
1- Mechanism - Item # 28571 • $11.99

1 pair - Hands - Item # 36889 • $1.29

The fall-off pieces from the front taper make perfect clamping cauls to exert equal pressure on the sides. Pilot-drill, then nail the bottom and top to the sides, leaving a ¹/₁₆" setback. Set the nails.

Through-tenons

Cut, chamfer, then glue the applied through-tenons as located on the diagrams. Cut, chamfer and glue the fake square pegs to cover the nail holes. Rout a ¹/₄" by ³/₈"-deep rabbet in the clock's back edges. Then fit the back into the rabbet.

The Block and Face

Cut the dial support block and glue the clock face to the block, centered and 2¹/₂" down from the top of the block. Apply two coats of clear finish to the block and face, which is typically paper.

Attach the Hands

Drill a hole in the center of the clock face for attaching the hands to the clock mechanism and attach the movement to the back of the support block.

Apply Glaze and Finish

To finish, first apply warm brown glaze to the clock case. Apply a few coats of clear finish.

Last Things Last

Screw the dial support block to the inside of the face. Shorten and attach the pendulum, then pilot-drill the back and attach using No.4 × ³/₄" brass screws.

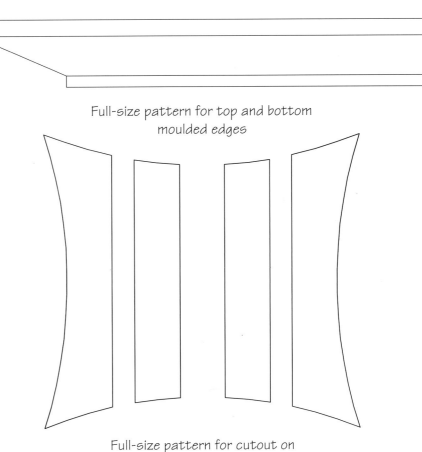

Full-size pattern for top and bottom moulded edges

Full-size pattern for cutout on clock face

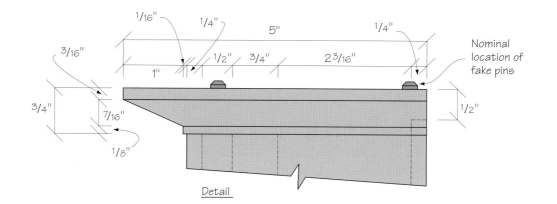

1/16"   1/4"   5"   1/4"

Nominal location of fake pins

3/16"   1/2"   3/4"   2 3/16"

1"

3/4"   7/16"

1/8"

1/2"

Detail

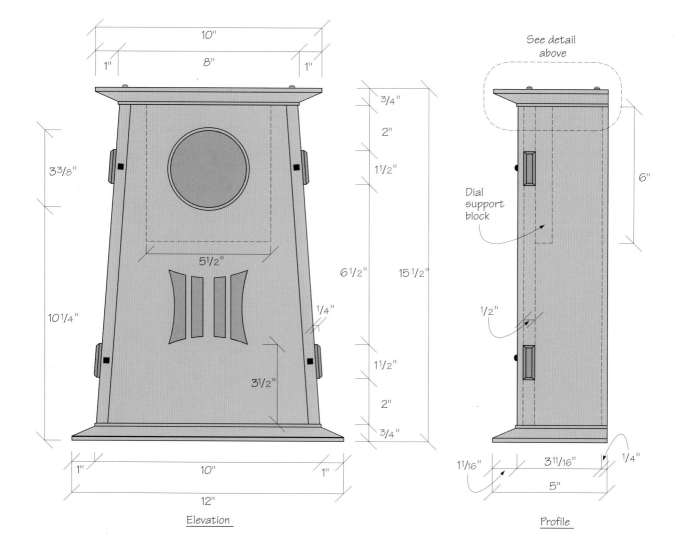

10"

1"   8"   1"

3/4"

2"

3 3/8"

1 1/2"

5 1/2"

6 1/2"   15 1/2"

1/4"

10 1/4"

3 1/2"

1 1/2"

2"

3/4"

1"   10"   1"

12"

Elevation

See detail above

6"

Dial support block

1/2"

11/16"   3 11/16"   1/4"

5"

Profile

Wastebasket

BY THANE LORBACH

A simple wastebasket — not so fast! This piece is more complicated than it looks. Building this wastebasket teaches you about tapered frames and panels, how to cut parallel and opposite angles, how to resaw and bookmatch wood grain. In addition, you'll learn a simple mortise-and-tenon technique and a fast and simple way to cut miters on a jointer.

More reasons to love this project: It's small so it doesn't require a great deal of wood and requires no hardware. It's also beautiful, a little challenging and makes a great finishing touch for a home office.

REFERENCE	QUANTITY	PART	STOCK	THICKNESS	(mm)	WIDTH	(mm)	LENGTH	(mm)	COMMENTS
A	8	stiles	white oak	$3/4$	(19)	$1^3/4$	(45)	$15^3/16$	(386)	angled cut both ends
B	4	top rails	white oak	$3/4$	(19)	$1^3/4$	(45)	$9^1/2$	(241)	$1/2$" (13mm) tenons both ends
C	4	bottom rails	white oak	$3/4$	(19)	$1^3/4$	(45)	$7^3/4$	(197)	
D	4	panels	white oak	$1/4$	(6)	9	(229)	$11^1/2$	(292)	
E	4	bottom	white oak	$1/4$	(6)	$9^1/4$	(235)	$9^1/4$	(235)	

Supplies

wood glue

stain

polyurethane finish

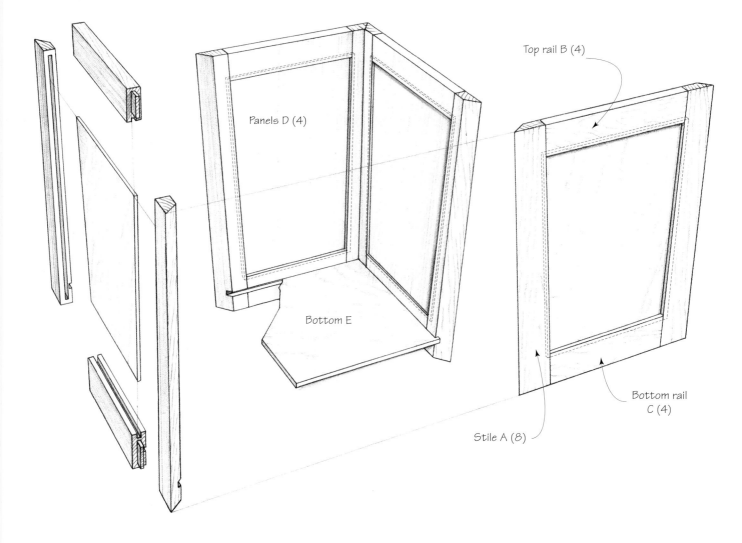

Top rail B (4)

Panels D (4)

Bottom E

Stile A (8)

Bottom rail C (4)

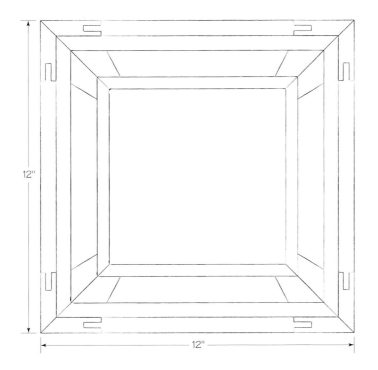

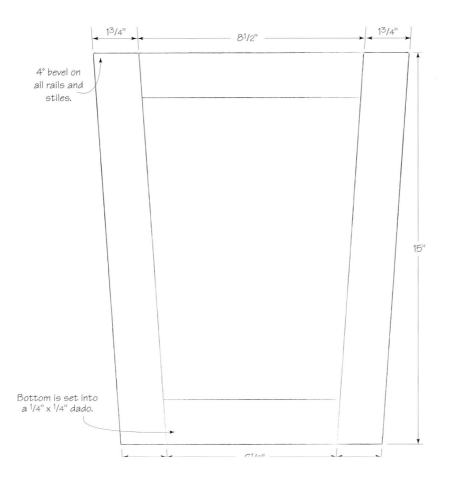

12"

12"

1³/₄"   8¹/₂"   1³/₄"

4° bevel on
all rails and
stiles.

15"

Bottom is set into
a ¹/₄" x ¹/₄" dado.

6¹/₂"

1 Set the miter gauge to 4° and make a cut on one end of all of the rails and stiles.

2 Leave the miter gauge at the same setting and set the fence to the stile length, then flip the stile over end for end, reference the cut end flat against the fence and make the second cut. This will make the two parallel cuts. When one end of a stile is placed flat on the table, the stile will stand at a 4° angle. Cut all eight stiles to length.

3 Set the fence for the length of the bottom rails. (Don't forget to add the length of both tenons before cutting the rails to length.) Flip the rail end for end (but not over). Note that the cut end will not sit flush against the fence, only the tip will touch the fence. Make the second cut on the four bottom rails. Reset the fence to the length of the top rails and make the cuts.

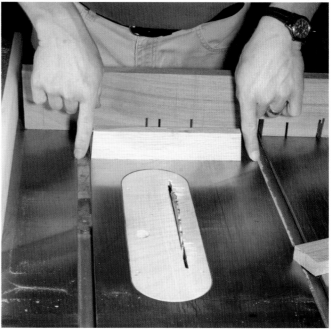

4 The rails will have opposite angles and the stiles will have parallel angles. I'm showing exaggerated opposite angles on the rails using my fingers.

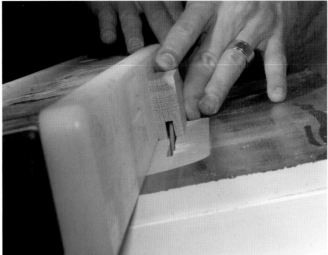

5 Mark the center of one of the rails. Using a square tooth blade, position the fence so the blade will cut to one side of the centerline. Raise the blade to ½" (13mm) high and cut a through groove in one edge of all of the rails and stiles. For the stiles, choose either edge for your groove. For the longer top rail, make the groove in the tapered, shorter edge. For the shorter bottom rail make the groove in the wider edge. This can get confusing, so mark the edges to be grooved.

6 To assure the groove is centered, make the first cut, then turn the rails and stiles 180°, referencing the other side against the fence and make the second cut. This centers the groove in the parts to accept the floating side panel. Make fence adjustments if necessary so the groove is ¼" (6mm)-wide. After your final pass leave the blade at the same height in order to cut your tenons.

7 I find it helpful to use a shop-made push block when cutting the tenons. This allows you to clamp the rails to the push block at the appropriate angle. If you don't use a push block or a tenon cutting jig here, the piece could move during a cut — and that can be dangerous. The push block is shown on its side. For the tenons, it is used standing upright with the small block on top.

8 Cut the tenons by clamping the rail to the push block with the cut end on the rail resting flat on the saw's table. Set the fence so the blade will cut the outer part of the tenon.

9 Turn the rail 180°, making sure the end is flat on the table saw (it will angle the opposite direction), and cut the other side of the tenon. Repeat these two cuts on both ends of all eight rails before moving your fence.

10 Move the table saw fence slightly toward the blade and make another pass. Turn the rail and make the second pass. Cut both ends of all eight rails at this setting before moving your fence. Continue this process, easing the fence in just slightly, until the tenons fit snugly into the grooves in the stiles. Remember, the distance the fence is moved is double the amount of material being removed. Make small adjustments.

11 Because you used the same blade height when cutting the grooves for the floating panels and the tenons, the tenons will be the correct length to fit perfectly in the groove. (The grooves for the floating panels also serve as the mortises.)

12 The tops of the stiles will be visible when the wastebasket is finished. Fit the end of the tenons so they bottom out in the grooves. It's not necessary to leave a space for glue.

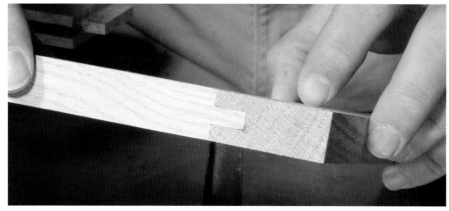

13 I chose to resaw and bookmatch the quartersawn white oak to make the floating panels. (This technique requires you to slice a board in half, opening the two pieces like a book. When glued together, one piece is a mirror image of the other.) The graining in the bookmatched panels for this particular piece looks very similar to the stems of a large leaf. You can also make the panel with multiple hardwood boards glued together or a piece of ¼" (6mm)-thick plywood. If you choose to use plywood, find a piece that is veneered on both sides because both sides will be visible.

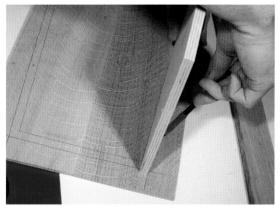

15 I used a piece of scrap that was just under ½" (13mm) thick to trace the final size for the panel. The panel shouldn't bottom out in the grooves. Keep the width slightly narrower, which allows the panel to "float" inside the grooves. This will allow the board to expand and contract over the seasons with little risk of warping or cracking.

16 Cut all the panels to size by cutting on the *outside* line. It might be helpful to erase or sand off the inside line so you don't cut on the wrong one.

14 Place a dry-fitted frame on top of each panel and trace a line around the inside of the frame.

17 If you don't have access to a jointer, it's easier to cut the long miters on the stiles before gluing everything together. Set the table saw blade at 45° and set the fence so the blade will take only enough stock to allow the edge to come to a point. These edges are fragile, so pad the edges during glue up and use very little clamping pressure to avoid damaging the edges.

18 If you have access to a jointer, after gluing up the frames, set the jointer fence to 45° and set the infeed table so it takes no more than a 1/16" (2mm)-deep cut. Make as many passes as necessary to complete the miter (until the face and edge meet at a point). While making the miter, count the number of passes you make on the jointer and cut the remaining miters, making the same number of passes for each one.

19 Set the table saw blade angle at 4° and cut the dado to accept the bottom. It is important to cut the long miters before cutting this dado. Otherwise, the jointer could cause the small piece of wood at the bottom of the dado to splinter off.

20 Move the saw's fence and cut the dado to final width.

21 Using the same 4° blade angle, cut the bevel on the top edge of the frame assemblies. This bevel will allow the completed wastebasket to sit flat on the floor. When cutting the top angle, the inside of the panel faces up (for a left-tilting saw) or down (for a right-tilting saw).

22 Reset the fence to cut the bevel for the bottom edge. The top and bottom bevel cuts should be parallel to each other.

23 Dry fit the frames together and measure for the bottom. After cutting the bottom to fit, lay all four frames on a flat surface with the outsides facing up. Butt the sharp edges of the miters together and tape the three joints.

24 Turn the taped assembly face down. Use a brush to spread glue on all of the miters. To keep the bottom from moving and rattling, put a dab of glue in the center of two opposite bottom dadoes.

25 Insert the bottom, fold the parts together and tape the final joint. I chose to use an oil stain on this wastebasket. Use scrap to try different colors until you come up with one you like. I created my color by mixing five parts red mahogany and one part dark walnut oil-based stains. I applied three coats of wipe-on polyurethane since this piece will be treated like "trash."

Stickley Mantel Clock

BY GLEN HUEY

A few years prior to his brothers taking over the furniture business, Gustav Stickley, the grandfather of the Arts & Crafts movement, produced what might at first glance appear to be an ordinary mantle clock. A closer look reveals many remarkable details. It's the details that make this project more than just a box containing a clock movement.

Take a look at where the top of the clock meets the sides. Is Stickley over the top with the number of pins and tails? I guess. But that's a detail that influences the overall look of the clock. Through-tenons that have chamfered ends is another small detail, as is the leaded-glass window that reveals the swinging pendulum. And the 12-sided clock-face opening certainly grabs your attention; but it's not as easy to cut as a simple circle. At the end of the project, you'll have a clock worthy of a sacred spot on your mantle.

Plan Your Dovetails

To be faithful to the original (an example of which recently appraised for $4,000), I set out to cut a total of 13 pins and tails. I wasn't so lucky. In fact, I had to abandon my 12°-dovetail marking gauge in favor of a 1:8 dovetail ratio. Even then, I only managed to arrive at five tails, four pins and two half-pins. The idea is to leave enough width in the pins to hide the groove for the backboard.

After you've established the baseline of your dovetails, layout begins on the top's face with two ¼" sections that become the half pins, one on each edge of the piece. Squeezed between those smaller sections are nine ½" spaces. These wider spaces become the full pins and tails.

Place marks on the face to form the sections. This makes the dovetail layout easier. Use a dovetail saddle marker, or a 1:8 layout jig, to transfer the layout and create the appropriate angled line – each line receives an opposing angled line. Designate the waste area with scribbled lines to ensure accuracy as you work, then repeat similar steps for the other end to complete the pin layout of the top.

Measure and mark. Layout on the dovetails begins with accurate sizing. Work from the face to the angled lines on the board's end.

Band Saw is Better

I generally cut my dovetails with a 12° angle. That measurement prevents me from using a band saw for the majority of my work without a jig; on most band saws it's not possible to get a 12° setting left of zero. If you use a 1:8 ratio, or 7° angle, that option is back in play so the band saw is my tool of choice.

Set the band saw table to 7° or align the saw blade with the layout mark as shown (above right). The first setting is easily attained with a simple tilt of the table. Make your cuts on the waste side of the lines. (Take a look at the layout in order to figure which line the angle is set for.) Once that's determined, cut every other line to your baseline. Remember to cut both ends of the top piece with the saw's table positioned at this setting.

Handsaw-free pins. Pin cuts are easy if you use a band saw set at an angle to match your layout lines. Tilt the table once for each pin direction.

Sharp lines, tight fit. Align the top onto the clock sides, use a sharp pencil to transfer the lines and mark the waste area to be removed. The extra marks assure that you'll waste the correct area.

Next you have to change the tilt of the band saw table. This time the table must be tilted toward the post of the saw. Set the angle of the table, then make the remaining cuts to delineate the pins and tail sockets. Remove the waste area to form your pins.

Transfer the pin layout to the tailboard then remove the waste of the tailboard to form the tails. Set the band saw table back to 90°, then make the cuts along the layout lines on the waste side of the lines. Remove the waste and check the fit. Make any adjustments to achieve a snug, but not a tight, fit. The rule of thumb is: The more dovetails you have and the more dense the wood, the closer to your layout lines you can cut and still achieve a nicely fitted joint.

REFERENCE	QUANTITY	PART	STOCK	THICKNESS	(mm)	WIDTH	(mm)	LENGTH	(mm)	COMMENTS
A	1	top	QSWO	5/8	(16)	5	(127)	8 1/2	(216)	
B	2	sides	QSWO	5/8	(16)	5	(127)	14	(356)	
C	1	bottom	QSWO	5/8	(16)	5*	(127)	8 7/8	(225)	13/16" tenon both ends
D	1	door	QSWO	3/8	(10)	7 1/4	(184)	12 1/8	(308)	
E	2	supports	QSWO	5/8	(16)	1 1/4	(32)	12 1/8	(308)	rabbeted for dial back
F	1	back	QSWO	1/2	(13)	7 5/8	(194)	13 1/4	(337)	
G	1	dial back	plywood	1/4	(6)	7 1/4	(184)	7 1/4	(184)	

QSWO = quartersawn white oak. *Oversized, cut to fit.

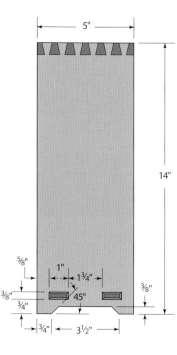

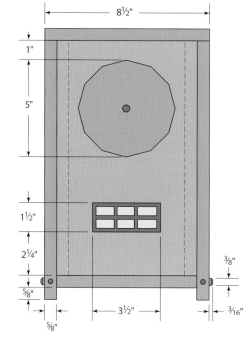

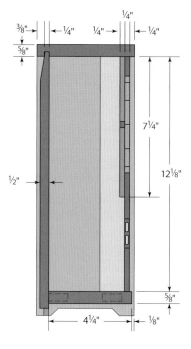

Supplies

woodcraft.com
1 - standard quartz movement
   #3722X,
   (includes 4802X hands)
1 - rare earth magnets
#128473

rockler.com
1 - narrow cabinet hinge
#32908

clockprints.com
1 - clock face
   #AC9 PWW

Easy Mortise for Through-tenons

Once the dovetails are complete and fit, determine the position of the mortises for the through-tenons of the clock bottom. The bottom is 5/8" thick, but the tenons are 3/8" in thickness. There are a number of methods you can use to create the mortises. You can cut them by hand, use a router and jig or use a dedicated mortise machine with a 3/8" mortise chisel and bit installed (that's the easiest way I've found).

Due to the position of the mortises, you'll need to cut the stock moving front to back, instead of side to side as is normal. Place a scrap piece beneath the side to reduce any blowout as the chisel plunges through the workpiece. Locate the mortise area under the chisel. Align the bit with both sides of the layout and position the fence so the front edge of the chisel is in line with the near edge of the rear mortise. Place a stop-block at the bottom end of the side that's 90° to the fence. You'll also need two spacers, one 5/8" thick and one 1/4" thick.

Place the side against the fence and the stop-block, then plunge the first hole. Next, slide a 5/8" spacer between the fence and the workpiece. This positions the chisel to cut the opposite end of the rear mortise. Plunge that hole. Replace the thick spacer with a 1/4" spacer, which

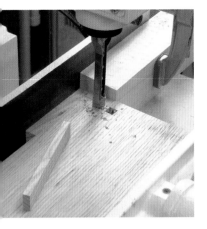

Spacers make quick work. Once the mortise chisels are positioned to the workpiece, it's a matter of changing spacers to complete the mortises.

Watch that cut. Don't push your groove through the dovetail or it will show from the top.

Stand tall. Simple feet are cut at the bottom edge of the sides. The best tool is a band saw.

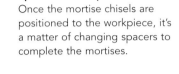

Accuracy counts. Mark the tenons on your bottom off the mortises cut into the sides. Be sure to accurately transfer the layout once the edges of the pieces are aligned.

Simple and straight. Tenons made at the table will be straight, which makes for a tight fitting mortise and tenon.

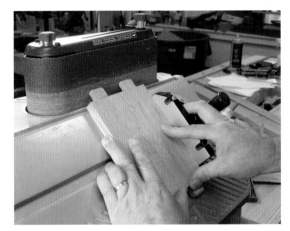

Hybrid woodworking. This sander's table adjusts to 45°. Another way to chamfer the tenon edges is with a miter gauge at a disc sander. No matter which method you use, the ends of the tenons require handwork.

removes the balance of the waste material from that mortise.

To cut the second mortise in the same side, simply flip the workpiece and repeat the same steps. It's best to change the scrap with each new mortise to keep the exiting face crisp. Complete all four mortises, two per side.

The sides are then grooved to accept the clock's back. A ¼" groove is carefully positioned to fit to the dovetail layout. As you can see in the top center photo on the next page, the ¼"-deep groove is aligned with the rear dovetail socket in the clock top and cut with a spiral upcut router bit at a router table. Groove the top from side to side, but for the sides, a stopped groove terminates before exiting the dovetail.

To complete the milling of the sides, form the feet of the clock using your band saw.

Tenons Complete the Joint

After the tenons are created, the piece is reduced in width at the front and back edges. It's easier to locate and form tenons with the workpiece the same width as the top and sides.

Begin by forming a full-width tenon on each end of the bottom. I use a two-step approach at my table saw. Make the shoulder cuts with the workpiece flat on the table, then with the workpiece vertical, make the cheek cuts to form the tenons. Look for a snug fit.

Position the clock's bottom (with the ⅜" tenons formed and fit to the mortises) onto the clock's sides, then transfer the layout lines to the tenons. Take care to accurately transfer these marks. The tenons should be snug on all sides when fit to the mortises.

Use a table saw to define the tenons. Match the saw blade height to that of the formed tenons. Use a tall auxiliary fence and clamp the bottom in position to cut the tenons at your layout lines. Be sure to work on the waste side of the tenons.

Remove the end waste areas using a band saw or nibble the material away at your table saw. The center section can be cut and/or nibbled, but I find it more efficient to use a chisel to remove the waste. Work partway through the material, then flip the stock and remove the remaining waste. Work with your chisel at a slight angle so you undercut the area. Any material extending beyond the shoulder of the tenon will cause problems when fitting the pieces.

These tenons extend through the clock sides by ³⁄₁₆" and are chamfered on all four edges, with a portion at the center remaining flat. You can use an edge sander or disc sander to chamfer the long portion of each tenon, but the work on the ends of the tenons has to be completed by hand with a rasp due to

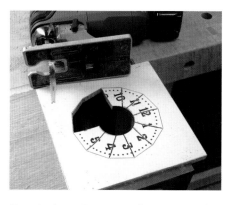

Hour by hour. To remove the waste inside the dial cutout, make cuts from the center out , then trim closely to the 12-sided opening.

Raspy detail. Small variations in the faceted edges are magnified when viewed as a whole. Spend some time to bring the edges to your layout lines.

Ramping up a hinge mortise. Installation of the hinges is tricky because the door is slightly recessed into the clock. A ramped mortise allows you to bury the hinge leaf and keep the barrel aligned as needed.

the fact that you'll nip the corner before you reach the tenon's edge.

Once the tenon work is complete and the fit is accurate, make the cuts to reduce the width of the bottom. The front edge is trimmed ⅛" to create an offset at the front of the clock. (Arts & Crafts designers were always looking for shadow lines.) The back edge of the bottom is trimmed ⅝" to allow the clock back to slide past the bottom when slid into the grooves.

The Focus of the Clock

There's no way around the fact that the door of this project is the focal point. The faceted cutout for the dial is a real eye-popper while the art glass is no

small feature. The point here is to find and use a very nice piece of lumber for your door.

Assemble the clock – without glue – to get the height and width of your door, then mill the piece to ⅜" thick. Affix a paper pattern of the dial cutout to the door front with spray adhesive to begin the work. (The pattern is available as a free download at popularwoodworking. com/dec08.) Find your largest-diameter drill bit, chuck it into a drill press and hog out as much of the center of the cutout area as you can, without cutting beyond the facets. The hole size needs to be at least large enough for a jigsaw blade to pass through and the more you remove, the easier the jigsaw work.

Precise transference. Mark the door-hinge location off the mortises made in the side. Make sure to keep the door aligned as you transfer the layout.

Just like the tenon cuts. Remove the waste from the hinge area on the doors at the table saw. This is the same setup I used to define the tenons for the bottom.

Fit tight or fit right. There's a fine line between your door fitting exactly and fitting sloppy. Make the piece fit, then angle the back edge with a block plane. If the gap needs to be enlarged, a simple pass or two with a sanding block should do the trick.

Secure the door in a vise or at your bench, then use a jigsaw to cut from the center hole to each facet junction. Next, cut close to each facet line without touching the line. As you reach each center-to-facet junction line, the waste falls away, allowing you to line up the next length of cut. A good jigsaw blade is a must.

Now use a rasp to straighten your cuts. Work tightly and accurately to the lines. If you're off even a small amount, the symmetry of the design will visually intensify any inconsistencies.

Next, lay out the opening for the art glass and again use a jigsaw to hog out the majority of the waste. Fine-tune the opening with your rasp. When these two areas are cut, shaped and finished, use a card scraper to remove the paper from the dial area.

The Door: Hang and Fit

The door's position is slightly back from the front edge of the clock, so it's not possible to install butt hinges as you would normally. The leaf mortise on the case side has to be ramped and the barrel of the hinge is on or at the surface.

Establish the mortise locations according to the plan. Mark both the front edge and rear edge of the door. It's from the front edge of the door that you'll ramp the mortise area. The idea is to create a ramp so the hinge leaf is flush to the surface where the outer edge of the leaf meets the case.

To make this ramp, set the inner hinge line with a chisel to a depth equal to the hinge-leaf thickness. At each end of the hinge area, plunge a ⅜" chisel into the waste area while it's set at an approximate angle that matches the ramp. All that's left is to create the ramp.

Begin with your chisel resting on the outer-most hinge line and slice downward as you move toward the inner layout line. Work slowly until the leaf

edge is just flush and the ramp is straight and flat.

Next, install the clock bottom to the hinge side piece. This creates a 90° corner and a place to fit the door. Align the door to the assembled pieces, hold a small gap at the bottom and transfer the hinge location onto the edge of the door.

Because the door thickness matches the length of the hinge leaf, it's possible to cut the recess at a table saw. One method to achieve the necessary depth of cut for the recess is to hold the hinge so the leaves are parallel, measure that thickness, then subtract 1/16" (for a reveal) and set the depth of cut at that figure. I think it's best to install the hinges on the clock body and create a test piece to arrive at the accurate depth of cut.

Once the blade is set for the correct depth of cut, add a tall auxiliary fence to your miter gauge, position the door to cut at the transferred marks and make a pass over the blade with the door clamped to the fence. Cut both ends of the recess on the waste side to define the hinge area; nibble away the balance of the material.

Install the door on the hinges. Add the top to the hinge side/bottom assembly. Mark at the tenon shoulder as well as the baseline of your dovetailed top to establish the exact width of the door.

The first of two steps. Form a notch in the supports that will eventually accept the dial back. A number of passes over the saw blade will carve out an area that makes finishing the rabbet a breeze.

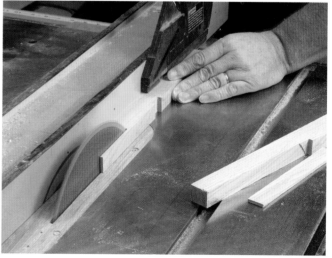

The second of two steps. The support rabbets are finished when you rip the material up to and including the notch. A small amount of waste needs to be cleared prior to the addition of the dial back.

Where to position the supports. Hold the door closed and tight to a square, then mark the edges of the door. Use a folded business card to position the supports behind those lines.

Cutting to that line will make the door fit, but it will be far too tight. Take a look at the reveal at the hinge side and adjust your cut to match.

Finally, turn a door knob from matching hardwood. Form a ⅜" tenon on the end of the knob to fit a ⅜" hole drilled into the door. A small amount of glue secures the knob in place.

Finishing Construction

After you've assembled all the parts of the clock and fit the door to the case, it's time to finalize construction. You have to add supports for the door and dial back, and make then install a backboard.

The two supports pull double duty. First, they act as a stop for the door and

second, they hold the plywood dial back. Mill the material for these supports according to the cut sheet. At the table saw, raise the blade height to match the thickness of your plywood dial back. Set the fence to cut at the 7¼" mark. Use your miter gauge with the auxiliary fence to cut a small notch into each support. Make the first cut with the end of the support tight to the fence, then pull away from the fence making a number of cuts until you've removed about ¾" or more of waste.

Raise the blade to just below its full height. In this position, the cut will be more vertical and the pressure applied from the blade helps hold the stock to the table. Position the fence to rip the

Pegged joint. The mortise-and-tenon joint is held together with a dowel that extends well into the first tenon. I made this matching-hardwood dowel by driving the stock through a series of graduated holes in a dowel plate until I reached the ¼" diameter.

Know your period. I found myself stuck in the 18th century when I made the clock back. If you're positioned differently, you might just want to mill your stock to a ¼" thickness and do away with the bevels.

Fuming the finish. Fuming the clock in a clear tub allowed us to see the difference in the way the wood changed. We pulled the door and back out after two hours. The clock case stayed put for another 16 hours. Remarkably, the color achieved was nearly identical.

A trick to install magnets. A brad driven into the center of a hole sized for a magnet will locate a second hole location by simply closing the door.

area for the dial back, then make the second cut.

The supports are added to the interior of the clock sides, just behind the door. To figure the placement, hold a square to the door and hinge side. Draw a line up both edges of the door. Add a thin bead of glue along the support's length, then attach the support just behind that line with a few small brads.

At this time, if everything is checked and fits, assemble the clock for the last time. Add glue to the dovetails and slip the parts together. I choose not to add glue around the tenons so as not to have any glue squeeze-out to clean up. Besides, the front edge of the tenons gets pegged through the face edge of the sides, which can also be completed as you assemble the clock. And don't forget to cut and fit the plywood dial back. It attaches to the supports with four small screws.

The back on my clock speaks volumes of the builder. Ordinarily, this back would be a piece that's ¼" in thickness. But because I usually build pieces from the 18th and early 19th centuries, I found myself making this piece as I would a drawer bottom in Queen Anne furniture. If you choose to copy my project, mill the back to size and thickness and set up at the table saw to complete the piece.

Set the fence (with a height extension added) spaced ³⁄₁₆" from the blade, just as a tooth passes below the table's surface. Raise the blade so you can just slide the panel between the blade and the fence. Use a push stick to make the cuts, as shown on the next page. The first cut is at the end grain, while the other two cuts are along the long-grain edges. This results in a near-perfect fit of a backboard into a ¼" groove.

If you choose to make the piece traditionally, mill the back to size and thickness the part to just slip into the groove.

Finish-sand the entire project to No.120 grit. There's no need sand go any further unless you plan to use a different finishing method.

The door is held in a closed position with a pair of rare-earth magnets, one in the door and one in a support. After the finish is complete, drill a hole in the support that's sized to accept your magnet. Cut off a small brad, then install the brad into the center of the hole. Close the door onto the brad a few times to mark the location for the second magnet. Install the magnets with a drop or two of thick cyanoacrylate glue and make sure to keep the polarity of the magnets in the correct orientation.

I turned to our resident Arts & Crafts expert, Senior Editor Robert W. Lang, for his help on the finish. He suggested this piece is the perfect size to fume, as was done on period pieces. Visit popularwoodworking.com/dec08 for additional information about fuming quartersawn white oak.

Also there, you'll find information on the paper dial (clockprints.com created a custom design for us that matches the original in most details). And you'll find information about the art-glass insert for the door.

This project was a venture into Arts & Crafts detail and the finish had me fuming, thanks to Mr. Lang. But the end result sits proudly on my mantle. I'll bet your results will be equally as impressive.

Step Stool

BY THANE LORBACH

A step stool is a necessity in every home. Most aren't very attractive. Until I built this design, mine was always hidden in a closet. At my house, this piece functions as both a step stool and a place for my kids to sit. It is, in fact, a piece of furniture. You can build this project in a weekend or less and it's not difficult to do. If you want to build a piece of furniture but need to hone your woodworking skills, this is a great project to take on.

The construction is straightforward, and you can complete the entire piece using basic tools. Buy your wood already surfaced (flat and square) and the main power tools you will need are a table saw, jigsaw or band saw, and a drill. In the course of this project you will make matching risers, learn a fun way to draw a curve and use dowels to hide screws and lend a decorative look to your work. So, step right up...

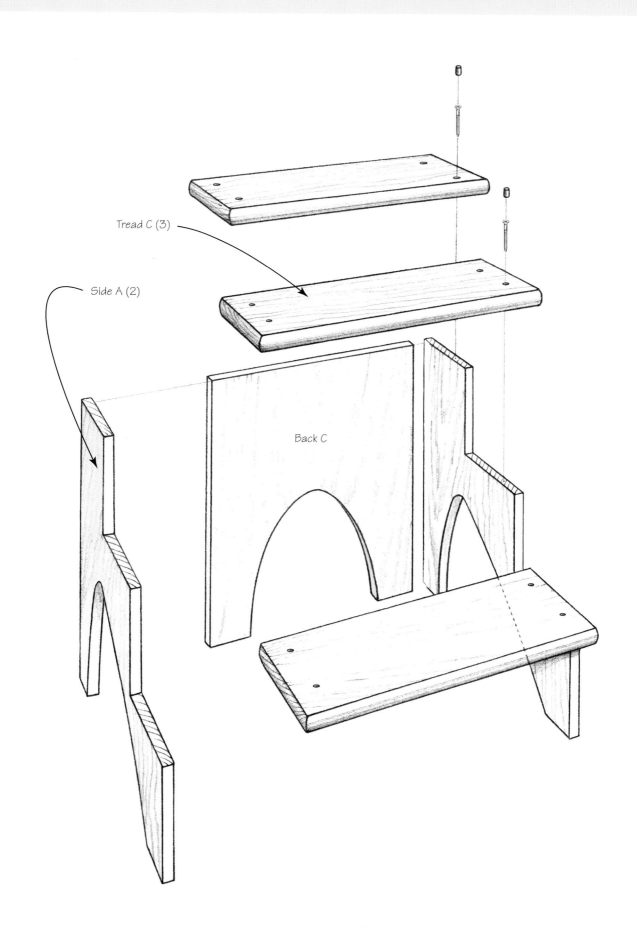

Tread C (3)

Side A (2)

Back C

STEP STOOL ■ INCHES (MILLIMETERS)

REFERENCE	QUANTITY	PART	STOCK	THICKNESS	(mm)	WIDTH	(mm)	LENGTH	(mm)
A	2	sides	white oak	3/4	(19)	18	(457)	18	(457)
B	1	back	white oak	3/4	(19)	15 1/2	(394)	18	(457)
C	3	treads	white oak	3/4	(19)	7	(178)	18	(457)

Supplies

24—No. 8 × 2" (50mm) flathead
wood screws

wood glue

stain

polyurethane finish

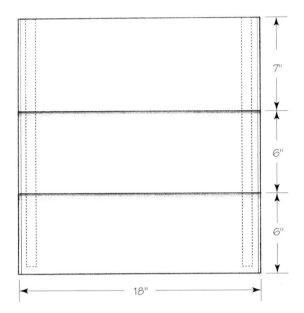

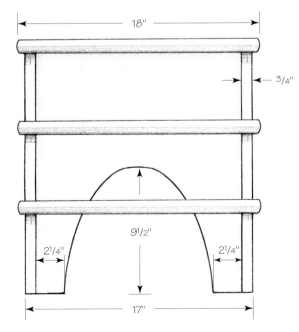

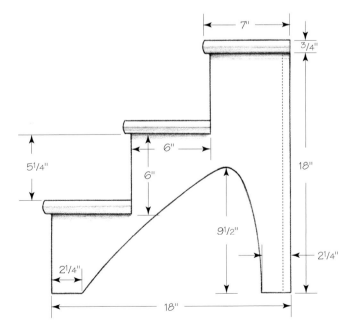

2 Square up one end of each board and mark that end using a pencil.

1 After purchasing or milling all of the stock, rip all parts to width. To make the back, edge glue as many pieces of wood as needed to achieve the final width.

3 The sides are made of three boards glued together to create the notches for the steps. Reference the squared end of the side boards against the fence. Cut the two longest side boards and the back boards to length. Move the saw fence and cut the middle side boards. Set the fence again and cut the shortest side pieces.

4 I found it easiest to glue up the sides two boards at a time using a spacer cut to step height.

5 Glue the short sideboard in place to complete the side assembly. (The bottom board square, so make sure the grain runs vertically.)

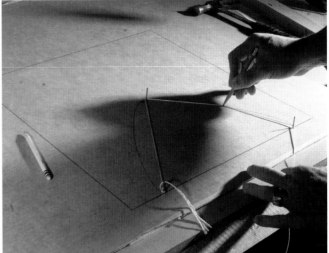

6 To visually lighten the step stool and to add some personal creativity to the project, I cut curves in the back and both sides. After gluing the boards together to make the back, lay the back on a piece of cardboard a couple inches from the bottom edge and draw a line around the perimeter. Determine how tall and wide you want your curve to be. Place a sacrificial board (plywood or medium density fiberboard [MDF]) under the cardboard and drive a nail at the curve's tallest point in the center (left to right) of the back. Drive nails on the bottom line at the curve's widest point, one on each side. Tie a string onto the bottom left nail, bring it over the top nail and loop it twice around the bottom right nail. Place a pencil inside the string and draw the curve. Loosen or tighten the string to form the curve you want. The looser you have the string, the wider and rounder your curve will be. For the curves in the sides, follow the same procedure, but offset the top nail instead of centering it. Once you have your desired curves drawn on cardboard, cut them out with a utility knife and use them to draw the curves onto the back and sides of your project. Using a jigsaw or band saw, cut out the curves in both sides and the back. Then use a file and sandpaper, or a spindle sander, to clean up the saw marks.

7 Lay the sides back edge to back edge. Mark the screw hole locations for attaching the sides to the back.

8 Because the back is ¾" (19mm) thick, drill the holes ⅜" (9mm) from the back edge of each side using a countersink bit. Drill the holes so the countersink bit creates a ¼" (16mm)-deep hole that will accept a plug to hide the screw head.

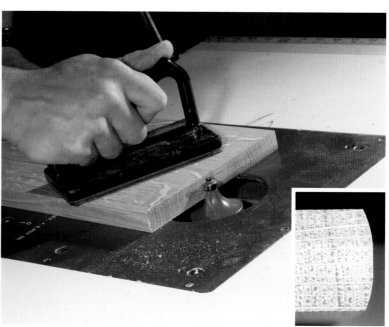

9 Sand the inside of the back. Then clamp the back and sides together and install the screws. You can use glue in addition to screws but it's not necessary.

10 Using part of a roundover router bit, ease the front edges and ends of the treads. Rout the end-grain first, taking a very light pass. Routing the long-grain after routing both ends cleans up any tear-out caused by routing the end-grain. Mark the back edges of the treads so you don't accidentally roundover the back edges. A file, rasp, sandpaper or block plane can also be used to create the roundover on the treads.

11 After sanding the entire piece (sides, back and treads), attach the treads to the base assembly using screws and wood plugs. Cut a scrap piece of wood the same width as the back and place it between the two sides at the bottom step so the sides will remain parallel. Start with the bottom tread. For a more dramatic look, choose a contrasting wood for the plugs. My kitchen has a white oak floor with a natural finish so I chose not to stain this piece. Since this piece will get a lot of wear, I applied four coats of polyurethane, rubbing with No.0000 steel wool between each coat — including the final coat — for a nice semigloss look. Applying stain and polyurethane can change the wood's color and appearance, so use some scrap wood from your project as a test piece. Experiment with different stains and finishes.

Isaac Youngs' Wall Clock

BY CHRIS SCHWARZ

It's difficult to open a book about Shaker furniture or to page through a woodworking catalog without coming face to face with a clock similar to this one. It seems that nearly every woodworking magazine and catalog has published plans for a clock with Isaac Newton Youngs' name on it.

So what possessed us to do the same thing?

Well, the goal of this project was to create a version of Youngs' clock that looked very much like the classic original but was built with joinery that a beginner would be comfortable with.

As I began drawing up our plans, I made an interesting discovery. Other plans for this clock that I consulted didn't look exactly like the original 1840 wall clock at the Hancock Shaker Village in Pittsfield, Mass. Many of these other plans made slight alterations to the size of the clock's case or the visual weight of the doors' rails and stiles.

In a few instances, these changes looked good. In others, however, it seemed that the designer — in seeking to make the project easier to build — made the clock a little chunky or squat. So John Hutchinson, *Popular Woodworking's* project illustrator, scanned in a photo of the original clock and scaled the parts using his computer-aided design (CAD) software.

Suddenly the clock got a little taller, a little skinnier and the top door's stiles became narrower. After we "built" the project with CAD and compared it to the original, we knew we were on the right track.

Of course, we did make changes, but they are mostly invisible to the naked eye. To make the clock easy to build, the case is joined using rabbets and dadoes. The back piece is plywood, instead of solid wood. And the moulding on the top and bottom is a bead instead of a roundover. All the changes can easily be undone for those seeking Shaker purity.

Finding Rift-sawn Wood

Youngs built his original using mostly rift-sawn butternut. All of the grain in that clock is arrow-straight without any of the arching cathedral patterns that are common to this somewhat-uncommon wood.

To reproduce that look I sorted through a 4'-high stack of butternut at the lumberyard but came up empty-handed. Rift-sawn butternut, according to the guys at the lumberyard, is hard to come by. So I went with Plan B: rift-sawn red oak, which is plentiful and inexpensive.

Three things are important when choosing wood for this project: Pick boards where the grain is dead straight, the growth rings are close together and the grain is rift-sawn — not flat-sawn or quartersawn. Flat-sawn oak exhibits the cathedrals you see on every red oak kitchen cabinet in every suburban sub-

Sacrificial fence

With the sacrificial fence in place, this setup will allow you to cut the rabbet in one pass. This eliminates the need for multiple saw setups and you don't need to stand your work on edge to make the cut.

division. Quartersawn oak shows off the medullary rays of the wood as shiny bits of what we call "ray flake." (Ray flake isn't desirable on a Shaker piece.) Rift-sawn oak generally has tight grain lines but no cathedrals or ray flake.

How do you find rift-sawn wood? Some lumberyards sort the wood for you. But if they don't, you can pick out the rift-sawn stuff by looking at the end grain. In rift-sawn wood, the growth rings intersect the face of the board at an angle between 30° and 60°. If the angle is less than 30°, the board is flat-sawn. If it's more than 60°, the board is quartersawn. Look over a few boards with this in mind and the difference will be obvious.

I bought 50 board feet of 4/4 red oak for this project. While that's more than I needed, it ensured that I would be able to choose the wood for the rails, stiles and panel with extra care.

As you joint and plane your wood to its final thickness, set aside the straightest, tightest-grained boards for the rails, stiles

Don't change your saw's setup any more than you have to. By shifting the rip fence ¼", you can make the rabbets that hold the back piece by running the sides on edge.

A standoff block clamped to the fence as shown allows you to use the rip fence and miter gauge in tandem and reduces the chance of a nasty kickback.

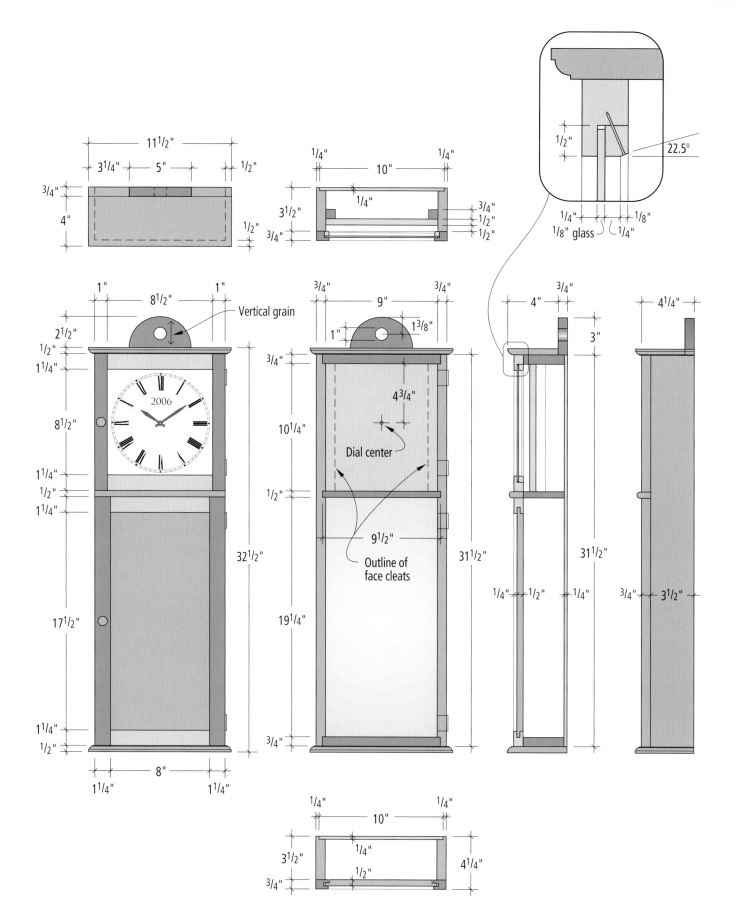

Vertical grain

2006

Dial center

Outline of
face cleats

1/8" glass

REFERENCE	QUANTITY	PART	STOCK	THICKNESS	(mm)	WIDTH	(mm)	LENGTH	(mm)	COMMENTS
A	2	sides	red oak	3/4	(19)	3 1/2	(89)	31 1/2	(800)	
B	2	interior top & bottom	red oak	3/4	(19)	3 1/4*	(83)	9 1/2	(241)	
C	1	divider	red oak	1/2	(13)	4 1/2	(114)	10 1/2	(267)	
D	1	back	red oak	1/4	(6)	10	(254)	31 1/2	(800)	
E	1	hanger	red oak	3/4	(19)	5	(127)	3	(76)	
F	2	exterior top & bottom	red oak	1/2	(13)	5**	(114)	11 1/2	(292)	
G	1	dial	red oak	1/2	(13)	9	(229)	10 1/4	(260)	
H	2	cleats	red oak	3/4	(19)	3/4	(19)	10 1/4	(260)	
UPPER DOOR										
I	2	rails	red oak	3/4	(19)	1 1/4	(32)	9 1/2	(241)	1/2" TBE
J	2	stiles	red oak	3/4	(19)	1	(25)	11 1/2	(292)	includes 1/4" horns
K		glazing moulding	red oak	3/8	(10)	1/2	(13)	48	(1219)	
LOWER DOOR										
L	2	rails	red oak	3/4	(19)	1 1/4	(32)	9	(229)	1/2" TBE
M	2	stiles	red oak	3/4	(19)	1 1/4	(32)	20 1/2	(521)	includes 1/4" horns
Nn	1	panel	red oak	1/2	(13)	8 3/4	(222)	18 3/8	(467)	

*Finished size after machining will be 4 1/4".

**Finished size after machining will be 4 3/4".

TBE = tenon both ends

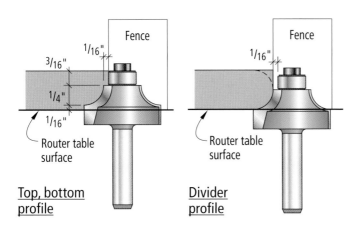

Top, bottom profile

Divider profile

Supplies

Lee Valley Tools
800-871-8158 or leevalley.com

1 - 1/2"-quartz movement
#46K0115

1 - pair of black clock hands
#46K0303

2 - pairs of no-mortise hinges
#00H5123

1 - package of #5 x 5/8" screws,
#01Z5305, pkg. of 100

Rockler
800-279-4441 or rockler.com

1 - pair of oak Shaker knobs
#88840

You could wait until the carcase is assembled to glue the detail back in place, but I find that you can get a tighter joint if you do this before the case is glued up. If your joint is smooth, you should be able to use painter's tape to position the detail to the remainder of the divider before clamping.

and panel. Not only will these "look right," they will be more stable and less likely to twist out of shape during machining.

The Clock's Carcase

Here's how the basic skeleton of the clock goes together: The interior top and bottom pieces are secured in shallow rabbets in the side pieces. The ½"-thick divider that separates the doors rests in dadoes in the side pieces. The back fits in a rabbet cut in the sides. The exterior top and bottom are merely glued to the top and bottom of the assembled case.

It's a bit of a trick to cut notches in the divider so that its front edge runs the entire width of the case. And you'll employ that same trick to notch the exterior top piece around the half-round hanger piece. But it's simple stuff.

Once you've cut the parts for the carcase to the sizes shown in the cutting list, the first step is to cut the ¼"-

deep × ¾"-wide rabbets on the ends of both side pieces. I like to perform this operation with a dado stack set in my table saw. As you can see in the photo above, I've added a "sacrificial" wooden fence and a featherboard to my saw's rip fence. This setup allows me to cut right up against the rip fence without leaving a little waste piece on the end of the board. The featherboard keeps the work pressed to the saw's table.

To make the cut, place a side piece against the miter gauge with the end of the board touching the sacrificial fence. Move the work forward into the cut and keep firm downward pressure on the piece. Check your work with a dial caliper to make sure the height of the blades is correct. When you're satisfied, cut this rabbet on both ends of both side pieces.

To complete the joinery necessary on the side pieces, cut the ¼"-deep ×

Using a folding rule — I like the ones where you can extend a 6"-long "finger" from the end — compare the diagonal measurements you make from corner to corner. If they're the same, your case is square. If not, place a clamp across the two corners that produced the longer measurement and apply a small amount of clamping pressure until the two measurements are identical.

½"-wide rabbets on the sides that will hold the back. To cut this joint, keep the height of your dado stack the same that you had for your first cut. But shift the rip fence so that you expose only ½" of the dado stack's cutters. Then cut the rabbets on the side with the parts run on edge as shown in the photo above.

Finally, cut the ¼"-deep × ½"-wide dado in the side pieces for the divider. Leave the height of the dado stack alone. In fact, lock the arbor of the saw in place. Then remove the dado stack and put enough chippers and wings on the arbor to make a ½"-wide cut. Also, remove the sacrificial fence from your rip fence.

Clamp a 1"-wide "standoff" block to your table saw's rip fence in the location shown in the photo on page 48. Set your rip fence at the 12" mark — this will put exactly 11" of space between your standoff block and the dado stack. That's right where you want the divider to be. Put a side piece against your miter gauge and against the standoff block. Cut the dado in the side piece and repeat the procedure for the other side. The joinery for your sides is now complete.

Tricky Notches

As you look at the cutting list for this project, you might notice that the divider is longer than the interior top and bottom pieces. It also runs the entire width of the clock's case and stands proud of the doors when they're closed. To make the divider do this, you need to notch the ends so they fit inside the dadoes and the front rounded-over edge then extends to the edges of the carcase.

This is actually easy. Here's the trick: First rout the ¼"-radius roundover on a long edge of the divider, as shown in the drawing below. Next, using your table saw, rip 1" of this detailed edge off of the divider. Crosscut the remaining piece to 9½" long — the same length as the interior top and bottom pieces. Now glue the 1"-wide strip back to the divider.

If you do it this way you will have perfect notches on both ends and the grain will match all the way across the

width of the board. (You'll use this same trick to notch the exterior top around the hanger piece.)

Before you assemble the carcase, plane or sand the interior surfaces so they are ready to finish. If you are using sandpaper, sand up to #220 grit. Then perform a dry run without glue to make sure you have the clamps you need and your joints close tightly.

When you're satisfied, spread a thin film of glue in the rabbets and dadoes and put the interior top, bottom and divider in place. Clamp the second side in place and ensure all the parts of the carcase are flush at front and back.

Compare the diagonal measurements of the clamped-up case to ensure it's square and wait for at least 30 minutes for the glue to dry. Then take the case out of the clamps and secure the joints with nails. (Tip: If you drive the nails in at slightly different angles, you'll wedge the parts together.)

Adding the Top and Bottom

The exterior top and bottom pieces are merely glued to the completed carcase. But before you can do this, you need to

do some machining to add the beaded detail on three edges and create a notch in the exterior top piece for the half-round hanger.

Begin by ripping a ¾"-wide strip off the back edge of your exterior top piece. Take this narrow strip and crosscut 3¼" off each end. Now you can tape and glue these pieces back to the exterior top piece to create a notch in the center for the hanger.

Next you can rout the beaded detail on the ends and front edge of the exterior top and bottom. First rout the bead on the ends and use a backup block behind your work to control tear-out and add stability to this machining operation.

Once the ends are routed, cut the same detail on the front edge of both pieces. Before you attach these pieces, plane or sand the exterior of your carcase so it's ready for finishing.

With that done, you want to fit the exterior top and bottom pieces. These must fit tightly to the case, so it pays to clamp them in place without glue first. Note where any gaps are, then remove material with a block plane from any

When you glue the strips onto the exterior top piece, tape them in place so they don't slide around as you add clamping pressure.

area that won't ever show to get the pieces to mate tightly. Don't rely on clamping pressure to close up gaps — you should be able to get a tight fit using hand pressure only.

I've found that the best way to attach each piece is to lay it on your bench, then spread a thin film of glue on the mating surface of the carcase and put the carcase in place. Before you clamp the two parts together, secure the pieces with a couple of nails.

Last Carcase Details

Cut the 5"-diameter half-round hanger to shape on your band saw and bore the 1" hole that's 1⅜" from the top edge of the hanger. First glue it in place in the notch in the exterior top piece and secure it with screws through the back of the hanger.

To hold the dial in position, you need to nail in two ¾" × ¾" cleats in the top section of the case. When you position them, be sure to allow for the thickness of the dial (½" in this case), and the length of the stem of your clock's movement. Otherwise, the top door won't close.

Then cut the dial to fit the opening in the top and attach your movement to the rear. When you drill the hole for the stem of the movement, note that it is not in the center of the dial board. To center it in the upper door, you need to drill this hole ⁷⁄₁₆" up from the center point of the board.

I used a quartz movement to keep the clock simple and inexpensive. A mechanical movement with a pendulum is another option. If you choose this, be aware you'll have to cut a clearance hole for the pendulum in the divider.

You can download a file from our web site (click on "Magazine Extras") for the face of the clock if you want it to look like the one featured here. Otherwise, you can find 8" faces at a variety of supply houses or web sites.

Affix the paper face to the dial using a spray adhesive (I use 3M's Super 77 Multipurpose Spray Adhesive) and screw the dial to the cleats using four brass screws. Cut the plywood back to size, prepare it for finishing and screw it to the back of the case.

Building the Doors

Because the stiles and rails of these doors are narrow, there are some useful tricks to machining and assembling them.

The first trick is to cut the rabbets for the top door on wider pieces, then rip the rails and stiles free from these wider boards. This makes cutting the rabbets a much safer operation.

Second, I like to cut all my rails and stiles ¹⁄₁₆" wider than called for in the cutting list. Then I like to cut my stiles ½" longer than the finished size of the door. All this creates a door that is slightly oversized for its opening so that I can then trim the door to be square and perfectly sized after it's glued up. It takes a bit more time, but it saves a lot of frustration when doing the final fitting.

Begin by working on the upper door. Set up a dado stack set and sacrificial fence for your table saw much like you did to cut the rabbets for the carcase. Set the height of the blade and the position of your rip fence to make a ½" × ½" cut. After confirming that your setup is correct, cut this rabbet on the inside edge of the rails and stiles for the upper door.

Above, you can see how a couple of well-placed nails keep everything in line as I apply the clamps. Whenever you can, use your bench to assist your clamping (right). It helps spread clamping pressure over a wider area.

Cleat for dial

Cringe if you want, but I like quartz movements. They're reliable, require little upkeep and are simple to install. I know this from installing and adjusting several mechanical movements in clocks over the years. Do whatever makes you happy on this point.

Before you switch over to your rip blade to cut the rails and stiles free of their wider boards, it's a good idea to go ahead and cut the rabbet on the ends of the rails. These end rabbets create the lap joint that joins the rails and stiles together for the upper door (see the illustration on page 70). This lap joint, when properly executed, is satisfactory for a small door. To cut this joint on the ends of the rail pieces, leave the saw's rip fence as it is and lower the saw blade so it makes a ¼"-deep cut. Then make the cuts on the ends of the rail boards.

Set these boards aside for a moment and get your rails and panel for your lower door. This saw setup is exactly what you need to cut the stub tenons on the ends of the rails for the lower door and the rabbet on the backside of the panel so it will fit in the door's groove. Cut this joint on both faces of your lower rails. Then cut this rabbet on all four edges of your panel stock.

Finally, install a rip blade in your table saw and rip the rails and stiles of the upper door free to their final width plus ⅟₁₆".

To complete the joinery on the lower door, you need to plow a ¼"-wide × ½"-deep groove in the rails and stiles for the panel and for the stub tenons on the rails. Keep the rip blade in your saw and set the fence ¼" away from the blade and set the height to ½". Now plow the groove in two passes. The first pass has one face of the board against the fence; the second pass has the other face

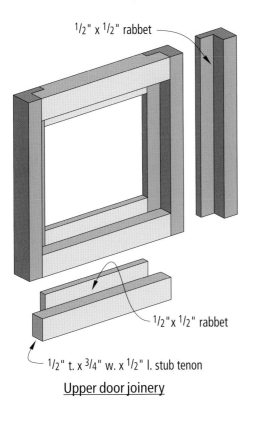

½" x ½" rabbet

½" x ½" rabbet

½" t. x ¾" w. x ½" l. stub tenon

Upper door joinery

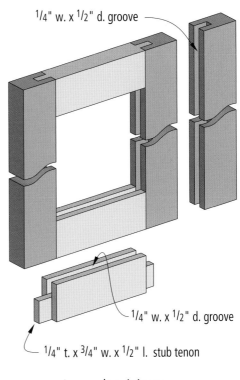

¼" w. x ½" d. groove

¼" w. x ½" d. groove

¼" t. x ¾" w. x ½" l. stub tenon

Lower door joinery

A Closer Look at Isaac Youngs

The Shaker faith arrived in the United States from northern England in the late 18th century. One of the earliest communities existed in New Lebanon, N.Y., and it was there that Isaac Newton Youngs made a name for himself in the early 19th century.

Born in 1793, Youngs joined the Shakers when he was just 14 years old. While the Shakers didn't permit watches (they were deemed "an unnecessary indulgence"), they did value clocks to support punctuality. Many clocks were kept in dining areas and common rooms.

Youngs would grow to become one of the group's chief clockmakers, building more than 20 of these projects over the course of his lifetime, as well as numerous other pieces for the New Lebanon community. His clocks clearly illustrate the Shaker principles of simplicity, purity and utility. Many follow what has come to be known as the Shaker style — namely, they are straightforward, functional and modest.

Along with his clockwork, Youngs delved into another passion while at the community — music. He helped develop the guidelines of small letteral notation that included material on the importance of melody, rhythm and meter. He knew it was important to teach this system of notation, to provide examples for students to study and to encourage a uniform system for the entire community. Youngs died in 1866.

At its peak in the mid-19th century, there were about 6,000 Shakers living in the United States. But after a long, slow decline in membership throughout the late 19th and 20th centuries, there now exists only one active village, located in Maine.

— MICHAEL A. RABKIN

When working on narrow stock such as the door rails, it's safer to cut your joinery on a slightly wider board (this one is about 4" wide) and cut the part free when the joinery is complete.

against the fence. Cutting the groove in two passes ensures that it will be centered on the edge.

Next, prepare all your door parts for finishing. Don't worry about cleaning up the outside edges of the rails and stiles because they'll be trimmed after assembly. Clamping the upper door is a bit trickier than most doors because of the lap joinery. First clamp the stiles against the rails like you would a traditional door. Don't forget to position the rails to accommodate the ¼"-long horns on the ends and don't use a lot of clamping pressure. Clamp each of the joints with a bar clamp positioned like you would compress a sandwich, as shown on page 77.

The lower door is easier to assemble. Paint glue in the grooves where the stub tenons will go (but not the panel), assemble the parts and clamp things up. Allow the glue to dry and remove the doors from the clamps.

Fitting and Fussing

Now it's time for the detail work. Your goal is to trim the doors so they fit on the carcase with a ¹⁄₁₆"-wide gap between the doors and the carcase. This gap, called the "reveal," must be consistent. If it's not, other woodworkers will quickly notice.

Here's how I trim my doors, though there are many ways to do it: First true one stile on your jointer and rip the door to width, taking equal amounts of material from each stile. Then crosscut the door so it's just a hair longer than necessary. Finally, after installing the hinges, plane the top and bottom of the door to get that perfect ¹⁄₁₆"-wide reveal.

The hinges are a snap to install because they require no mortise. If you lack confidence when installing hardware, here's a simple trick you can use: Screw the hinges in place on the carcase.

You need to compress the joint vertically as well as join the pieces horizontally, so you need to clamp both simultaneously as shown.

Mix up some five-minute epoxy and put a few dabs on the hinge leaf that attaches to the door. Position the door right where you want it, tape it to the carcase with painter's tape and allow the epoxy to set. Open the door and drive in the hinge screws for the door.

After your project is finished, install the ⅛"-thick glass. The most handsome way to do this is with glazing moulding that you machine yourself. This moulding is simply ⅜"-thick × ½"-wide moulding with a chamfer machined on it. Because you'll finish the project before installing the moulding, now is the time to machine and sand it.

Install the Shaker knobs and the catches for the doors (I used a simple hook and screws), then disassemble the project for finishing. Break all the sharp edges with No.120-grit sandpaper.

To give the piece an aged look, I chose to finish it with two coats of garnet shellac. Then I followed that up with two coats of a dull-sheen spray lacquer (shellac is very glossy). This finishing process mimics the look of the original clock quite well.

With the project finished, you can install the glass with a bead of silicone in the rabbet, then miter the glazing moulding and secure it with silicone and brads as shown in the construction drawing.

The original clock is hung on a traditional Shaker peg. You could build yourself a "peg board" and array it with a number of Shaker-like accessories. Another authentic option is to hang the clock on a single forged iron hook.

No matter how you hang it, whenever you check the time, you'll be reminded that it takes a little perseverance and (yes) time to get any project designed and built so it's just right.

Spiral Staircase Table

BY ROBERT BELKE

Some years ago, my wife and I spent a week cross- country skiing in Stowe, Vermont. While there, we stayed at the Trapp Family Farm (as in *The Sound Of Music*). In the library of the main lodge, we discovered what I call a spiral staircase table. I had never seen another like it. Subsequently, I learned the original use of such a piece was as a step stool to reach books located high out of reach in a formal library; however, this one was used as a table to hold a lamp and various small items of interest. Over the years, the memory of this table remained with me. Recently, I decided to design and build one. The only caution I can give about this piece is, if you decide to build it, don't use it as a step stool! This attractive table is made from cherry wood and has a natural finish to showcase the beauty of the wood. For those who like to do wood turning, this project features lots of spindle turning on the lathe.

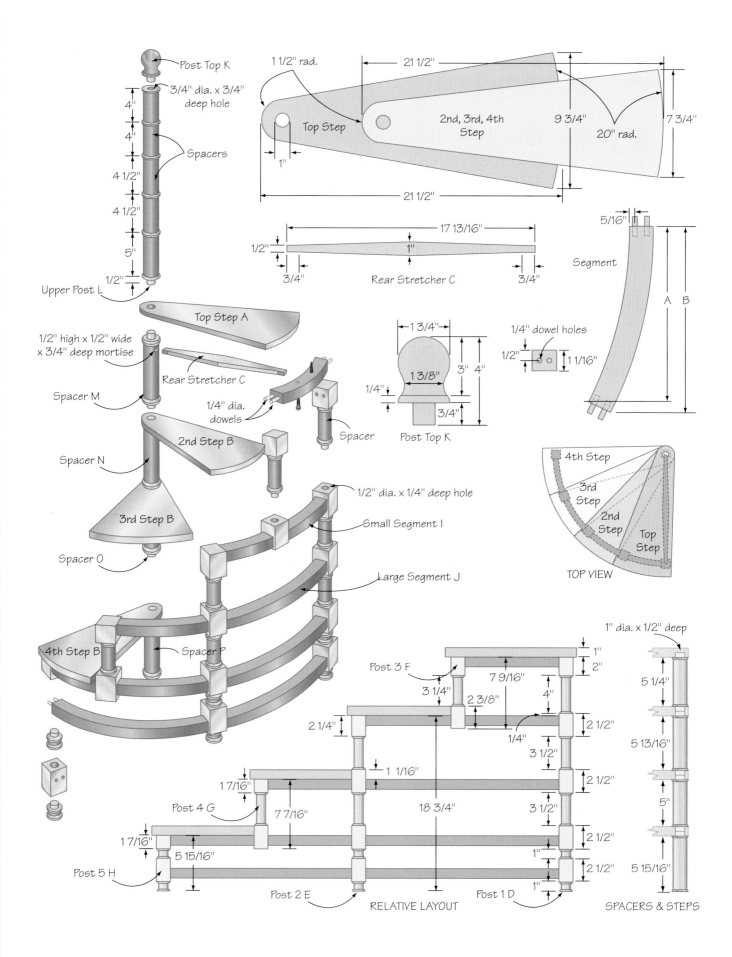

Post Top K

3/4" dia. x 3/4" deep hole

4"

4"

4 1/2"

4 1/2"

Spacers

5"

1/2"

Upper Post L

1 1/2" rad.

21 1/2"

Top Step

2nd, 3rd, 4th Step

9 3/4"

7 3/4"

20" rad.

1"

21 1/2"

17 13/16"

1/2"

1"

3/4"

3/4"

Rear Stretcher C

5/16"

Segment

A   B

1/2" high x 1/2" wide x 3/4" deep mortise

Top Step A

Spacer M

Rear Stretcher C

1/4" dia. dowels

Spacer N

2nd Step B

Spacer

1 3/4"

3"   4"

1 3/8"

1/4"

3/4"

Post Top K

1/4" dowel holes

1/2"

1 1/16"

3rd Step B

Spacer O

1/2" dia. x 1/4" deep hole

Small Segment I

Large Segment J

4th Step   3rd Step   2nd Step   Top Step

TOP VIEW

4th Step B

Spacer P

1" dia. x 1/2" deep

1"

2"

Post 3 F

7 9/16"

3 1/4"

2 3/8"

4"

1/4"

2 1/2"

5 1/4"

2 1/4"

3 1/2"

5 13/16"

1 1/16"

2 1/2"

1 7/16"

Post 4 G

7 7/16"

18 3/4"

3 1/2"

5"

2 1/2"

1 7/16"

5 15/16"

1"

2 1/2"

Post 5 H

1"

5 15/16"

Post 2 E

Post 1 D

RELATIVE LAYOUT

SPACERS & STEPS

SPIRAL STAIRCASE TABLE ■ INCHES (MILLIMETERS)

REFERENCE	QUANTITY	PART	STOCK	THICKNESS	(mm)	WIDTH	(mm)	LENGTH	(mm)	COMMENTS
A	1	top step	cherry	1^{1}/$_{16}$	(27)	5^{3}/$_{4}$	(146)	22	(559)	
B	3	2nd, 3rd & 4th steps	cherry	1^{1}/$_{16}$	(27)	7^{3}/$_{4}$	(197)	22	(559)	
C	1	rear stretcher	cherry	1	(25)	1	(25)	17^{13}/$_{16}$	(452)	add an additional ^{1}/$_{2}$" for lathe work
D	1	post No.1	cherry	1^{1}/$_{2}$	(38)	1^{1}/$_{2}$	(38)	25	(635)	
E	1	post No.2	cherry	1^{1}/$_{2}$	(38)	1^{1}/$_{2}$	(38)	18^{3}/$_{4}$	(476)	
F	1	post No.3	cherry	1^{1}/$_{2}$	(38)	1^{1}/$_{2}$	(38)	7^{9}/$_{16}$	(192)	
G	1	post No.4	cherry	1^{1}/$_{2}$	(38)	1^{1}/$_{2}$	(38)	7^{7}/$_{16}$	(189)	
H	1	post No.5	cherry	1^{1}/$_{2}$	(38)	1^{1}/$_{2}$	(38)	5^{15}/$_{16}$	(151)	
I	1	small segments	cherry	1^{1}/$_{16}$	(38)	1^{1}/$_{2}$	(38)	6^{1}/$_{4}$	(159)	blank dimensions
J	1	large segments	cherry	1^{3}/$_{4}$	(45)	2^{3}/$_{4}$	(70)	13^{1}/$_{2}$	(343)	blank dimensions
K	1	post top	cherry	1^{3}/$_{4}$	(45)	1^{3}/$_{4}$	(45)	4	(102)	add an additional ^{1}/$_{2}$" for lathe work
L	1	upper post	cherry	1^{3}/$_{4}$	(45)	1^{3}/$_{4}$	(45)	22^{1}/$_{2}$	(57)	
M	1	spacer, top & 2nd step	cherry	1^{3}/$_{4}$	(45)	1^{3}/$_{4}$	(45)	6^{3}/$_{16}$	(157)	
N	1	spacer, 2nd & 3rd step	cherry	1^{3}/$_{4}$	(45)	1^{3}/$_{4}$	(45)	6^{3}/$_{4}$	(171)	
O	1	spacer, 3rd & 4th step	cherry	1^{3}/$_{4}$	(45)	1^{3}/$_{4}$	(45)	5^{15}/$_{16}$	(151)	
P	1	spacer, 4th step & floor	cherry	1^{3}/$_{4}$	(45)	1^{3}/$_{4}$	(45)	6^{7}/$_{16}$	(164)	

Hardware

40   ^{1}/$_{4}$" x 1" Dowels
8   No.8 x 1^{3}/$_{4}$" Wood Screws

Supplies

Carpenter's glue
Gloss polyurethane
Satin polyurethane
No. 400 wet/dry paper
Cabinet wax
No. 0000 steel wool

Required Tools

Lathe
Spindle sizing jig
Drill
Band saw or saber saw
Dowel centers
Sander (or sandpaper and block)

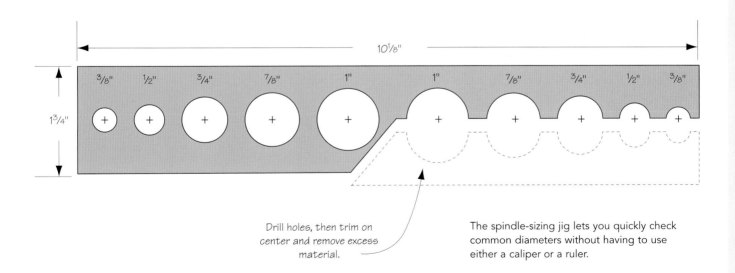

Drill holes, then trim on
center and remove excess
material.

The spindle-sizing jig lets you quickly check
common diameters without having to use
either a caliper or a ruler.

Lathe Work

There are 12 different spindles that have to be turned on a lathe. With the exception of the post top, most of the turning work is between center spindles. To quickly check the sizes of the spindles as you work, see the simple spindle-sizing jig as described on page 81.

Before turning the spacer between the fourth step and the floor, bore a centered ½"-diameter hole, ¾" deep, 2¾" up from the floor. This hole will be used during final assembly of the rear stretcher.

Turning the Spacers

With a roughing gouge, and referring to the dimension chart below, turn all the spacers to an overall 1¾" diameter. With the exception of the spacer between the fourth step and floor, where there is only a stub on one end, turn 1" × ½" stubs on both ends of each spacer. These 1" diameter stubs should be turned using the actual measurement taken from the 1" Forstner bit that will be used later in the project. The reason for this is to obtain a snug fit between the spacers and the steps. Mark the C and D dimensions on the spacers and turn the G dimension (1½"). With a ⅜" beading and parting tool, round over the edges of C and D. Sand each spindle.

Turning the Upper Post

Mount the upper post blank on the lathe, and as was done with the spacers, turn the upper post blank to an overall 1¾" diameter (see photo 1). Mark all the dimensions on the blank and turn the 1"-diameter, ½"-long stub, again taking the 1" measurement from the Forstner bit selected for this project. Using a skew chisel, score a mark in the center of the four interior beads. Turn the 1½" diameters as indicated in the technical drawing (there are five such areas). Round over the beads with a parting and beading tool. Sand the post, and bore a ¾" × ¾" hole on the top end with a Forstner bit (see photo 2).

1 Mount the upper post blank on your lathe with all the dimensions marked.

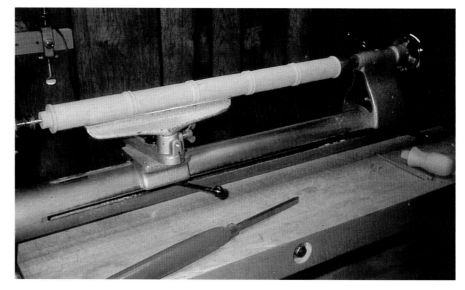

2 Here you see the upper post after turning is completed.

Spacers

SPACERS FROM	TOP & 2ND STEP	2ND & 3RD STEP	3RD & 4TH STEP	4TH STEP & FLOOR
A	1	1	1	1
B	½	½	½	½
C	¼	¼	¼	¼
D	¼	¼	¼	¼
E	½	½	½	N/A
F	1	1	1	N/A
G	1½	1½	1½	1½
H	1¾	1¾	1¾	1¾
I	5³⁄₁₆	5¾	4³⁄₁₆	5¹⁵⁄₁₆
J	6³⁄₁₆	6¾	5¹⁵⁄₁₆	6⁷⁄₁₆

Dimensions in inches

Turning the Post Top

The post top can be turned using between-the-centers turning or a combination of between the centers and a chuck. I chose the latter method. Holding the stock between-the-centers, turn the blank to a 1¾" cylinder. Lay out and mark all the dimensions as shown in the technical drawing. Cut the 1⅜" cove and round over the half bead. Transfer the stock to a three-jawed chuck and finish turning the ball end. Finally, sand the post top and glue it to the upper post (see photo 3).

3 Transfer the stock for the post top to a three-jawed chuck and turn the ball end. Finally, sand it smooth.

Turning the Lower Posts

There are five different lower posts that require some turning. Each of these starts out as a 1½" square blank of the various lengths specified in the materials list. Mount each of these on the lathe and turn the 1" diameters as indicated in the technical drawing (see photos 4 and 5).

4 Here you see the longest of the lower posts while it is still mounted on the lathe.

5 The completed lower posts.

Turning the Rear Stretcher

This is made from 5/4 stock, turned to a 1"-diameter cylinder. Starting at the middle, taper the blank to both ends. Turn ½" × ¾" stubs on both ends. Sand the piece (see photo 6).

Building the Steps

Use 5/4 stock to make the steps all to the same length of 21½". The top step is somewhat wider than the others to provide a larger platform for a lamp.

To make the shape of the step, first draw a 3" circle (1½" radius) on your stair blank. Then with a beam compass, draw a 20" arc from the center point of that circle. Mark the end points of 9¾" for the wider top step, and 7¾" for the other steps, and then draw lines connecting the smaller 3" circle with those end points.

With a band saw or a saber saw, cut out each of the steps, and smooth all edges. With a Forstner bit, bore a 1" hole in each step, and with your router, round over all the edges with a ½" roundover bit. Sand all parts (see photo 7).

Making the Segments

With the exception of the length, both types of segments are made in the same manner. The table below lists the exact dimensions. Lay out each of the segments, in the quantities specified, and cut out on a band saw or saber saw. Smooth all curves.

Lay out and bore ¼"-diameter holes, ½" deep in all the segments. Sand all parts. Select four of the small segments and designate them No.1, No.3, No.4 and No.6. These require countersunk holes to accommodate the No.8 × 1¾" wood screws that will secure the steps during final assembly (see photo 8).

Segment and Post Assembly

Assembly of the segments to the posts requires the use of ¼" dowel centers to locate the ¼" holes in the segment ends to the posts. It is important that the segments be located with their respective post positions in this sequence:

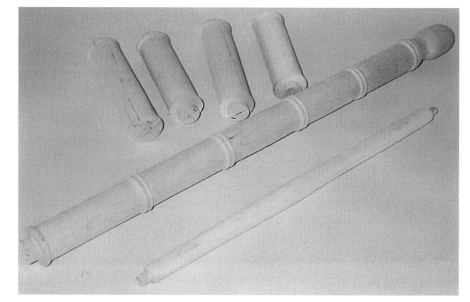

6 The completed rear post with mounted end ball, spacers and stretcher.

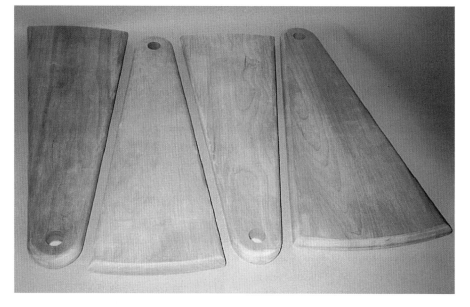

7 The completed stair treads. Remember that the top tread is slightly wider to accommodate a lamp.

Segments

SEG	QTY	A	B	C	D	WOOD THICKNESS
Small	6	5⁹⁄₁₆	6	19" radius	18" radius	5/4
Large	4	12⅝	13½	19" radius	18" radius	5/4

Dimensions in inches

1. Place the dowel centers in one end of small segment No.1. Center on the 7⁹⁄₁₆" post and press the segment to the post, thus leaving two indentation marks on the post. Bore two ¼" × ½"-deep holes in the post. Using two ¼" × 1" dowels, test fit the segment to the post. Do not glue in any dowels at this time.

2. For segment No.2, shift the dowel centers to the other end of the small segment No.1 and do the same operation as before for segment No.1.

3. Repeat the same operation for small segment No.3 to the 18¾" post.

4. Repeat the same operation for small segment No.3 to the 7⁹⁄₁₆" post.

5. Repeat the same operation for small segment No.3 to the 7⁹⁄₁₆" post and then to the 25" post.

6. Repeat the same operation for small segment No.4 to the 7⁷⁄₁₆" post and then to the 18¾" post.

7. Repeat the same operation for large segment No.1 to the 18¾" post and then to the 25" post.

8. Repeat the same operation for small segment No.6 to the 5¹⁵⁄₁₆" post and then to the 7⁷⁄₁₆" post.

9. Repeat the same operation for small segment No.5 to the 7⁷⁄₁₆" post and to the 18¾" post.

10. Repeat the same operation for large segment No.2 to the 18¾" post and to the 25" post.

11. Repeat the same operation for large segment No.4 to the 5¹⁵⁄₁₆" post and to the 18¾" post.

12. Repeat the same operation for large segment No.3 to the 18¾" post and to the 25" post.

Gluing the Joints

Since there are so many joints to keep track of, it's a good idea to number the joints on the posts and on the segment ends.

Glue the dowels to the segments (two dowels per side). In gluing the segments to the posts, it should be done in a couple of time spans as follows:

1. Glue small segments No.1 and No.2 to the 7⁹⁄₁₆" and 25" posts respectively. Set aside to dry.

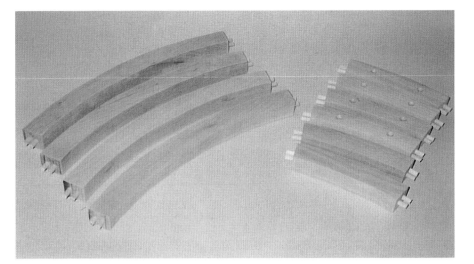

8 The completed segments with attached mounting dowels.

2. Glue small segment No.3 and large segments No.1, No.2 and No.3 to the 18¾" post. Set aside to dry.

3. Glue small segments No.4 and No.5 to the 7⁷⁄₁₆" post. Set aside to dry.

4. Glue small segment No.6 and large segment No.4 to the 5¹⁵⁄₁₆" post. Set aside to dry.

5. Glue the four segments attached to the 18¾" post to the 7⁹⁄₁₆" post and the 25" post.

6. Small segments No.4 and No.5 to the 18¾" post.

7. Finally, glue small segment No.6 and large segment No.4 to the 7⁷⁄₁₆" and 18¾" posts respectively.

Final Assembly

Before final gluing, temporarily assemble the table and mark the locations on the bottom of the steps where the No.8 × 1¾" wood screws will go. Drill the pilot holes. Begin final assembly by assembling and gluing the bottom spacer to the fourth step as well as gluing the rear stretcher to the 25" post and the bottom spacer. Don't screw down the stairs until all the gluing is finished. Continue assembling and gluing spacers and steps starting from the bottom. Screw each of the steps in place. Finally, glue the upper post in place.

Finishing

Since I used cherry for this project, I chose a clear finish to allow the wood to darken to its own natural beauty. To duplicate this finish, apply one coat of gloss polyurethane and two coats of satin polyurethane. Between coats, lightly sand with 400-grit wet/dry paper, wiping with a tack rag after each sanding. Once the finish is dry, apply a good grade of cabinet wax and buff with No.0000 steel wool.

Shoji Lamp

BY CHRIS SCHWARZ

Believe it or not, the idea for this lamp came to me while scrutinizing some flea-market lamp shades made from used popsicle sticks. The concept, I decided, was sound. But I wanted to make some changes.

So instead of gorging myself on 100 Dreamsicles, I decided to use ¼" maple strips. And instead of creating a true oddity of Americana, I chose to look to the Far East to create a lamp that would be at home in a Japanese household.

SHOJI LAMP ■ INCHES (MILLIMETERS)

REFERENCE	QUANTITY	PART	STOCK	THICKNESS	(mm)	WIDTH	(mm)	LENGTH	(mm)
A	88	sides	maple	¼	(6)	¼	(6)	6⅛	(156)
B	2	feet	maple	¾	(19)	1	(25)	8½	(216)
C	1	base	maple	½	(13)	8½	(216)	8½	(216)
D	4	dowels		⅛	(3)			13	(330)

Supplies

Shoji paper - Highland Woodworking, www.highlandwoodworking.com, 800-241-6748. Item No. 216401

Light fixture available from Lowe's or other home improvement center.

STEP ONE: First you need to cut the 88 sticks that make up the sides. Rip some ¼"-thick maple into ¼"-wide strips. I found that a board that's ¼" thick, 6" wide and 4' long makes one lamp. Now crosscut the strips to 6⅛" long.

STEP TWO: Now drill the 176 holes in the side pieces for the four dowels that hold the lamp together. I made a jig to hold a side piece in place on my drill press while I drilled the holes. The center of each ⅛" hole is located 3⁄16" in from each end. Now sand all the pieces.

STEP THREE: Build the base. First cut the base to size and cut two ¼"-deep by ¾"-wide grooves in the bottom of the base. These should be located ⅞" from the edges. Glue the feet in place. Now mark on the base where the four dowels will be located. Here's how: Draw two lines between the opposite corners of the base. This creates an "X" at the center of the board. Measure out 4¹⁄16" from the center on each of these four lines. Drill a ⅛" hole at each location.

STEP FOUR: Sand your four ⅛" dowels a bit and put some wax on them. Slide the side pieces onto the dowels. When you've reached your final height, glue the four dowels into the base. Glue the top two side pieces to the dowels and cut them flush to the top.

STEP FIVE: Glue the shoji paper to the inside of the lamp. I cut out four pieces of paper and glued them to the inside using yellow glue sparingly. Add your light fixture and you're done. No finish is required.

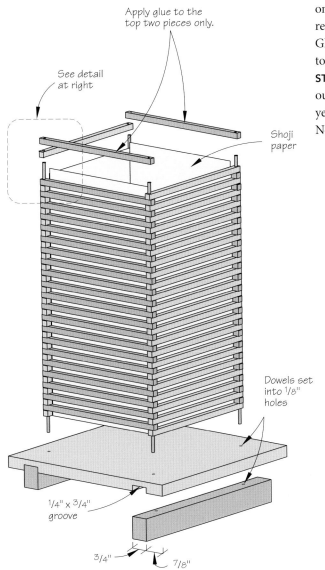

Apply glue to the top two pieces only.

See detail at right

Shoji paper

Dowels set into ⅛" holes

¼" x ¾" groove

¾" ⅞"

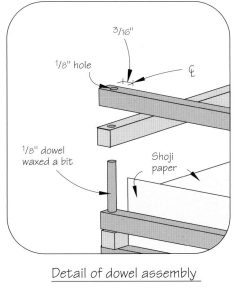

3/16"

⅛" hole

℄

⅛" dowel waxed a bit

Shoji paper

Detail of dowel assembly

Pendulum Wall Clock

BY DANNY PROULX

A wall clock is an enjoyable project to build, and one that I like doing but never seem to have the time — pun intended. When I was designing the projects for this book, I realized that pocket hole joinery could be used to make the clock, as well as adding a unique decorative element. The finished project is beautiful, and the wood-filled pocket holes are drawing a lot of positive comments.

I used my favorite hardwood and installed contrasting wood plugs. The red oak with walnut plugs is a nice combination of woods, and the appearance isn't overpowering. In some furniture designs, the decorative trim is so obvious that it becomes the focus. These two woods, after being finished with spray lacquer, are a nice gold and brown mixture.

A wall clock would be a great addition to any room in your house. It's functional and isn't all that expensive to build. The hardware, including the glass, totals less than $35. A single AA battery powers the quartz clock and pendulum mechanism.

This wall clock is unique and would be a nice gift for someone on that special occasion. It's something that will be used every day and will be passed down to future generations. I've had three or four family members remark, "Oh, that's nice. Can you make me one?" So, be sure to note all the measurements and construction steps, because you, too, will be building a few more clocks.

Purchase a clock kit that allows you to change the pendulum length to suit your cabinet size. My kit doesn't have chimes, but I did notice two or three slightly-higher priced kits that were equipped with that feature. Some people, myself included, don't appreciate the chimes sounding every hour, but many like the sound, so the choice is yours.

Take your time building the wall clock, and try a few different trim combinations. This is one project you'll be looking at for many years, so be sure you're satisfied with the results. And if you sell woodcrafts, this clock would be a big seller at any show.

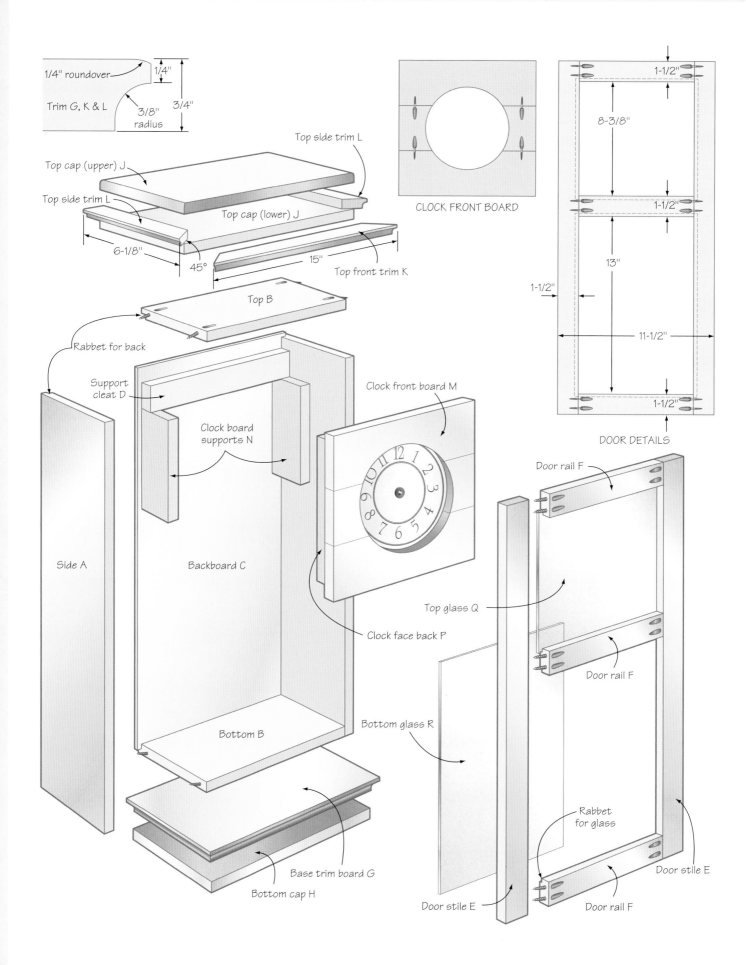

1/4" roundover

1/4"

3/4"

Trim G, K & L

3/8" radius

Top cap (upper) J

Top side trim L

Top side trim L

Top cap (lower) J

6-1/8"

45°

15"

Top front trim K

CLOCK FRONT BOARD

Top B

Rabbet for back

Support cleat D

Clock board supports N

Clock front board M

Side A

Backboard C

Clock face back P

Bottom B

Bottom glass R

Base trim board G

Bottom cap H

Clock front board M

Door rail F

Top glass Q

Door rail F

Rabbet for glass

Door stile E

Door stile E

Door rail F

DOOR DETAILS

1-1/2"

8-3/8"

1-1/2"

13"

1-1/2"

11-1/2"

1-1/2"

REFERENCE	QUANTITY	PART	STOCK	THICKNESS	(mm)	WIDTH	(mm)	LENGTH	(mm)	COMMENTS
A	2	sides	hardwood	$3/4$	(19)	$4^1/2$	(115)	26	(660)	
B	2	top and bottom	hardwood	$3/4$	(19)	$4^1/2$	(115)	10	(254)	
C	1	backboard	veneer ply	$1/4$	(6)	$10^3/4$	(273)	$25^1/4$	(641)	
D	1	support cleat	hardwood	$3/4$	(19)	$1^1/2$	(38)	10	(254)	
E	2	door stiles	hardwood	$3/4$	(19)	$1^1/2$	(38)	$25^7/8$	(657)	
F	3	door rails	hardwood	$3/4$	(19)	$1^1/2$	(38)	$8^1/2$	(216)	
G	1	base trim board	hardwood	$3/4$	(19)	$5^1/4$	(133)	13	(330)	
H	1	bottom cap	hardwood	$3/4$	(19)	$4^3/4$	(121)	$12^1/16$	(307)	
J	2	top caps	hardwood	$3/4$	(19)	$5^1/4$	(133)	13	(330)	
K	1	top front trim	hardwood	$3/4$	(19)	$1^1/2$	(38)	15	(381)	
L	2	top side trim	hardwood	$3/4$	(19)	$1^1/2$	(38)	$6^1/8$	(155)	
M	1	clock front board	hardwood	$3/4$	(19)	$9^{15}/16$	(253)	$9^{15}/16$	(253)	
N	2	clock board supports	hardwood	$3/4$	(19)	$2^1/2$	(64)	6	(152)	
P	1	clock face back	particleboard	$5/8$	(16)	$7^1/2$	(191)	$7^1/2$	(191)	
Q	1	top glass	glass	$1/8$	(3)	$9^1/4$	(235)	$9^1/8$	(232)	
R	1	bottom glass	glass	$1/8$	(3)	$9^1/4$	(235)	$13^5/8$	(346)	

Supplies

Pocket hole screws: $1^1/4$" (32mm)

Wood screws: $1^1/4$" (32mm), 1" (25mm)

$1^1/4$" (32mm) decorative wood screws

Brad nails

Glue

Pocket hole plugs

1	Clock face kit	item #46K05.17	Lee Valley
1	Clock mechanism	item #46K01.09	Lee Valley
2	No-mortise hinges		

Glass retainer clips

Door latch

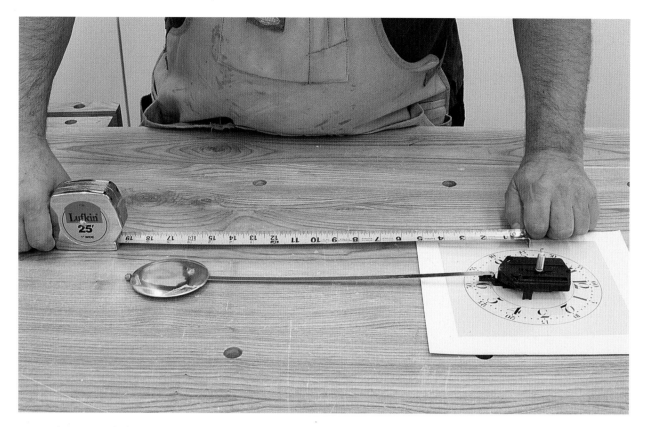

1 Purchase your clock and pendulum kit prior to finalizing the cabinet dimensions to ensure a proper fit. My clock face is 6" in diameter, painted on a 7½" square plate. These kits are popular and available at many woodworking hardware supply stores.

2 Cut the two sides A, as well as the top and bottom B, to the sizes shown in the materials list. Form a rabbet with your table saw, ¼" deep by ⅜" wide, on the rear inside face of each board. These rabbets can be cut along the full length of each board, because they will be covered by other trim pieces.

3 Drill pocket holes on both side edges of the top and bottom boards. Secure them to the clock sides using glue and 1¼"-long pocket hole screws.

Shop Tip

There has to be enough room to properly install wood filler plugs in the holes. I experimented with a couple of pocket hole drill setups, and found that setting my stop collar on the drill bit to drill a deeper hole worked best. I set the stop about ⅛" deeper than my standard ¾" material setting. The large heads of the pocket hole screws could then be driven a little deeper in the hole, providing more room to seat the wood plugs.

4 The backboard C is attached to the clock cabinet with brad nails and glue. The backboard should sit in the rabbets on all four panels.

5 Install the support cleat D, using glue and 1¼" wood screws through the top board. A hole can be drilled in the center of this cleat, through the backboard, which can be used to hang the clock. I will be putting a 3" screw into a wall stud to mount the clock.

6 The door is 25⅞" high by 11½" wide. The two stiles E (vertical members) and the three rails F (horizontal members) are 1½" wide. The rails are joined to the stiles with two 1¼" pocket hole screws and glue at each joint. I used walnut plugs to contrast with the oak door frame, in the pocket holes on the front face of the door frame. Carefully align and drill the pocket holes if they are to be on the front face of the door. If you prefer, the pocket holes, filled with matching wood plugs, can be on the back face of the door. Position the rails and stiles as shown in the illustration.

7 Use glue to install the wood pocket hole plugs, and sand them smooth once the adhesive has set.

8 Cut a recess on the back of both frame openings, using a rabbeting router bit. The rabbet should be ³⁄₁₆" deep to hold the glass panels. The rabbet width is dependent on your router bit, but should be at least ¼" wide. Square the corners with a chisel.

9 Complete the machine work on the door by rounding over the outside profile with a ¼"-radius router bit.

10 The first trim board is attached to the bottom of the wall clock cabinet. Cut base trim board G to the size indicated in the materials list. Use a ⅜"-radius cove router bit to cut a profile on the bottom edge of the front and sides of this trim board. The top face of the board's front and side edges are rounded over with a ¼"-radius router bit. Trim board G overhangs each side, as well as the front edge of the cabinet, by ¾". Attach this trim board to the bottom of the clock cabinet with glue and 1¼" wood screws.

11 The bottom cap H has the front and side edges of its lower face rounded over with a ¼"-radius bit. All the edges on this trim board should align with the edges of the coved trim board G. Note that the dimensions of your bottom cap may be slightly different from mine because of the profile on the cove bit you own. Verify the exact dimensions of cap board H before cutting to size. Use glue and clamps to secure the bottom cap H to the underside of G. Once the adhesive has set, sand the G-to-H edges smooth.

12 The lower top cap J is installed with glue and 1¼"-long wood screws. Round over the bottom face edges on the sides and front with a ¼" router bit. This cap overhangs the sides and front edge by ¾". Use a cove bit to profile the lower edges of the three top trim boards K and L. Attach them to the lower top cap with glue and brad nails. The cove cuts on these three boards face toward the clock. There should be a ¼" straight lip on each board after completing the cove profiles. Align the trim boards so their back edges are ½" in from the front edge of the lower cap J. Join the two corners with 45° miter cuts.

13 Attach the upper top cap J. The top face edges are rounded over with a ¼"-radius bit. This cap is aligned with the lower top cap and secured with glue and brad nails.

14 Glue up enough boards to achieve the final size for the clock front board M, as detailed in the materials list. You can use a single board if you have one that's large enough, or join a number of narrower boards. If you are joining boards, carefully position the pocket holes to leave room for a 6⅛"-diameter hole in the center.

15 Cut the 6⅛"-diameter hole in M, or to a size that's suitable for your clock face, in the center of this panel. Use a jigsaw or scroll saw to cut the hole and sand smooth after completing the cut. Profile the front edge of the hole with a ¼"-radius router bit.

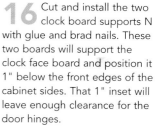

16 Cut and install the two clock board supports N with glue and brad nails. These two boards will support the clock face board and position it 1" below the front edges of the cabinet sides. That 1" inset will leave enough clearance for the door hinges.

17 The clock face is attached to the support boards with 1¼" decorative wood screws. They can be easily removed when the clock battery needs replacing. One on each side, threaded into the supports N, will secure the face.

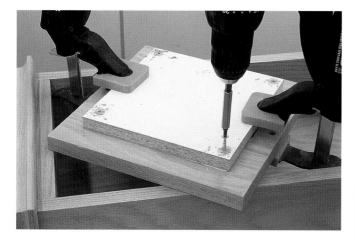

18 My clock face is 6" in diameter, painted on a 7½"-square sheet of thin metal. The clock motor assembly I purchased is designed for mounting on a ⅝"-thick piece of material. I used double-stick tape to attach the clock face to a ⅝"-thick sheet of melamine-coated particleboard (PB). Once the clock face is attached to the clock face back P, center the assembly in the hole on the clock front board M. Use four 1"-long wood screws to join the boards.

19 Drill a hole for the clock motor shaft and test fit the mechanism. When you're satisfied that the clock assembly is working correctly, remove the hardware and apply a finish to the wood. I used three coats of polyurethane, sanding with 220-grit paper between coats.

20 Dozens of hinge styles can be used to hang the cabinet door. I used no-mortise hardware mounted 4" on center from the top and bottom to install my door.

Construction Notes

I always remind woodworkers about using their favorite wood species, and this project is no different. I used red oak because it's reasonably priced in my area, and I like working with that type of wood. However, this wall clock can be built with any type of wood, and the choice is often dictated by existing room furniture. The project would be very striking if it were made of walnut with visible oak pocket hole plugs.

The size of this clock was based on the dimensions of my hardware. That's the reason I suggest you purchase your clock kit before cutting any wood. I looked through a few woodworking catalogs and found kits with similar dimensions, so I'm sure it won't be too difficult to get one that's sized close to the one I used.

One of the main design features of this project was the use of filled pocket holes on the front face of the clock cabinet door. It's an interesting effect and has drawn a lot of positive comments. However, you can just as easily drill the pocket holes on the back face of the door.

The cabinet box is simple and consists of two sides, a bottom and top, with a 1/4" back. The upper and lower trim details define the style, and it's here where you can create your own special look. Experiment with different store-bought and shop-made mouldings until you find a combination that suits your furniture style.

I considered putting hinges on the clock front board, but decided that a battery change every six or eight months wasn't enough to justify the added hardware cost. As it turns out, I found I could change the battery by reaching behind the clock board, so I didn't have to remove it. However, I would still recommend using the removable decorative screws in case the mechanism requires replacement.

The building steps for this wall clock can be used to build a floor model, if desired. I'd suggest a larger clock face, a longer pendulum and some minor design changes on the base. The clock case can be smaller or larger, with a few minor dimensional changes, so it's a versatile project.

I also thought about purchasing a better mechanism, possibly a plug-in powered model, and installing a light behind the clock face board to illuminate the case. It would be a dramatic effect, and one that might be worth researching. Clocks are fun to build and will usually remain in the family for years, so it's well worth trying a few design ideas until you get one that's right for you.

21 The two glass panels Q and R are secured with small plastic clips that are readily available in hardware stores. Be sure to position the clips so they won't hit the cabinet side boards.

22 I installed a spring latch to hold the wall clock door closed. However, a number of other latches are available, including the common magnetic type. Use whichever style of latch hardware you prefer.

Barrister Bookcases

BY STEVE SHANESY

Even if you're not a lawyer and don't wear a powdered wig, these bookcases are a smart addition to your home or office.

Not too far from our workshop here in Cincinnati, Globe Furniture made thousands and thousands of these so-called "barrister bookcases" for lawyers and bureaucrats across the nation. Many were made of oak, but the company also made them from other species of wood and even made a steel version.

REFERENCE	QUANTITY	PART	STOCK	THICKNESS	(mm)	WIDTH	(mm)	LENGTH	(mm)	COMMENTS
A	1	top or bottom	cherry	$3/4$	(19)	$12^5/8$	(321)	$34^1/4$	(870)	
B	2	sides	cherry	$3/4$	(19)	12	(305)	$13^1/4$*	(337)	
C	1	back	cherry	$1/2$	(13	$33^1/4$	(845)	$13^3/4$*	(349)	
D	2	door rails	cherry	$3/4$	(19)	$1^1/4$	(32)	$30^3/8$	(772)	
E	2	door stiles	cherry	$3/4$	(19)	$1^1/4$	(32)	$13^1/16$*	(333)	
F	1	base front	cherry	1	(25)	$3^1/2$	(89)	$34^3/16$	(868)	
G	2	base sides	cherry	$3/4$	(19)	$3^1/2$	(89)	$11^7/8$	(302)	
H	1	base back	plywood	$3/4$	(19)	3	(76)	$32^{11}/16$	(830)	
J	1	glass	glass	$1/8$	(3)	$12^1/4$*	(311)	$30^5/16$	(770)	
		glass stops		$3/8$	(10)	$7/16$	(11)	96	(2438)	

* Subtract 2" (51mm) for shorter unit.

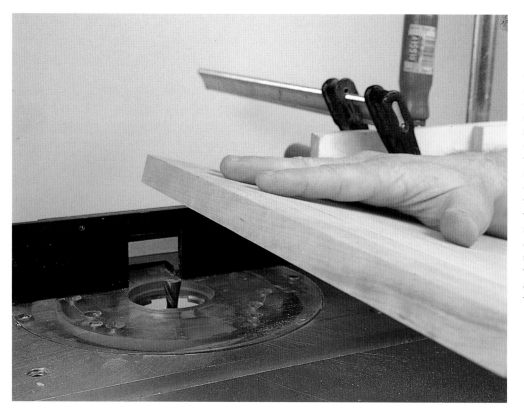

Door slide. With a $1/2$" straight bit set in a router and mounted in a router table, set the height of the cutter to make a $3/8$"-deep cut. Now set up a fence on the router table so that the cut starts $5/8$" from the edge (see the diagram). Next set a stop on the fence so that the cut you make stops $3/8$" from the front edge of the sides. (Remember that you will have to change the stop when switching from right to left sides.) Because the peg used is $1/2$" thick, you'll need to create a very slight amount of clearance, say $1/32$", so that the peg moves easily through the dado. Do this by adjusting the fence away from the cutter. Then rerun the parts.

Though this style of bookcase was first used exclusively by attorneys and government-types, the stackable units are now extremely popular (and pricey) in antique stores. And no wonder. You can use them to store just about anything anywhere. While most people use them for books or their favorite collectibles, I know one person who uses them in her bathroom for toiletries.

I designed these bookcases so you can make any number of units that can be stacked on top of one another and side-by-side as well. And there's a complete economy of material use because the top of one also serves as bottom of the case above it. In constructing the three cases shown, I used two different heights for the boxes. The shorter one accommodates books that are 9" tall or less; the larger case accepts books up to 13" tall.

Other than the extra time and the expense of more material, it makes a lot of sense to make several boxes because the set-ups to build the boxes are perfect for the "short production run" approach to building. That means setting up the machine — in this case a router in a table and a drill press — then running the parts. Because it can take longer to accurately set up the machine than run a part or two, running a few more parts makes real sense. Remember that accuracy is the key to the project because each unit has to be able to mate with all the other units.

After you've determined the quantity and size of the cases you want to build, prepare enough wood to glue up the

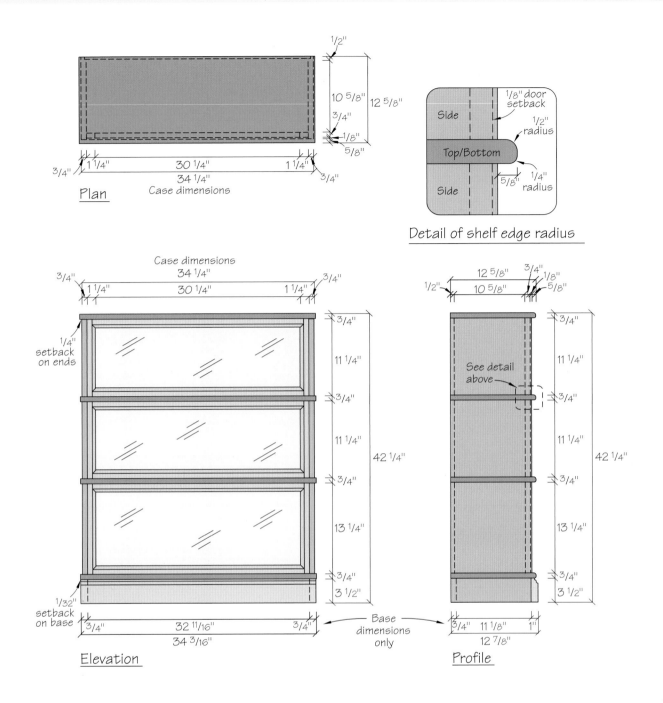

Plan

1/2"

10 5/8" 12 5/8"

3/4"

1/8"

5/8"

3/4" 1 1/4" 30 1/4" 1 1/4" 3/4"

34 1/4"

Case dimensions

1/8" door setback

Side

1/2" radius

Top/Bottom

5/8" 1/4" radius

Side

Detail of shelf edge radius

Case dimensions

34 1/4"

3/4" 1 1/4" 30 1/4" 1 1/4" 3/4"

1/2" 12 5/8" 3/4" 1/8"

10 5/8" 5/8"

1/4" setback on ends

3/4"

11 1/4"

3/4"

See detail above

3/4"

11 1/4"

11 1/4"

3/4"

11 1/4"

42 1/4"

3/4"

13 1/4"

42 1/4"

3/4"

13 1/4"

1/32" setback on base

3/4"

3 1/2"

3/4"

3 1/2"

3/4" 32 11/16" 3/4"

34 3/16"

Base dimensions only

3/4" 11 1/8" 1"

12 7/8"

Elevation

Profile

panels you need. Glue up your panels, then sand the joints flush, making sure to keep all the panels the same thickness. Cut the panels to the finished sizes indicated in the Schedule of Materials.

Mill the Cases

The joinery for the cases is straightforward. The plywood back is captured in a rabbet made on the sides and bottom (although the bottom rabbet is stopped 1/2" from both ends so you can't see it from the outside). Then the bottom is

biscuited to the sides. The cases stack on one another using dowels in the tops of each case and holes on the bottom. Begin construction by chucking a straight or rabbeting bit in a router mounted to a table and make the 1/2" × 1/2" rabbets in the sides and bottoms.

Now it's time to do some additional routing to make the groove in the sides for the sliding doors and some hole drilling. While you can purchase special slides for barrister bookcases, my homemade method is cheaper, works just as

well and is almost as easy as installing slides. Each of these steps requires real accuracy, and you must pay attention to which parts are for the right and left sides, fronts and backs, tops and bottoms. The best way to keep this straight is to organize your parts by type, then stack them so they are oriented the way you want them. Marking them with a pencil adds another measure of insurance.

Begin by routing the stopped dadoes in the case sides that make up part of the sliding door mechanism (the other part of the mechanism is simply a peg inserted into the edge of the door).

Make Perfect Holes

Now drill the holes in the case bottoms. These holes are used to receive the indexing pins that are inserted in the top edges of the sides. This interlocking quality keeps the cases from sliding while stacked atop one another and holds the sides in position. Remember that the holes are drilled in the bottom piece and line up with each case's sides. Set up the drill press with a ⅜" diameter bit, using the fence and a stop block, and drill the holes as indicated in the diagrams to a depth of ⅜". Bear in mind that the holes are a different distance from the front and back edge so the fence set-up must change accordingly.

Now drill the corresponding holes in the top edges of the sides, again to a depth of ⅜". These holes are for the dowel pins. Again, accuracy is key. I used a self-centering doweling jig for drilling these holes. Mark the drilling locations carefully. Refer to the diagram for drilling locations.

Biscuit the Sides

Next cut the biscuit slots for joining the sides to the bottom. I used three biscuits in each side, a No.20 size in the middle and back, and a No.10 in the front. I used the No.10 so the slot didn't interfere with the hole drilled in the bottom. The last thing to do before final assembly is to run a roundover detail on the front edge of the bottoms. To make my profile, I used a ½" radius bit on the top edge and a ¼" radius bit on the bottom edge. Again, use the router table and fence for the cut, even if you have router bits with guide bearings on them. You can rely on the bearing for the first cut. But on the second cut the bearing would ride on the previously cut radius, which sweeps away from the edge.

1 If you want your cases to mate correctly, accuracy is key. Use stop blocks on your drill press when drilling the bottom and use a doweling jig when drilling holes on the sides.

2 After cutting the slots for the biscuits, assemble the cases. I used polyurethane glue. While not necessary, it does provide a stronger joint because of its ability to provide some glue strength to the end grain/cross grain joint where the sides join the bottom.

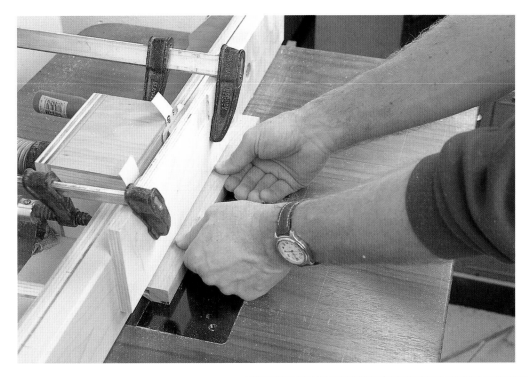

3 First run the ogee detail on the inside edges of both the stiles and rails. Set the height of the cutter so that it leaves just a slight bead on the face of the parts, say $\frac{1}{32}$". After running the parts, switch to the "coping" cutter and cut the matching opposite detail on the ends of the rails only. Make sure you use a back-up block, also called a coping block, to stabilize the narrow part while running it across the router bit.

4 A simple block made to index off the top edge of the side along with a dowel center marks the drilling center for the dowel pivot guide. Use the dowel center's point to insert a $\frac{1}{2}$" brad point drill point and make the hole.

Assemble and glue the sides to the bottoms. I set the case backs in place to help keep the assembly square during the glue-up. Here's how I glued these up: Put glue on the mating parts and set them in place. Then set the back in and clamp across the back and sides. Next, while making sure the back edge of the side is flush to the back edge of the bottom, clamp the side and bottom from top to bottom. With all the clamps in place, check for square and adjust as needed. Do not attach the backs until after finishing.

Next I made the base of the bookcases. Rout the ogee profile on the top edge of the front piece only before biscuiting and gluing the base together. The sides simply butt to the back side of the front piece, and the plywood back piece butts into the sides. The back piece is narrower than the sides and front so leave some space at the floor for any base moulding on your floors. Attach the back piece flush to the top of the base assembly. I also elected not to attach the base permanently to one of the cases. Instead, I screwed indexing blocks to the case bottom that allow the lower case to nest into the base. This allows you to level the base when you install it and then simply stack the cases on top.

Frame and Panel Doors

The frames for the glass doors were the last chore to tackle before moving on to sanding and finishing. Because I wanted the relatively small doors to have a delicate appearance, I made my stiles and rails just 1¼" wide. For a strong corner joint and a pretty detail on the inside edge of the frame, I used a matched stile-and-rail router bit set normally used for frame-and-panel doors. The nice ogee detail I used echoed the detail on the base and complemented the rounded front edge of the case bottoms.

Again, make sure you cut your stiles and rails to the exact length needed using a stop block. This will help ensure you make a frame that's square. Because

Diagram of indexing pin, door peg, door-stop peg and dado layout.

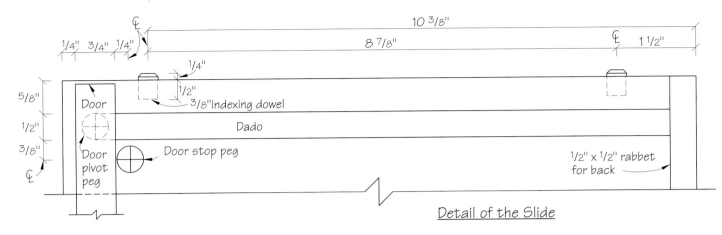

10 3/8"

8 7/8"

1 1/2"

1/4" 3/4" 1/4"

1/4"

1/2"

3/8" indexing dowel

5/8"

Door

Dado

1/2"

3/8"

Door pivot peg

Door stop peg

1/2" x 1/2" rabbet for back

Detail of the Slide

5 To install the glass, use wood stops with mitered corners cut to fit in the rabbets. An easy way to hold the stops in place is using 1/8" fender washers and screws. Simply screw them into the frame with part of the washer lapping over the stop. I clipped the ones on the door sides so they didn't hit the dowel on which the door rests when slid back into the cabinet.

the router bits are intended to be used with fixed panels, and the glass needs to be removable, it's necessary to cut away part of the edge detail on the back, changing it from a groove to a rabbet. Using a table saw, it's a simple procedure for the rails because you can run the part all the way through. For the stiles, however, you need to make a stopped cut because the piece you leave at the ends is part of the "mortise" joint made by the matching router profiles. Mark the stiles from the ends where you want to stop the cut (it can vary slightly depending on the cutters you use), then mark the table saw's fence at the point where the blade projects above the table when it is set to the correct height for the cut you're making. While holding the part firmly to the fence, slowly lower it onto the blade with the motor running, then cut the part to the matching lines on both the part and the saw fence.

Now you can glue up the stile and rail assembly, making sure you check for square and adjust as needed. When dry, chisel out the corner of the back of the stile where the waste piece remained from the stop cut you just made.

Critical Dowel Location

Check the fit of the doors. You should have a $\frac{1}{16}$" gap on the sides and bottom and a $\frac{1}{8}$" gap left for the top (this allows the door to pivot up without touching the piece above it). If the fit is good, drill a $\frac{1}{2}$" hole in the door's edge that's $\frac{1}{2}$" deep. Locate the hole in the center of the edge so that the hole centers $1\frac{3}{16}$" down from the top edge. Use your combination square as a marking gauge and a doweling jig for accurate drilling. Drill these holes on both edges of each door. Insert a $\frac{7}{8}$" length of dowel or other $\frac{1}{2}$" rod into the door edge (I used a nylon rod). Place the doors in the side grooves of the case (this is easily done with the top open). Bring the doors forward and gently lower them down into position.

Glass Installation and Finishing

The last bit of fussing with the doors is setting the pin below the groove where the doors slide in their grooves. Carefully positioning the pin provides not only the spot where the doors rest when open, but also coaxes them into the proper location at the top when closed. Lastly, cut and fit the $\frac{3}{8}$" $\times$ $\frac{7}{16}$" strips that will hold the glass in place on the back side of the frames.

Next sand your parts with 120 and 150 grit paper using a random orbit sander. Also make sure no glue was left behind that would splotch a nice finish. For the final finish, I tried something I'd never done before. I added a slight amount of oil-base stain to boiled linseed oil. Linseed oil on cherry brings out the grain of the wood more than a film finish like varnish, shellac or lacquer does. The wee bit of color added (I used about a thimbleful of stain to 10 ounces of oil) gave the new cherry a bit of "maturity," which new cherry always lacks. I tend to think that new cherry without any color added looks anemic. But too much color causes cherry to blotch if applied full strength.

If you choose to use an oil-only finish, apply a couple more coats of boiled linseed oil, making sure you thoroughly wipe off all excess oil after applying. For my bookcases, I allowed the oil to dry overnight then sprayed the pieces with clear lacquer. Brushing on varnish, shellac or polyurethane will work as well. Finally, put your doors back into the cases and screw the backs into the sides and bottom.

When it comes time to set up your barrister bookcases, their modular construction and variety of arrangements should prove a real asset. That is, unless you can't agree with your "significant other" about how they should be arranged. In that case, you might just need a barrister to settle the bookcase dispute.

Knockdown Bookcase

BY DAVID THIEL

The Arts & Crafts movement was part of an interesting social change in America — the advent of mail-order purchases. Catalogs from Sears, Roebuck and Co. and Montgomery Ward were all the rage, and many companies took their cue and offered their wares for sale through catalogs rather than set up expensive retail establishments throughout the country. While it was a great idea, it raised a difficult problem with furniture. The majority of space in any piece of furniture is air. While air is very light, it's also bulky and expensive to ship. So furniture makers perfected a style of furniture that continues today — knockdown furniture. Finished disassembled, the furniture could be shipped flat, then assembled by the owner. Through-tenons with tusks were the turn-of-the-20th-century answer, while hidden cam-locking hardware is the answer today.

Slanted Construction

This project is actually a very simple bookcase made challenging by slanting the sides. Many of the knockdown bookcases had straight sides, but why do things the easy way?

Start construction by preparing the panels for the sides and four shelves. If you aren't fortunate enough to have oak that's wide enough to make your sides using a single board, glue up the shelves or sides using two boards, but make sure the joint falls in the center of the finished panel. This is less important on the shelves; but since the sides come to a peak at the center, the joint becomes obvious if you're off the mark. Also, you can cut the top and bottom shelves to length, but leave the two center shelves

long at this time. When the through-tenons are cut and fit, you can measure for the exact length of the center shelves.

Critical Pencil Lines

With the sides prepared, lay out the shelf locations, mortise locations and the overall shape in pencil on one of them. To allow you to do a minimum of angled or beveled cutting on the pieces, the shelves all fit into ¾"-wide by ⅜"-deep dadoes cut at a 5° angle in the sides using the table saw. Because of this, the location of the shelves actually falls at an angle on the sides. A ¹⁄₁₆" difference in shelf height one way or the other won't dramatically affect the use of the bookcase, but you must make sure that the dadoes are cut at the same locations on each side.

If you happen to have a sliding table on your table saw, you're in great shape. Most people don't, so the next best option to cut the angled dadoes is to use your miter gauge. If you don't have a substantial wooden fence attached to your gauge, now is a good time. A fence that is 18" to 24" long and about 3" high will work fine. You'll need to determine which way to orient the sides on your saw depending on the way the arbor of your saw tilts. With some of the cuts, the majority of the side will be supported by the miter gauge, and you can use your rip fence to guide your cut. When the larger section of the side will be between the blade and rip fence, this is an unsafe cut. The board can twist and bind against the blade and cause a kickback. Move the rip fence out of the way, mark the sides and make the next cuts with only the miter gauge fence. With the dadoes complete, swap the dado with a crosscut blade, and bevel the bottom edge of each side at that angle.

Angled Mortising

The next step is the through-mortises. For these to work correctly, they also need to be cut at a 5° angle, and they must fall directly in the dadoes you just cut on the saw. You could cut them by hand, but the 5° angle is tricky to maintain. You could also set up a mortiser to do the job, but I got a little smarter and came up with a router template.

By using a piece of ½" Baltic birch with a strip added beneath one end, I made a router template that would make cuts at a 5° angle. It takes some rearranging of the guide for the different cuts, but the results work rather well.

REFERENCE	QUANTITY	PART	STOCK	THICKNESS	(mm)	WIDTH	(mm)	LENGTH	(mm)	COMMENTS
A	2	sides	white oak	3/4	(19)	12	(305)	48*	(1219)	
B	1	bottom shelf	white oak	3/4	(19)	11¹/₈	(283)	24¹/₂	(623)	
C	1	top shelf	white oak	3/4	(19)	10	(254)	19³/₈*	(492)	2" TBE
D	1	third shelf	white oak	3/4	(19)	9⁷/₈	(251)	19*	(483)	2" TBE
E	1	second shelf	white oak	3/4	(19)	8¹¹/₁₆	(221)	17*	(432)	
F	8	tusks	white oak	3/4	(19)	3/4	(19)	3¹/₂	(89)	

*Oversized for fitting; TBE = tenon both ends

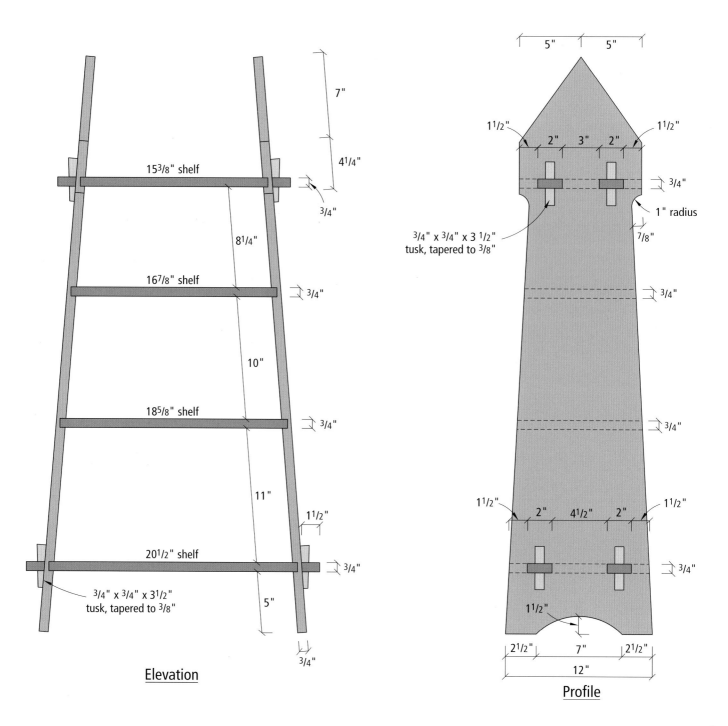

15³/₈" shelf

16⁷/₈" shelf

18⁵/₈" shelf

20¹/₂" shelf

³/₄" x ³/₄" x 3¹/₂"
tusk, tapered to ³/₈"

7"

4¹/₄"

³/₄"

8¹/₄"

³/₄"

10"

³/₄"

11"

1¹/₂"

³/₄"

5"

³/₄"

Elevation

5"   5"

1¹/₂"   2"   3"   2"   1¹/₂"

³/₄"

1" radius

7/8"

³/₄" x ³/₄" x 3 ¹/₂"
tusk, tapered to ³/₈"

³/₄"

³/₄"

1¹/₂"   2"   4¹/₂"   2"   1¹/₂"

³/₄"

1¹/₂"

2¹/₂"   7"   2¹/₂"

12"

Profile

After carefully laying out the shelf locations, use a dado stack (set at a 5° angle) and the saw's miter gauge to cut the angled dadoes.

This simple scrap-wood jig made angled mortises a fairly simple task.

Careful layout lines are critical here. To make the 5° ramp, I used a scrap piece of ½" material for the back strip, nailed to the template 14" from the end. Check this dimension carefully on your materials to get as close to 5° as possible.

The rest is fairly simple. Check the offset on your router template guide from the bit, and add this to the ¾" × 2" dimension for the mortise. Mark that size on the template and use a drill and jigsaw to make a square hole.

Clamp the template in place over the mortise locations and cut your through-mortises using two or three depth settings. Depending on the router bit you're using, you may want to use a backing board behind the side to reduce tear-out. I used a jigsaw and chisel to square up the corners.

Shaping up the Sides

The next step is to cut the sides to their "spade" shape. I used my band saw for most of this work, but used a jigsaw to cut the radii under the top shelf and the arch at the bottom. Cut a little wide of your layout lines, then clamp the sides together, aligning the sides by the shelf grooves on the inside surface. Plane and sand the sides to matching shapes.

Fitting the Through-Tenons

Now it's time to fit things together. Start by checking the fit of your shelves in the dadoes in the sides. Mine were a hair thick, so I was able to run them down on the planer to make an almost-perfect fit. Check the width of the bottom shelf against the width of the sides at the shelf location, now that the sides are shaped. Rip the shelf to size. Next, fit the shelf into the dado and, from the outside, mark the tenon location through the mortise on the end of the shelf. Remove the shelf and mark off the 2" length of each mortise, then head for the band saw again. The width of the tenons is the critical cut. The shoulder of the tenons should be neat, but that edge is buried in the side's dadoes, so it doesn't have to be perfect.

With the tenons cut for the bottom shelf, fit the shelf and sides together. You want a snug fit, but not too loose and not too tight. A chisel, file or rasp and some sanding should do the job. Take your time and get it right.

With the bottom shelf fit, check the dimensions on the top shelf, mark the tenons and repeat the fitting process. When that task is complete, fit the two center shelves and slide them into position. These shelves are designed to be left loose, but if they slide a little more than you like, a nail through the side into the center of the shelf will make a permanent solution, or you can drive a short wedge into the joint under the shelf for a temporary fix.

Tusks and the Home Stretch

To hold the top and bottom shelves in place — and the whole case together — disassemble the case and mark the ¾" × ¾" through-mortises on the shelf tenons as shown in the diagrams. I used my mortising machine to cut these holes. Another option is to use a drill press to cut the mortises and then square up the corners using a chisel.

Reassemble the case, then cut the eight tusks. Appropriately, the tusks should seat with their center at the shelf tenon. Fit the tusks as necessary, and tap them into place to make the whole case rigid. Now take it all apart one last time and sand everything to 150 grit.

For a finish, I used a simple dark-colored gel stain, wiping off the excess until I was happy with the depth of the color. I then top-coated the case with a couple of coats of lacquer.

The nicest thing about moving this bookcase is that after you knock out the eight tusks, everything fits in the trunk of a compact car.

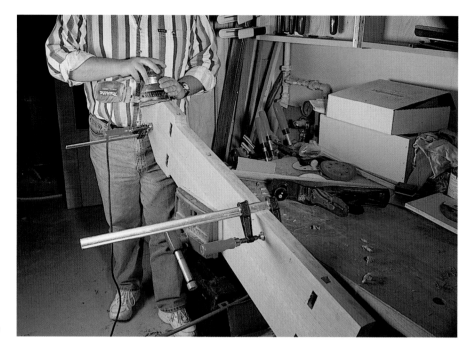

With the sides clamped together and mounted in my vise, shaping the sides simply took some sanding and planing.

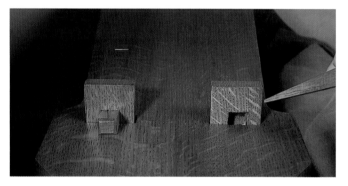

A close look at the wedged through-tenons shows the recess behind the side that allows the wedge to pull the sides tight.

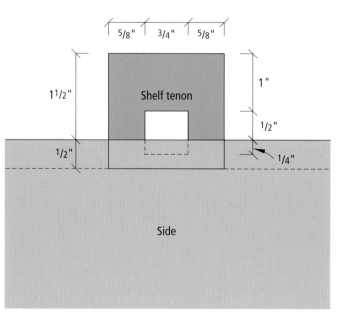

Detail of shelf joinery

5/8" 3/4" 5/8"

Shelf tenon

1 1/2"

1 "

1/2"

1/2"

1/4"

Side

Basic Bookcases

BY DAVID THIEL

In almost every home in America there's the odd corner that not a single piece of furniture looks right in. You know what I'm talking about: The weird space beside the fireplace, the interior corner in the solarium, the space next to the sliding glass door. You've probably thought to yourself that a custom built-in cabinet would do the trick. In my home, that space was next to the fireplace. Here's how I turned that liability into an attractive asset that adds value to my home.

Rabbets & Dadoes

Face frame cabinets are one of the easiest types of cabinets to build. Start by cutting the carcase sides and bottom. To support the bottom, cut a $\frac{3}{8}$"-deep × $\frac{3}{4}$"-wide dado on the inside of each side so the top of the dado is 3" up from the bottom. Next, cut a $\frac{1}{2}$"-deep × $\frac{3}{4}$" rabbet on the inside top edge of each side to accept the support rails.

The first step in making this cabinet built-in rather than free standing is rout-

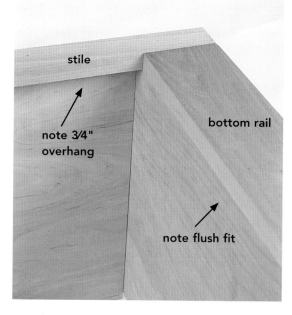

Face frame. Mill the facing rails and stiles to size and then glue the frames together with biscuits, remembering to check for square. When the glue has dried, sand the inside frame surface flush, and then glue and clamp the frames to the front of the cabinet carcases.

stile

note 3/4" overhang

bottom rail

note flush fit

Fitting strips. Both pieces of the fitting strip were made of solid ½" cherry. For the inset doors, the fitting strip is flush. For overlay doors, attach the strip forward to match the overlay (see below).

fitting strip

REFERENCE	QUANTITY	PART	STOCK	THICKNESS	(mm)	WIDTH	(mm)	LENGTH	(mm)	COMMENTS
LOWER CABINET										
A	2	sides	cherry plywd	$3/4$	(19)	$21^{1}/2$	(546)	$30^{1}/4$	(768)	
B	1	bottom	cherry plywd	$3/4$	(19)	$20^{1}/2$	(305)	$29^{1}/2$	(749)	
C	2	support rails	cherry plywd	$3/4$	(19)	3	(76)	$29^{3}/4$	(756)	
D	1	back	cherry plywd	$1/2$	(13)	30	(762)	$27^{1}/4$	(692)	
E	2	fitting strips	cherry	$1/2$	(13)	$1^{1}/2$	(38)	$30^{1}/4$	(768)	
F	2	facing stiles	cherry	$3/4$	(19)	$1^{1}/2$	(38)	$30^{1}/4$	(768)	
G	4	facing rails	cherry	$3/4$	(19)	3	(76)	$27^{1}/4$	(692)	
H	4	door stiles	cherry	$3/4$	(19)	$1^{1}/2$	(38)	$24^{1}/4$	(616)	
J	2	door rails	cherry	$3/4$	(19)	$1^{1}/2$	(38)	$13^{5}/8$	(346)	
K	1	door panels	cherry plywd	$1/4$	(6)	$11^{5}/8$	(295)	$22^{1}/4$	(565)	
L	1	top	cherry plywd	$3/4$	(19)	$22^{1}/4$	(565)	$31^{3}/4$	(806)	
M	1	top edging	cherry plywd	$3/4$	(19)	$1^{1}/2$	(38)	$32^{1}/2$	(826)	
N	1	top edging	cherry plywd	$3/4$	(19)	$1^{1}/2$	(38)	23	(584)	
UPPER BOOKCASE										
P	2	sides	cherry plywd	$3/4$	(19)	9	(229)	54	(1372)	
Q	1	top	cherry plywd	$3/4$	(19)	9	(229)	$29^{1}/2$	(749)	
R	3	shelves	cherry plywd	$3/4$	(19)	$7^{3}/4$	(197)	$28^{3}/4$	(730)	
S	3	shelf facings	cherry	$3/4$	(19)	$1^{1}/2$	(38)	$28^{3}/4$	(730)	
T	2	facing stiles	cherry	$3/4$	(19)	$1^{1}/2$	(38)	54	(1372)	
U	1	facing rail	cherry	$3/4$	(19)	3	(76)	$27^{1}/4$	(692)	
V	1	back	cherry plywd	$1/2$	(13)	30	(762)	$53^{1}/4$	(1353)	
W	2	fitting strips	cherry	$3/8$	(10)	$1^{1}/2$	(38)	54	(1372)	
X	1	support rail	cherry	$3/4$	(19)	$2^{1}/2$	(64)	$28^{3}/4$	(730)	

The Doors. The doors are simple but classic flat panel construction using half-lap joinery at the corners. The 1/4" cherry plywood panels are captured in a 1/2" groove run in the stiles and rails prior to assembly. Since they are inset doors, check the sizes in the cutting list against your actual opening and allow the doors to be a hair oversized to allow for fitting.

ing a rabbet on one of the sides, (see photo at left). If your wall is perfect and square, you're in great shape and won't have to do any fitting.

In my corner cabinet, the interior side was ripped a second time to 20½". This allows the back to simply overlay the entire back edge of the interior side without the worry of a rabbet. If the cabinet were being mounted to a wall where both sides would be visible, both sides would be made with a rabbeted back edge.

Assemble the lower cabinet using glue and clamps, strategically placed nails, or for extra strength and less nails, cleats can be used to attach the sides to the bottom from underneath. Square up the cabinet and temporarily attach the back to support the cabinet.

The upper shelving section is built in the same manner, but with the dado this time cut at the top of the sides, 1½"

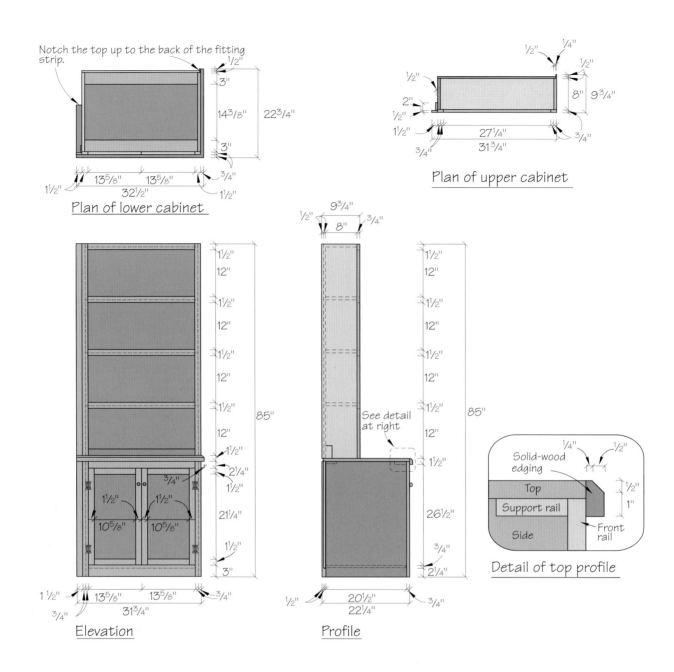

Notch the top up to the back of the fitting strip.

Plan of lower cabinet

Plan of upper cabinet

See detail at right

Elevation

Profile

Solid-wood edging

Top

Support rail

Side

Front rail

Detail of top profile

down from the top. The lower support rail at the bottom of the unit is biscuited between the sides, so run the same rabbet on the back edges of each side and temporarily attach the back for extra support.

Face Frames

Next, make the two face frames. The stiles of the lower cabinet overhang the inside of the cabinet by ¾", but the bottom rail overhangs the bottom only a fraction of an inch on the inside, (see photo above). The outside overhang

should be sanded flush to the cabinet after gluing.

The top for the lower cabinet is simply cut to size from plywood, and then a solid cherry edge is glued and biscuited to the two visible edges with a miter joint at the corner. I ran a ½" chamfer on the top edge to soften the edge of the top.

Fitting Strips

The most important piece of the built-in part of the cabinetry is next. Referred to as fitting strips, these are simply L-

shaped strips that are screwed to the wall side of the cabinet during installation, (see photo above).

The shelves are the next step in construction. Cut the shelves to size and biscuit and glue a ¾" × 1½" solid cherry rail to the front edge. This is called a "dropped edge" and not only gives the shelves a more substantial appearance, it keeps the shelves from bowing under the weight of books. The shelves are held in place with adjustable shelf pins which can be located and drilled to suit your needs.

Half-Lap Doors

The simple door construction is shown in the photo on page 114. The butterfly hinges I used don't require any mortising, but you do need to be careful to align the doors correctly when attaching the hinges.

The interior of the lower cabinet can be whatever you need. On the piece shown I installed three interior drawers compartmentalized for video tape storage.

I finished the piece using a cherry oil-based stain and two coats of satin finish lacquer, giving the piece a rich appearance.

Installation

Now it needs to be installed. At this point you might want to take a couple of minutes to consider how the cabinets are being used. If you're using any lighting or stereo components in the cabinets, consider your wiring options. Also consider ventilation for the stereo.

Start the installation by preparing the space where the cabinet will go. If the room is carpeted, the cabinet can sit right on top of the carpeting. This cabinet has been designed to work without a base moulding. If you've got hardwood floors with any grooving detail on the floor, the cabinet base against the floor will show off these grooves. If this offends you, a small quarter-round moulding can be added after installation. Any existing baseboard in the cabinet's location can be marked and cut in place with a backed saw so the cabinet will slip into place (from above if it's a corner cabinet). Or the baseboard can be removed and cut and reattached after the cabinet is installed. A third option is to cope the back of the cabinet and the fitting strip to match the base moulding and allow the cabinet to cover the baseboard.

With the space prepared, put the cabinet in place, allowing space for the fitting strip (or with the fitting strip attached), square it up and level it up front-to-back and side-to-side using shims. Then check the fit against the walls. If you're lucky you won't have to touch a thing, but more likely than not you'll need to use the scribing method

shown on the next page. This cabinet is of a size that the face frame could have been design to extend beyond the cabinet and serve as a fitting strip, but the removable fitting strip is a lot easier to remove, mill and replace than the whole cabinet.

Put the cabinet back in place and again check the fit. If everything looks good, the cabinet can be screwed in place against the wall. Locate the studs behind the cabinet. Hopefully you can catch two. If not, a molly bolt in the wall would provide a second attachment location. Then mark the stud locations on the cabinet back and drill a clearance hole, then screw the cabinet in place. Make sure you use a long enough screw, 3" is preferable. Don't over-tighten the screw, it needs only to pull the cabinet to the wall, not correct any bow in the drywall (that's what the scribing was for).

Before putting the top in place, drill clearance holes (two each) in the support rails to attach the top after fitting. Next put the top in place and check its fit

against the wall and plane or cut to provide the best joint. Then place the upper bookcase unit on the top, and again fit, scribe and plane or cut the back edge and fitting strip to match. With the bookcase fit to the walls, lightly mark the side location on the top and then remove the bookcase. Drill holes through the top (two per side), then remove the top from the lower cabinet and attach the upper case to the top with screws.

The upper assembly should fit into place with a few inches clearance on top. Screw the top to the lower cabinet through the support strips. A couple screws through the upper case's back at the very top will secure it to the wall. Hang the doors, put the shelves in place and you're ready to fill the cabinets.

Scribing. Take a compass, and with the legs separated to the width of the widest gap between wall and cabinet, scribe a line down the back edge and against the front of the fitting strip. Remove the cabinet and cut almost to the scribe line with a coping saw or jigsaw. Then clean the cut with a plane.

Two Traditional Hanging Shelves

BY TROY SEXTON

These shelves are quite popular with my two best customers: my wife and my daughter. We have them hanging in several rooms of our farmhouse where they hold plates and knickknacks.

Not surprisingly, these shelves are also popular with my paying customers. While many of them may dream of buying a custom corner cupboard, sometimes what they can best afford are the hanging shelves. So these small projects make everyone happy.

For the home woodworker, these shelves are a home run. These two traditional designs look great in most homes, and the woodworking part is so simple that almost anyone should be able to build these in a weekend.

Patterns and Dadoes

Both of these shelves are built using the same techniques and joints. The only significant difference is that the Shaker-style unit has three shelves and the 18th century "Whale Tail" project has four shelves and a more ornate profile that looks vaguely like a whale's tail. To me, it looks more like a goose.

Begin your project by selecting your lumber and planing it down to ½" thick. Using the supplied patterns and the construction drawings, draw the profile

on your side pieces and mark where the dadoes should go.

Now set up your dado stack in your table saw so it makes a ½"-wide cut that's ³⁄₁₆" deep. As you can see in the photo on page 120, I made this cut using only the fence. I feel real comfortable with this cut; but if you're not, I recommend you use your miter gauge and a stop block attached to your fence to guide the work instead.

Cutting the Details

I use a band saw to shape the sides. Begin by making several "relief" cuts along the profile of your side. These allow you to remove the waste in chunks so your blade and workpiece are easier to maneuver through the cut.

Once you've completed both sides, sand the edges using a drum sander that's chucked into your drill press. I recommend you tape the two sides together using double-sided tape and sand them simultaneously. It's faster and the sides end up identical.

Once that's complete, fit the shelves and sides together for a dry fit. Notice anything? The square edges of the shelves don't match the sides exactly.

Mark the shape of the sides onto the end of the shelves. Now, using a jointer with the fence beveled (or a hand plane), shape the front edge to match the side.

REFERENCE	QUANTITY	PART	STOCK	THICKNESS	(mm)	WIDTH	(mm)	LENGTH	(mm)	COMMENTS
A	2	sides	maple	1/2	(13)	4⁷/₈	(124)	25¹/₄	(641)	
B	1	bottom shelf	maple	1/2	(13)	3¹/₈	(79)	23¹/₂	(597)	
C	1	middle shelf	maple	1/2	(13)	4⁷/₈	(124)	23¹/₂	(597)	
D	1	middle shelf	maple	1/2	(13)	3	(76)	23¹/₂	(597)	
E	1	top shelf	maple	1/2	(13)	3	(76)	23¹/₂	(597)	

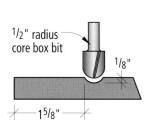

½" radius
core box bit

1/8"

1⁵/₈"

Plate rail groove detail

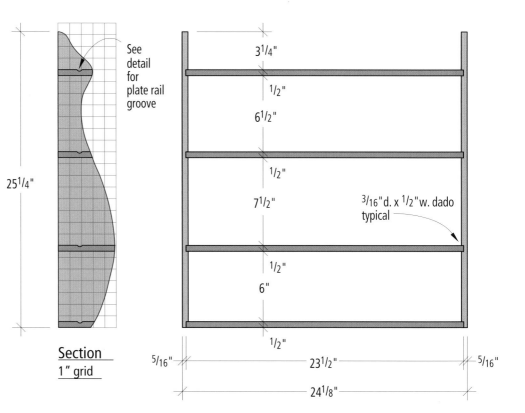

See detail for plate rail groove

25¹/₄"

Section
1" grid

3¹/₄"

½"

6¹/₂"

½"

7¹/₂"

3/16"d. x ¹/₂"w. dado typical

½"

6"

½"

5/16"

23¹/₂"

5/16"

24¹/₈"

Cut the dadoes in the sides using a dado stack in your table saw. If you're a beginning woodworker, I recommend you perform this operation with a miter gauge to guide the work instead of the fence. I've made a lot of these shelves and am quite comfortable with this method.

Notice the relief cut I made in the sides. By removing the waste in smaller hunks (instead of all at once), the blade is more maneuverable.

REFERENCE	QUANTITY	PART	STOCK	THICKNESS	(mm)	WIDTH	(mm)	LENGTH	(mm)	COMMENTS
A	2	sides	cherry	1/2	(13)	6 1/2	(165)	24	(610)	
B	1	bottom shelf	cherry	1/2	(13)	6 1/2	(165)	23 1/2	(597)	
C	1	middle shelf	cherry	1/2	(13)	6	(152)	23 1/2	(597)	
D	1	top shelf	cherry	1/2	(13)	4 1/4	(108)	23 1/2	(597)	

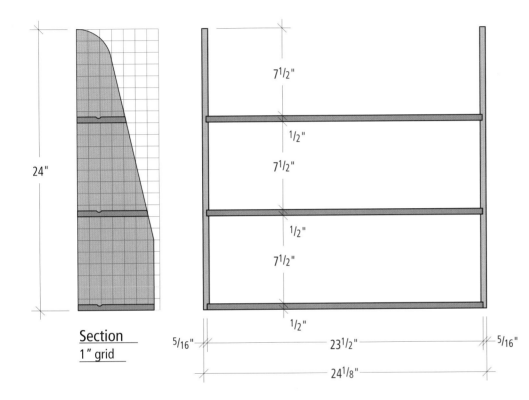

24"

Section
1" grid

7 1/2"

1/2"

7 1/2"

1/2"

7 1/2"

1/2"

5/16"   23 1/2"   5/16"

24 1/8"

Supplies

Picture Hooks
available from home-center
stores or from Lee Valley
Tools, 800-871-8158 or
leevalley.com
Item # 00D78.02, 50 picture
hooks

You just want to get in the ballpark; sanding can take care of the rest of the contouring job.

Now cut the plate rail groove in the shelves. I used a router bit with a core box profile and a router table. The plate rail is 1/8" deep and 1 5/8" in from the back edge.

Before you assemble the unit, finish sand all the surfaces except the outside of the sides. Begin with 100-grit sandpaper and work your way up to 120, 150 and finish with 180.

Assembly and Finishing

Put a small bead of glue in each dado and put the shelves in place. Clamp the shelves between the sides and check your project to make sure it's square by measuring diagonally from corner to corner. If the measurements are equal, nail the sides to the shelves using a few 18-gauge brads.

If your measurements aren't equal, clamp the project diagonally from one corner to another. Clamp across the two corners that produced the longest measurement. Apply a little pressure to those corners and keep checking your diagonal measurements. When they are equal, nail the project together.

After an hour, take the project out of the clamps and sand the outside of the side pieces and putty your nail holes.

Ease all the sharp edges of the project using 120-grit sandpaper. I dyed my project using a water-based aniline dye that I mixed myself from several custom colors. I recommend you use J. E. Moser's Golden Amber Maple dye for a similar effect. It's available from Woodworker's Supply, woodworker.com.

Finally, add a couple coats of your favorite top-coat finish and sand between coats. Hang your shelf using some common picture hooks, available at any home center or from the source listed in the supplies box.

Stickley Bookcase

BY GLEN HUEY

If you've perused the pages of our former sister publication, *Woodworking Magazine*, you might have seen this piece in the Spring 2005 issue. We dug through the archives to find a fine bookcase, then did a bit of construction modification to allow the design to better fit the "I Can Do That" column. And that's something you should be on the lookout for as you read woodworking articles or skim the pages of your favorite catalogs. Find a piece you like and see what changes can be made to match the construction to your skill set and tools.

For this piece, we eliminated the complicated shelf joinery, and we adjusted a few sizes to better accommodate the lumber dimensions found at home centers. But by and large, this bookcase is close to our original project and a great piece to build.

For material, you'll need an 8' piece of 1 × 10 for the sides and one shelf, and a 1 × 10 × 4' for two shelves, the braces and one toe kick. Crosscut the material to the required length, then rip the braces and toe kick.

Add Design to the Sides

The bookcase sides require the most work, so begin at the handle area. Measure down from the top 1¼", then square a line across the grain. Also, find the top center of the sides then square a line off the top edge that extends just across the first line.

The next layout step is to grab a compass that's set for a 2½" radius, position the point of the tool at the intersection of the two lines and mark a half-circle with the flat side parallel with the top edge of the sides. To soften the look,

round the sharp corners of the handle area. I used a pair of nickels placed at the corners to establish the radius.

To create the handle opening, use a ¹³⁄₁₆" bit to drill holes at each corner (the bit closely matches the diameter of the nickels). With the two difficult-to-cut areas done, use a jigsaw to remove the balance of the waste. Insert the blade through one of the holes then cut on the line from hole to hole. After that's complete, pivot the saw to cut the half-circle line. Stay close to the line, take your time as you cut and slow the blade speed if possible – a slower blade increases your control as you cut. Then clean up your cuts with a file and sandpaper.

Next, make the cutout at the base. This, too, is a half-circle with a 2½" radius. Because you can start the cut from the bottom edge of the sides, there's no need to drill a hole. Use your jigsaw to cut the area, then smooth the cut as you did before.

The last shaping step is to round the top corners. This step is a bit more

Look at projects with a different eye. Find a piece with great design, such as a Stickley No. 79 bookcase, then make adjustments to the construction to better match your skill set.

REFERENCE	QUANTITY	PART	STOCK	THICKNESS	(mm)	WIDTH	(mm)	LENGTH	(mm)	COMMENTS
A	2	sides	red oak	³⁄₄	(19)	9¹⁄₄	(235)	38	(965)	
B	3	shelves	red oak	³⁄₄	(19)	9¹⁄₄	(235)	12¹⁄₂	(318)	
C	3	support braces	red oak	³⁄₄	(19)	1¹⁄₂	(38)	12¹⁄₂	(318)	
D	1	toe kick	red oak	³⁄₄	(19)	2¹⁄₂	(64)	12¹⁄₂	(318)	

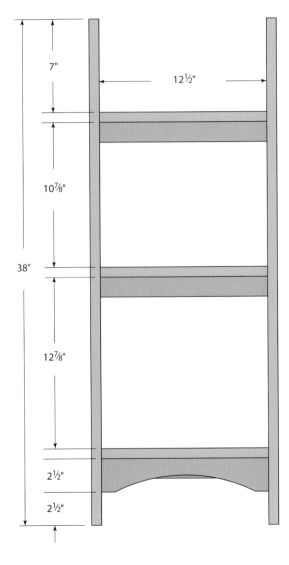

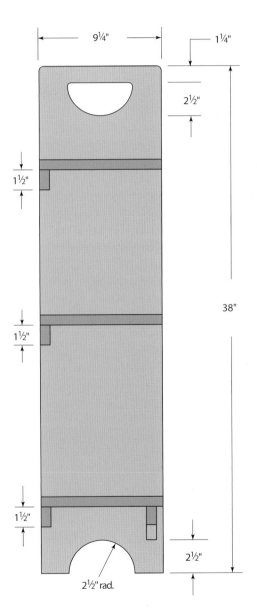

Quarters and nickels make great templates for rounding off corners. The larger the coin, the bigger the radius.

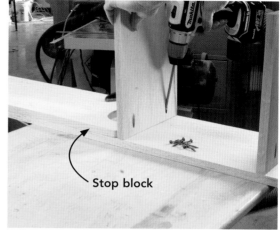

Use a clamp and stop block, or in this case, one of the bookcase sides, to keep your shelves from inching forward as screws are driven.

expensive; use quarters as a template. Draw the profile on your sides, then remove the material with your jigsaw, or use a file and sandpaper.

The only other shaping work required is on the toe kick. Make a mark 1" in from both ends along the bottom edge of the piece. At the top edge, find the center of the piece then add a vertical pencil line across the toe kick. Move down that line 1¼" and mark the location.

Next, instead of finding the appropriate radius with a trammel, bend a ruler or thin stick to create the curve. Hold the ruler at the two points at the bottom edge as you bend the piece to reach the center point of the curve. With the bend set as you like, have a friend mark a line following the bend in the ruler. Cut on the waste side of your line with your jigsaw, then smooth the curve with your file and sandpaper.

No Complex Joinery

Pocket screws make the joinery for this project a snap. Each shelf is drilled for four pocket screws, two at each end, spaced 1½" from the edges. The toe kick is drilled for two screws at both ends as well. And the support braces have one hole per end (with the braces held tight to the bottom of the shelves, you need only the two screws for a secure connection).

Set up your pocket-screw jig as directed and drill the pockets. Use 1¼"

screws for this project; fine threads are better because you're working with hardwood. Note: As you drill in your toe kick, stay toward the top edge of the workpiece. If you bore near the curved portion, it's possible to have a pocket extend into the curve and be visible in the finished bookcase.

Curtail Creepy Movement

As you install pocket screws, it's possible for your pieces to creep slightly. To reduce that possibility, use a stop block and a clamp to keep things in place. To begin, do a simple layout of the shelf locations on the inside face of your sides (a couple short lines set in from the edges is all that's needed).

Next, clamp a wide cutoff at a layout line that is the top edge of a shelf's location. As shown in the photo below, with the shelf pressed against that clamped-in stop block there is no problem with creeping pieces. Install the screws to affix all the shelves to one side of the bookcase, then align the second side and add the screws to complete the installation of the shelves.

One support brace fits tight to the bottom edge of each shelf and flush with the back edge of the bookcase. Align the pieces, then drive the screws to lock the braces in place. The toe kick also sits under the bottom shelf but is held back ½" from the front edge. A clamp added

after the toe kick is positioned holds the piece secure and tight to the shelf as the screws are installed.

A One-Two-One Finish

With the construction complete, take the time to knock off any sharp edges (especially around the handle area) and sand the piece to #120 grit. The finish is a coat of "Dark Walnut" Watco Danish Oil followed, when the oil is dry, by two coats of amber shellac. To complete the bookcase, lightly sand the piece with 320-grit sandpaper then apply one layer of paste wax for protection. All that's left is to put books, family photos or other knickknacks on display.

Pick a Furniture Style — It's in this Book

The projects in this book are based on several furniture styles: Arts & Crafts, Greene & Greene, Contemporary (which is ambiguous at best, but at least it provides us with a style for those projects that don't fit anywhere else), Shaker, American Country, Chippendale and a little of the Federal influence. The descriptions that follow of these styles hit just the high points of joinery usage, stylistic elements, wood usage and overall functioning of the furniture pieces. Each project affords the furniture maker a chance to explore the building and finishing techniques, thereby adding to your woodworking skills.

Each style has characteristics that separates it from the others. Part of the function of art is to reflect the period of time in which it was created — weather that art be in the form of painting, music, literature or furniture making.

 ARTS & CRAFTS uses lots of straight lines, basic mortise-and-tenon joinery (which is easily done by hand or power tools) and sometimes pegs are inserted into the mortise-and-tenon joints to keep them solidly connected. The wood of choice was/is quartersawn white oak, which is usually stained medium to dark.

 GREENE & GREENE is a complex style, which includes lap, mortise-and-tenon and dovetail joinery. Sounds simple enough, but the lap joints are made so the parts stand proud to each other and the edges of the parts have various bevels that create multiple shadow lines. One outstanding element is the use of square, dark-wood (usually ebony) plugs at the joints. So called cloud lifts are cut into rails, stretchers and legs to create visual movement and lighten the look of what would otherwise be a heavy-looking parts.

 CONTEMPORARY style includes (usually) basic joinery methods that include: biscuits, dowels, loose tenons, butt (using screws covered with plugs to hold the joints tightly) and mortise-and-tenon. The use of colorful woods such as paduak, purpleheart, redheart, white oak, red oak, hard maple, cherry, etc. — many times to contrast each other — veneers and clear finishes is common.

 SHAKER uses mortise-and-tenon joinery (many times including pegs) almost exclusively. Cherry, walnut and poplar (as a secondary wood) are the woods of choice. The lines are straight with the use of bevels on the edges of some parts and little else in the way of ornamentation. Many turned parts are also used.

 AMERICAN COUNTRY is another of those somewhat ambiguous styles in that the influences include Chippendale, Queen Anne and others. The joinery is mostly mortise-and-tenon with some being pegged. The use of mouldings and turned parts helps give this style some graceful lines. This furniture is made to be used on a daily basis and includes pieces for the kitchen, bathroom, parlor (dens or libraries) , bedroom and living room. Knotty pine, sugar pine, oak and poplar are commonly used.

 CHIPPENDALE uses mortise-and-tenon joinery, straight and gracefully-curved lines, carvings and turned parts. Many furniture makers consider it the ultimate woodworking challenge.

 FEDERAL uses lots of veneers, laid up in patterns and used as striking-looking design elements. Usually more straight lines and basic joinery are employed. With a clear, highly-polished finish, these furniture pieces are used as showpieces, with the utilitarian part secondary.

Chippendale Mirror

BY KERRY PIERCE

ALTHOUGH NOT A
REPRODUCTION OF ANY
SPECIFIC EIGHTEENTH-
CENTURY ORIGINAL,
THIS MIRROR DOES
EVOKE A NUMBER OF
CHIPPENDALE DESIGNS.

Shaper cutters and router bits come in a bewildering array of shapes and sizes and the exact configuration required for a particular project isn't always available. But often, through some imaginative blending of manufactured shapes (sometimes mixed with a little handwork), the woodworker can create the necessary forms.

This photo shows how the scrollwork, tack strip and cleat are assembled.

The moulding that frames the glass on this Chippendale mirror was produced through the use of two three-winged shaper cutters and a little rabbet work on the table saw. Although not a reproduction of any specific eighteenth-century original, this mirror does evoke a number of Chippendale designs.

Begin construction with the scrollwork background. After the pieces have been band sawn and sanded, assemble them with butt joints and hold in place wit a pair of cleats which are glued and screwed across the back of the scrollwork. At that time, take measurements for the large moulding that lifts and presents the glass.

Working with these measurements and the available shaper cutter and router bits, you can determine the moulding's profile. After the stock had been run, miter the four pieces of the moulded frame to length and screw into place. Complete finishing before installing the mirror to avoid sullying its surface. Tack four wood strips to the back, inside face of the moulding to hold it in place.

This makes stylistic attribution a slippery business. Even though almost all high-style American furniture of the late eighteenth and early nineteenth centuries exhibits characteristics of Chippendale, Hepplewhite and Sheraton designs, very little actually represents any specific published drawings. Further complicating the business of stylistic attribution is the fact that many pieces exhibit characteristics of more than one style. A sideboard might have a spade foot (a Hepplewhite signature) and a gallery of turned spindles (associated with Sheraton's designs).

A chair might have a balloon back and solid splat (Queen Anne) and ball-and-claw feet

(Chippendale). In the hands of a skilled craftsman, such blending is unimportant. A well-designed chair is a well-designed chair whatever the origins of its iconography.

But for the student of furniture, it can be useful to look at this matter of stylistic attribution-not to fasten a particular label on a particular piece but in order to reflect on the American designer/craftsman's handling of the forms and motifs with which he worked.

What Are the Characteristics of Chippendale Furniture?

In the strictest sense, the only furniture that can be identified as Chippendale is that to which Thomas Chippendale, the English carver and designer actually applied his tools. But there are few such pieces and many that are commonly (and usefully) referred to as Chippendale.

Another approach reserves the Chippendale name for those pieces that are exact representations of his published drawings. But this, too, is very limiting, particularly when discussing furniture made in North America. While there are a handful of American-made pieces which accurately represent specific Chippendale designs, the overwhelming majority of American-made Chippendale furniture does not — for some very good reasons.

Thomas Chippendale, George Hepplewhite and Thomas Sheraton — the English designers whose seminal books inspired much American period furniture — all designed for a different market than that served by most American craftsmen of the day. Many of the English designs were intended for placement in grand English homes and included, therefore, elaborate ornamentation that was inappropriate for less palatial American settings (and perhaps for less effete American sensibilities).

This doesn't mean that discriminating American buyers weren't concerned about the appearance of their furniture. Clearly they were, but what those buyers wanted was furniture that not only looked good but was also, and most importantly, useful. They wanted storage, serving surfaces, beds. In short, they wanted furniture in which function and form were more fully integrated.

To address this desire on the part of their customers, American designers/craftsmen reinterpreted the forms presented in the books of the English designers, restraining the decorative excesses of the originals, focusing on the usefulness of their furniture in the homes of their customers.

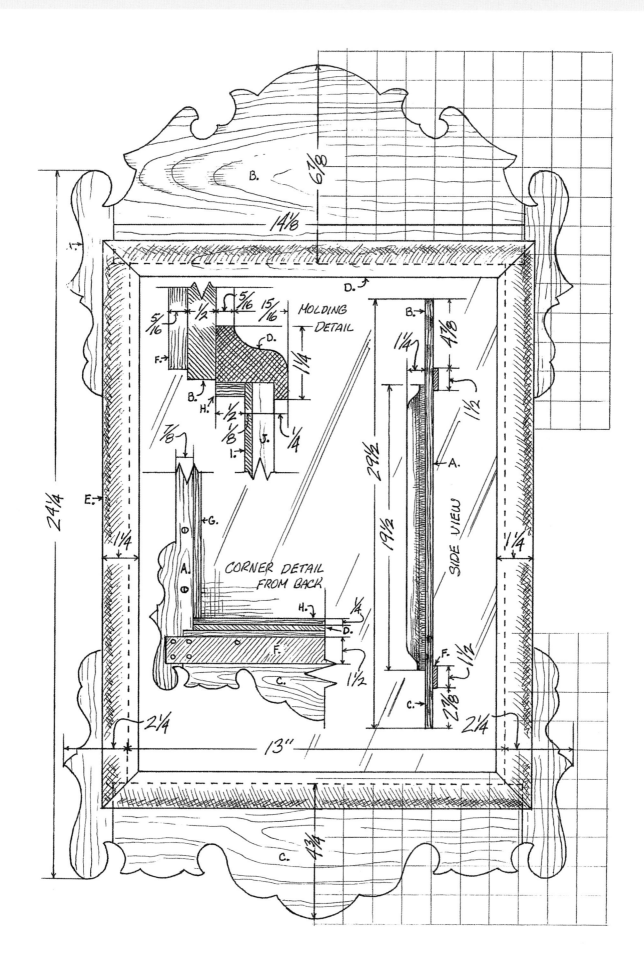

B.

6⅛

14⅛

D.

MOLDING
DETAIL

5/16 ½ 5/16 15/16

5/16

B.

F.

D.

H.

½
⅛

J.

I.

¼

⅛

E.

G.

A.

CORNER DETAIL
FROM BACK

H.

¼

D.

F.

C.

1½

24¼

1¼

B.

4⅛

1¼

½

A.

SIDE VIEW

29½

19½

1¼

F.

½

2⅛

C.

2¼

2¼

13"

C.

4¾

REFERENCE	QUANTITY	PART	STOCK	THICKNESS	(mm)	WIDTH	(mm)	LENGTH	(mm)	COMMENTS
A	2	vertical scrollwork	cherry	$\frac{1}{2}$	(13)	$2\frac{1}{4}$	(57)	$24\frac{1}{4}$	(617)	
B	1	top scrollwork	cherry	$\frac{1}{2}$	(13)	$6\frac{7}{8}$	(175)	$14\frac{1}{8}$	(359)	
C	1	bottom scrollwork	cherry	$\frac{1}{2}$	(13)	$4\frac{3}{4}$	(121)	$14\frac{1}{8}$	(359)	
D	2	horizontal moulding	cherry	$1\frac{1}{4}$	(32)	$1\frac{1}{4}$	(32)	$14\frac{7}{8}$	(378)	
E	2	vertical moulding	cherry	$1\frac{1}{4}$	(32)	$1\frac{1}{4}$	(32)	$19\frac{1}{2}$	(495)	
F	2	cleat	cherry	$\frac{5}{16}$	(8)	$1\frac{1}{2}$	(38)	$16\frac{1}{8}$	(410)	
G	2	vertical tack strip	cherry	$\frac{1}{4}$	(6)	$\frac{1}{2}$	(13)	$17\frac{9}{16}$	(446)	
H	2	horizontal tack strip	cherry	$\frac{1}{4}$	(6)	$\frac{1}{2}$	(13)	$12\frac{7}{8}$	(327)	
J	1	mirror back	hardboard	$\frac{1}{8}$	(3)	$12\frac{7}{8}$	(327)	$17\frac{9}{16}$	(446)	
K	1	mirror	glass	take measurements after frame is built						

Style Characteristics

This chart is not intended to list all the elements of any of these styles. It is meant only to illustrate ways in which one style might be differentiated from another.

	CHIPPENDALE	HEPPLEWHITE	SHERATON	EMPIRE
FORM	Cyma curve	Geometrical Curvilinear	Geometrical Rectilinear Delicate	Massive
ORNAMENT	Carving Scrollwork	Stringing Veneering Inlay	Turning Bandings Carving Reeding	Carving Veneering Ormolu
MOTIF	Cabriole leg Ball-and-claw foot	Spade foot Tapered legs	Turned and tapered legs Tapered legs	Animal feet Animal heads

Shaker Mirror

BY KERRY PIERCE

I began this mirror with the intent of reproducing a Shaker design. However, the more I studied the drawing of the original in John Kassay's *The Book of Shaker Furniture*, the less I liked certain of its features.

Its most appealing detail, the faceted edges at the top of the blade, weren't repeated anywhere else on either the mirror or the blade, so after a little reshaping of the shelf, I brought this faceted edge to the shelf front that holds the bottom of the mirror in place, hoping to make better use of this detail. I also made other changes. Although the original was constructed of cherry and pine, I chose curly maple and walnut in order to make a more dramatic presentation.

The mirror frame stock on the original measured only ½" × ⅞", which I thought was little light even for a mirror that would be supported, not by screw eyes turned into its frame, but by a shelf. I decided, then, to increase the dimensions of that frame stock to ¾" × 1¼".

Making the Shaker-style Mirror

Begin construction with the mirror itself. After thicknessing the frame stock, cut the ¼" × ⅜" rabbet on what will become the back, inside edge of the frame. (This rabbet will ultimately receive the glass and the glass backing.) Form a radius on the two front edges of the frame stock.

Then miter the frame parts. You can do this on a miter box or a table saw or radial arm saw using a very fine-toothed blade. At this point, cut the slots for the feathers that will later join the frame parts. You can cut these by hand with a tenoning saw or on a table saw fit with a hollow ground planer blade, using a Universal Jig to control the stock as it is passed over the blade. Precision is important in the cutting of both the miters and the feather slots as these joints comprise the entire inventory of joinery in the mirror frame. Any error in these processes is very difficult to hide.

The feather stock is then thicknessed and slid into the slots, marked, and cut. The frame is assembled with glue.

The walnut wedges in the mirror frame corners are not only beautiful, they also add structural support.

The hanger consists of only three parts: the blade, the shelf and the shelf front.

Fashion the blade first. After cutting its shape on the band saw, facet the top edges. Do this by hand, guided by a marking system similar to that used in the hand manufacture of the raised panel in chapter one. First, draw a line down the center of each edge to be faceted. Then draw lines on the front and back faces of the blade adjacent to these edges. These lines should be placed about 3/16" from the corners. Then, by using a wood file to create planes, join the lines down the center of the edges and the lines on the blade's faces. You could create these planes freehand, but the reference lines make it much easier to produce regular shapes.

Cut a dado on the back edge of the shelf, and position the blade in that dado, holding it there with a bit of glue and two 1½" no. 12 wood screws.

Then profile the shelf front on the band saw and facet all except the top edges in the same manner as that used for the top edges of the blade. Glue this to the front edge of the shelf.

After sanding and finishing the wood parts, place the mirror glass and a matt board backing inside the rabbet cut in the backside of the mirror frame. Hold both in place with the protruding heads of a half-dozen wood screws turned into the sides of the frame rabbet.

Adhesives

A recent Woodworker's Supply catalog lists eleven different types of adhesives. Several of those-for example, hot melt glues-are available in different formulas for different applications. These differ-

1 Clamp a piece of mitered frame stock in the Universal Jig prior to passing it over the hollow-ground planer blade. Notice that the frame stock rests on its mitered tip and is clamped in the jig at a 45° angle.

2 The faceting at the top of the blade can be seen in this shot. The same faceting is used on all but the top edges of the shelf front.

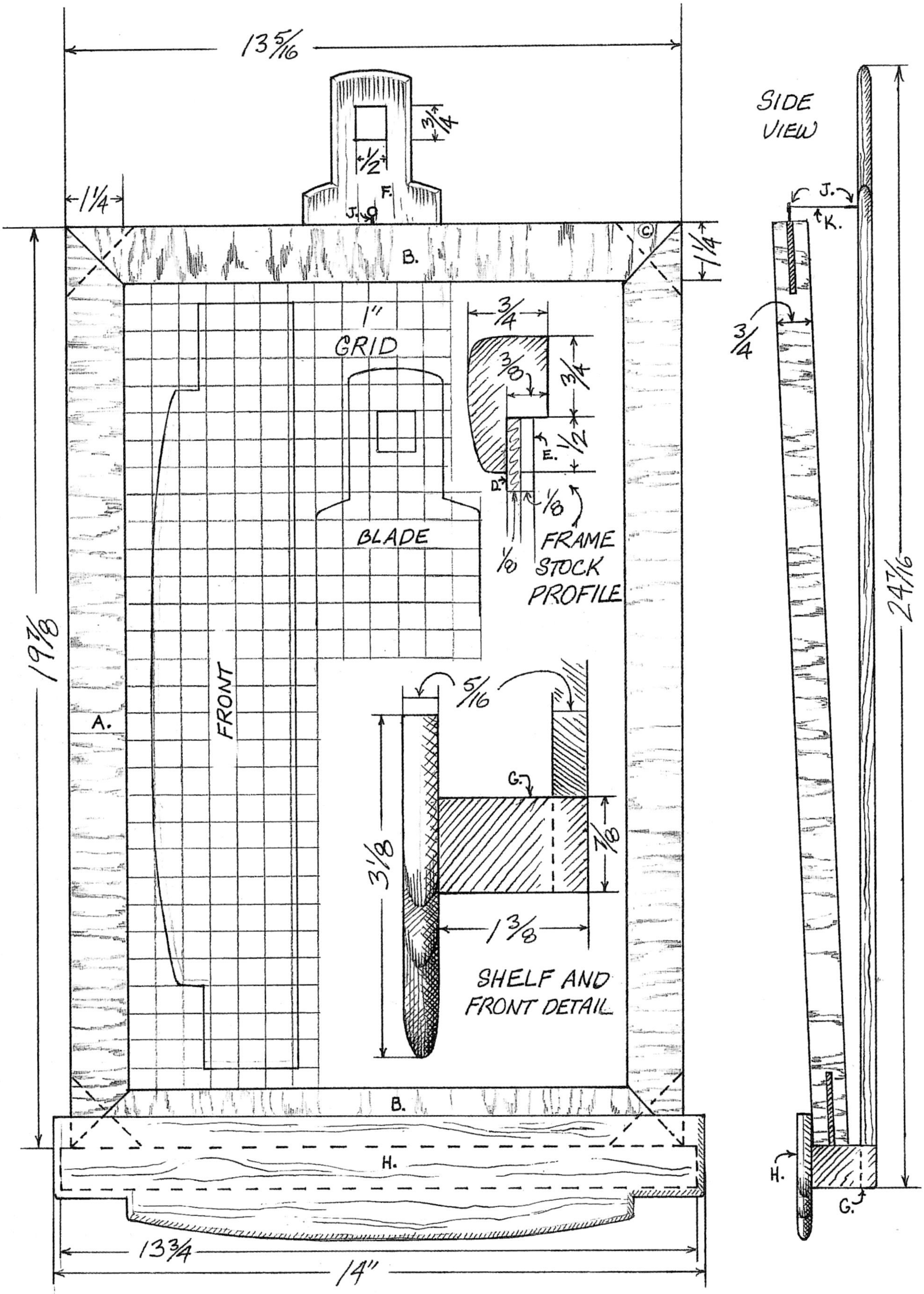

13 5/16
3/4
1/2
F.
J.
1 1/4
C
B.
1 1/4
1" GRID
3/4
3/8
3/4
1/2
E.
D.
1/8
1/8
BLADE
FRAME STOCK PROFILE
19 7/8
A.
FRONT
5/16
G.
3 1/8
7/8
1 3/8
SHELF AND FRONT DETAIL
B.
H.
13 3/4
14"
SIDE VIEW
J.
K.
3/4
24 7/16
H.
G.

REFERENCE	QUANTITY	PART	STOCK	THICKNESS	(mm)	WIDTH	(mm)	LENGTH	(mm)	COMMENTS
MIRROR FRAME										
A	2	sides	cherry	3/4	(19)	1 1/4	(32)	19 7/8	(505)	
B	1	top and bottom	cherry	3/4	(19)	1 1/4	(32)	13 5/16	(338)	
C	4	feather	walnut	3/32	(2.4)	1 1/8	(29)	2 1/8	(54)	
D	1	mirror	glass	1/8	(3)	11 11/16	(297)	18 1/4	(464)	
E	1	mirror backing	hardboard	1/8	(3)	11 11/16	(297)	18 1/4	(464)	
RACK										
F	1	blade	walnut	5/16	(8)	3	(76)	24 7/16	(621)	
G	1	shelf	walnut	7/8	(22)	1 3/8	(35)	13 3/4	(349)	
H	1	front	walnut	5/16	(8)	3 1/8	(79)	14	(356)	
HARDWARE										
J	2	brass eye hook								
K	1	brass chain								
L		various								

ent formulas increase the actual number of choices to sixteen.

Sixteen kinds of glue?

Without devoting significant time to study and experimentation, no woodworker is likely to make the perfect adhesive choice for any particular application. And who wants to spend hours studying adhesives?

In my shop, except for specialized applications (for example bonding Formica-like products to wood), I've reduced the adhesive inventory to three choices: white glue (plain old Elmer's), yellow glue, and hide glue, all of which are more or less appropriate for any wood-to-wood joint.

Each of these three types forms a bond that is stronger than necessary for wood furniture. The primary differences are the amount of working time they allow, the ease with which joints they've bonded can be disassembled, and the convenience of their application.

Hide glue allows for relatively easy disassembly when making repairs and also offers the woodworker the longest working time. It's available in two forms, each of which, unfortunately, has its own set of drawbacks. Traditional hide glue, which comes in flakes or pearls, must be mixed with water and kept heated to a temperature of 140-150' F. Then, after

a few days, it must be thrown out and a new batch mixed because, once mixed and heated, it quickly loses its strength. All of this is a significant inconvenience for the owner of a small shop.

The other form comes premixed in squeeze bottles just like white and yellow glues. Unfortunately, however, its shelf life is shorter than white or yellow glue and much shorter than the dry form of hide glue.

In terms of convenience, both white and yellow glue are clearly superior to hide glue. They come premixed in easy-to-use squeeze bottles. They have long shelf life if kept from freezing, and they form an all-but-unbreakable bond between two pieces of joined wood.

There are, however, drawbacks to their use. First, because the bond they form is all-but-unbreakable, a piece assembled with these glues is very difficult to repair. If a yellow- or white-glue-assembled chair comes into my shop needing a new rung, I have to explain to the customer that I can't predict the cost of the repair.

Whereas, a chair assembled with hide glue can be disassembled by applying warm water to a tight joint, thus allowing a fairly predictable repair time, the same chair assembled with white or yellow glue may resist my best efforts at disas-

sembly. On more than one occasion, I've broken the slab seat on an old Windsor trying to break loose parts that have been joined with white or yellow glue.

The second problem associated with the use of white and yellow glues is short assembly time. When using these products, a woodworker may have only ten or fifteen minutes to get parts aligned and clamped before the glue grabs and adjustments become all but impossible to make. The time constraints applied to the assembly process by white and yellow glues add stress to an already stressful procedure.

In my shop, I follow these guidelines when choosing an adhesive:

1. For large, complex pieces with a high dollar value (pieces for which one could justify the cost of making repairs), I use hide glue.

2. For pieces requiring lengthy assembly time, I use hide glue.

3. For all other applications, I turn to the ease and convenience of white and yellow glues. For example, all the pieces in this book were assembled with one of those two varieties, the choice being determined by the proximity of the glue bottle to my hand when it was time to glue something up.

Framed Mirror

BY DANNY PROULX

I designed this framed mirror for a couple of reasons. First, I needed a hall mirror for my home. Second, I was anxious to use the pocket hole filler plugs as a decorative element on a large frame, and this was the perfect project.

A wise old cabinetmaker that I knew, when speaking about joinery, said, "If you can't hide it, celebrate it." That's the case with these visible pocket holes. I could have put them on the back side of the frame but decided to show them off — and I think they look great!

This elegant mirror is simple to build and will be a useful addition for the hall, or any room in your home. It can be used in the bathroom as a vanity mirror, in a bedroom as a dresser mirror or as an accent piece in any small room that needs to look larger. A mirror always seems to enlarge a space, so it would be perfect in a small dining room.

One of the advantages of being a woodworker is the ability to custom design and build projects for a specific purpose. There are many framed mirrors available in the marketplace, but you'd have to settle for a standard size. A woodworker can build to any size, and that's a big plus with this project. It's a real bonus because buying a custom-size framed mirror would be an expensive proposition.

I used a visual trick with this project by making the top edge of the mirror appear curved. In reality, it's a straight-cut plate mirror that's much less expensive than a curved cut; only the top rail of the frame is arched. As I said, it's an easy project to build, so have fun making this popular framed mirror.

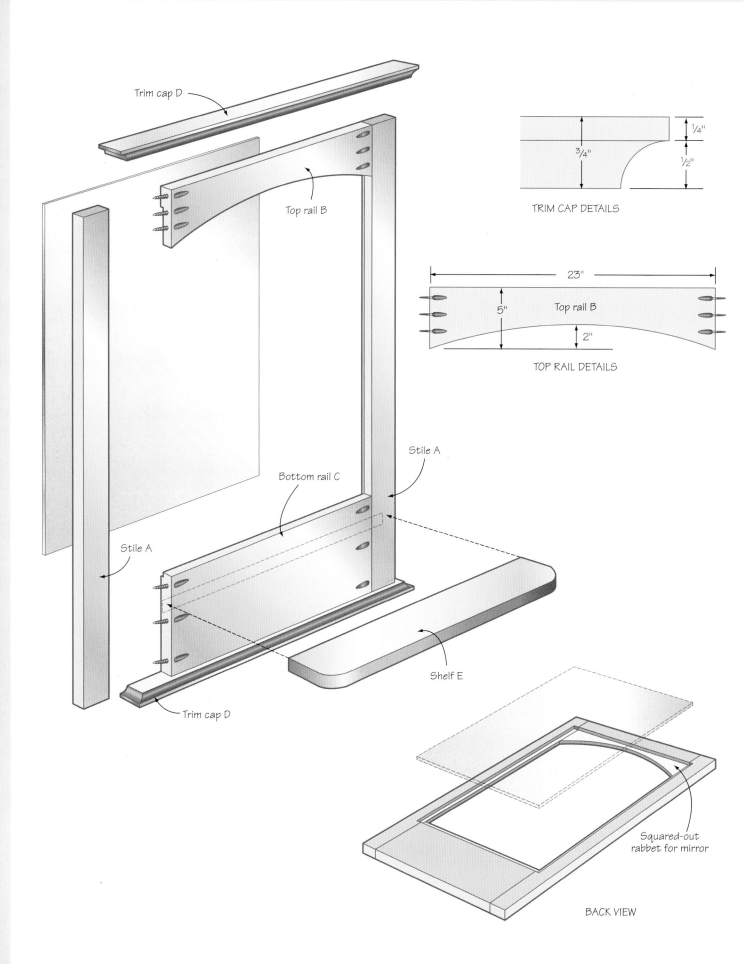

Trim cap D

Top rail B

TRIM CAP DETAILS

1/4"

3/4"

1/2"

23"

5"

Top rail B

2"

TOP RAIL DETAILS

Stile A

Bottom rail C

Stile A

Shelf E

Trim cap D

Squared-out
rabbet for mirror

BACK VIEW

REFERENCE	QUANTITY	PART	STOCK	THICKNESS	(mm)	WIDTH	(mm)	LENGTH	(mm)	COMMENTS
A	2	stiles	hardwood	3/4	(19)	2 1/2	(64)	38	(965)	
B	1	top rail	hardwood	3/4	(19)	5	(127)	23	(584)	
C	1	bottom rail	hardwood	3/4	(19)	7 1/4	(184)	23	(584)	
D	2	trim caps	hardwood	3/4	(19)	1 5/8	(41)	30	(762)	
E	1	shelf	hardwood	3/4	(19)	3 1/2	(89)	26	(660)	
F	1	mirror plate		3/16	(5)					approximately 23 5/8" (600) × 28 7/8" (733); cut to the size required

Supplies

Pocket hole screws: 1 1/4" (32mm)

Wood screws: 1 1/2" (38mm), 1/2" (13mm)

Glue

Pocket hole plugs

Mirror clips

Mirror hangers

1 Cut the four frame parts A, B and C, as indicated in the materials list. Draw an arc on the top rail B, following the dimensions shown in the illustration. Use a thin strip of wood, bent around finishing nails along the arc, to mark the pattern. Then, use a jigsaw or scroll saw to form the arc.

2 Drill three equally spaced pocket holes on the ends of each rail B and C. Set your drill bit stop collar so the pocket hole will be about 1/8" deeper than normal. These pocket holes will be filled with wood plugs, and I want to make sure they are seated deep in the hole without being limited by the screw head.

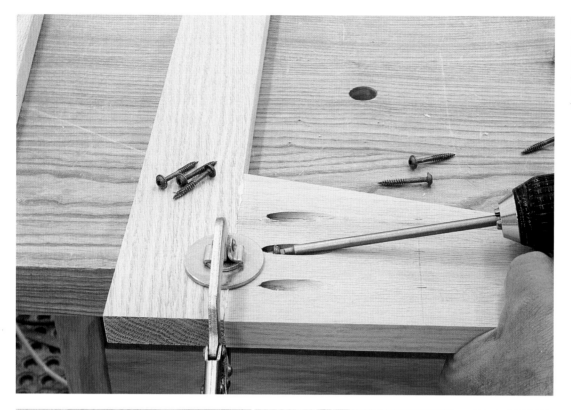

3 Join both rails to the stiles using glue and 1¼"-long pocket hole screws. The outside edges of the rails are set flush with the ends of each stile.

Shop Tip

I'm drilling my pocket holes on the front face of the frame members. However, you may want to skip the wood plug step and hide the holes on the back side of the mirror frame. Either option is acceptable.

4 Fill the pocket holes with wood plugs. I am using walnut plugs on this oak frame as a decorative element; however, any combination, including plugs of the same wood species, is fine and really a matter of personal taste. Use glue in the pocket holes, insert the plugs and, when the adhesive has cured, sand the plugs flat to the frame surface.

5 Ease the inside frame profile, using a ⅜"-radius router bit. Then complete the final sanding of the frame front face.

6 Use a rabbeting router bit to cut a ³⁄₁₆"-deep rabbet on the inside back profile of the frame. This will provide a place for the mirror plate to rest. Each rabbeting bit cuts a little differently because of the bit style and diameter of the guide bearing. The width is not critical as the mirror will be ordered to fit the cut you create.

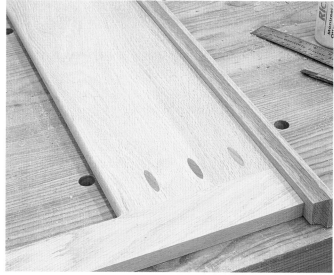

7 You can order the mirror plate cut with a curved top but that would be expensive. I want to use a plain, square-cut mirror, so I will have to square the rabbet on the curved top rail. Use a straight-cutting bit in your router, guided by a board, to clean out most of the wood. Remove the remaining material and square the corners, using a sharp chisel.

8 The upper and lower trim caps D are formed with a cove router bit. The cove is cut leaving a ¼"-high lip on the edge. Cove cut the front edge and ends of both pieces. The cove faces the frame on both bottom and top caps, and is centered on the frame. Use glue and 1½"-long wood screws to secure the trim caps. The back edges of D are flush with the back face of the frame.

9 Shelf E is attached with glue and 1½"-long wood screws driven through the back face of the frame. Round over the two outside corners of this shelf to minimize injury in case someone bumps into the mirror. I set my shelf board 2½" below the bottom rail's top edge and centered on the frame's width.

10 Use a ¼"-radius roundover bit to ease the outside edges of the frame stiles. The router base plate will strike the upper and lower trim cap, limiting its travel. However, that's the effect I want to achieve on those edges. Prior to installing the mirror, apply a finish to your frame.

11 I'm using metal clips to hold the mirror in place on the frame. The bent clips are installed in ⅛"-deep grooves that I've cut into the frame edge with a straight router bit. The clips are held in place with ½"-long wood screws. I also installed heavy-duty hanger clips on the frame for mounting on screws driven into the wall. If possible, attach the hanger clips to the stiles so the upper rail doesn't support the mirror's weight.

Construction Notes

This mirror can be any size, as previously mentioned. Different applications demand special sizing, so change the dimensions to suit your needs.

Any wood type can be used, and the pocket holes can just as easily be filled with matching or contrasting plugs. I applied three coats of polyurethane to the frame, but an applied stain, to match existing furniture color, is often necessary.

Be careful when installing the mirror clips, as too much pressure can crack the glass. You should also order the mirror ⅛" smaller than the overall width and height to accommodate any seasonal wood movement. My mirror supplier uses a standard 5mm-thick plate, and I'm sure that's a common thickness, but check with your supplier before cutting the rabbets in your frame.

The curved upper rail is a nice design element and adds a lot of interest to the mirror. However, it's not always suitable for some furniture styles. If your furniture has straight lines, as is the case for some styles like Shaker, you may want to eliminate the upper rail curve. As well, the coved caps may not suit the furniture style in your home. However, they can be almost any design, including straight line with cuts, bullnose or a simple roundover, so change them to meet your needs.

Mirror

BY KEN BURTON

Mirrors are fun (and often profitable) to make because they go together relatively quickly, they don't require a lot of material and their function is built right in. Because most people like to look at themselves, their interest in mirrors is almost automatic.

The mirror featured here is very definitely of the twenty-first century, but its roots can be traced backwards more than two hundred years. Its scalloped pediment is closely related to that found on many Queen Anne and Chippendale pieces, and its "carved" vertical moldings recall the Victorian era. These elements combine with the vertical symmetry to create a look that is at home in many formal settings. The painted highlights, however, keep the piece from becoming stodgy.

The mirror frame is made from mahogany and has curly maple accents. The corners of the frame are put together with lap joints, and the mirror fits into rabbets cut in the backs of the frame pieces. You'll have to drill the circular cutout in the pediment or cut it with a band saw.

One of the most compelling parts of this project is the harlequin pattern cut into the side pieces. This is accomplished on the table saw using a molding head equipped with a V-cutter. A simple carriage guides the pieces through the cut at the appropriate angle. A small key governs the spacing of the grooves much the same way the spacing of the cuts is controlled when making finger joints. Once all the grooves are cut, add paint, then sand the surface to clean up any errant color. The colored dots are inlays of epoxy mixed with acrylic paint. Vary the color scheme to suit your décor.

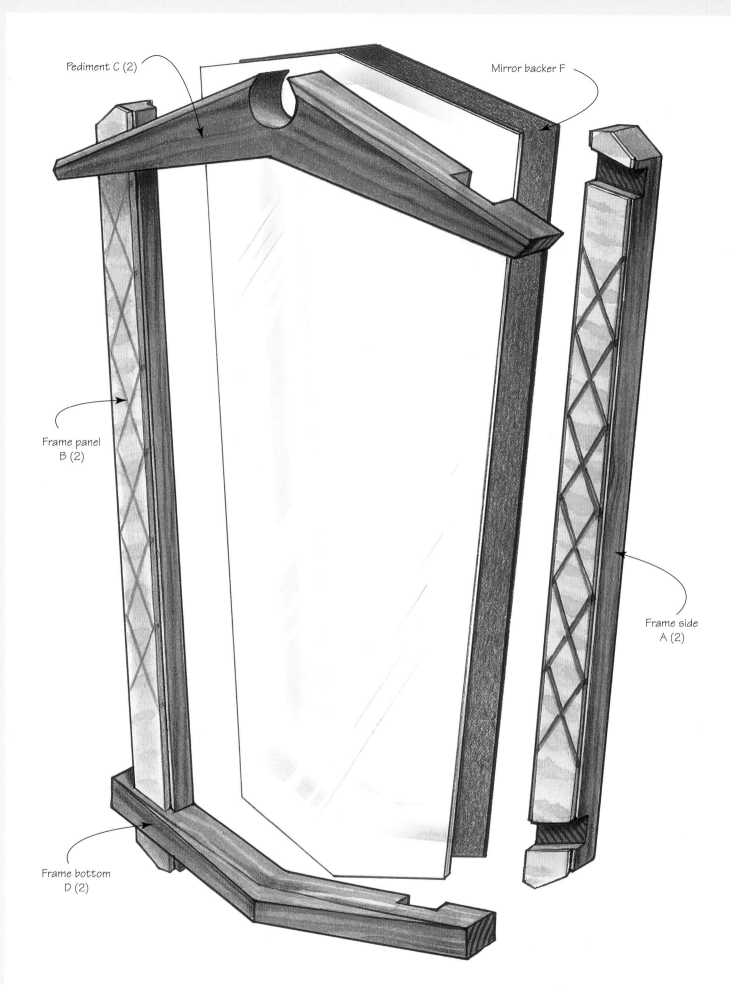

Pediment C (2)

Mirror backer F

Frame panel
B (2)

Frame side
A (2)

Frame bottom
D (2)

MIRROR ■ INCHES (MILLIMETERS)

REFERENCE	QUANTITY	PART	STOCK	THICKNESS	(mm)	WIDTH	(mm)	LENGTH	(mm)	COMMENTS
A	2	frame sides	hardwood	1	(25)	2¼	(57)	39¼	(997)	
B	2	frame panels	contrasting hwd	5/16	(8)	1⅞	(48)	39¼	(997	
C	2	pediment	hardwood	1¾	(44)	3¾	(95)	13⅝	(346)	
D	2	frame bottom	hardwood	1½	(38)	1⅝	(41)	10⅛	(257)	
E	2	spline	hardwood	5/16	(8)	1¾	(44)	1½	(38)	
F	1	mirror backer	hardboard	1⅛	(28)	18¾	(476)	42¼	(1073)	

Supplies

Mirror
Screw Eyes
Wire
Screws

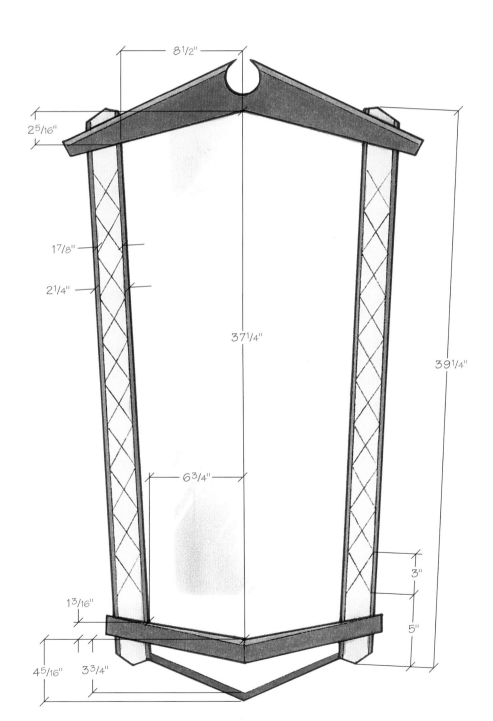

1 As with most projects that involve angles that are not 90° and pieces that taper, you'll find it much easier to measure and make your setups if you make a full-size drawing of the piece first. Start by drawing a center line, then use it as a reference for making the rest of the drawing.

2 Cut the frame sides to the sizes given in the materials list. Set up a dado and cut a ⅛"-deep × 1⅞"-wide (3mm × 48mm) channel down the center of each piece. This should leave ³⁄₁₆" (5mm) of material on either side of the channels.

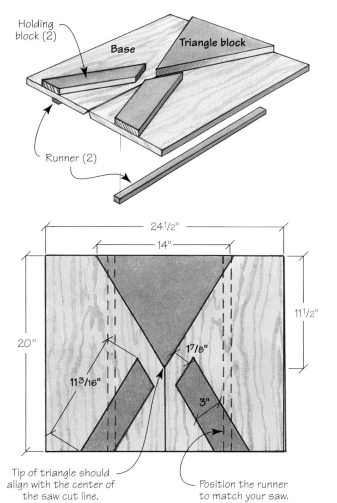

Holding block (2)

Base

Triangle block

Runner (2)

24½"

14"

11½"

20"

1⁷⁄₈"

11³⁄₁₆"

3"

Tip of triangle should align with the center of the saw cut line.

Position the runner to match your saw.

Drawing Materials

When I need to make a full-size drawing, I take a sheet of ⅛" (3mm) hardboard (or a portion thereof) and paint it white (or whatever leftover light color I happen to have). Then I make the drawing on the painted surface. If the piece is one I am likely to make again, I tuck the layout into my plywood rack for future reference. If the piece is one I am not likely to revisit, I paint over the drawing and save the sheet for a future drawing.

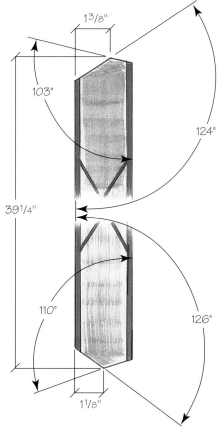

13/8"

103°

124°

39 1/4"

110°

126°

1 1/8"

3 Cut the side panels to the size listed. Be careful to get the width right—the panels should fit snugly into the channels you cut in the frame sides. The pieces are thin enough to be resawn from a single piece of 4/4 material. Resaw the pieces, then open them up like a book to get grain patterns that are a near-perfect match.

4 Make up a sled, then set up a molding head with a V-cutter. Use the molding head to cut the slot in the sled—make the cut in several passes, raising the cutter a little with each pass. Stop when the tip of the V is about 1/16" (2mm) above the sled's surface. Start cutting the panels from the lower end first. Measure and position the first cut 5" (13cm) from the end.

5 After you make the first cut in each panel, drive a small brad 3" (8cm) away from the cutter into the sled's surface. Leave the head slightly above the surface. This will serve to register each of the subsequent cuts. Make a total of 10 cuts across each of the panels. Be careful not to mar the pieces by dragging them over the brad.

6 Turn the pieces around for the second set of cuts. Remove the brad from the sled. Draw a perpendicular line across the panels from the end of the last cut to indicate where the second set of lines should begin. Make the first cut in each piece, then replace the brad and continue cutting.

7 Glue the panels in the channels cut in the frame sides. When the glue dries, cut the ends. Note: Be sure to make a right and a left side by cutting one frame side with the panel facing up and the second with the panel facing down. Position a stop along the miter gauge's fence to help maintain consistency.

8 Cut the pieces for the pediment to size. Crosscut one end of each at a 75° angle. Hold the pieces together and mark their outer faces.

9 Set up a 5/16"-wide (8mm) dado and adjust it to make a 3/4"-deep (19mm) cut. Clamp a pediment piece in the simple tenoning jig with its marked side out. Position the rip fence so the dado will be centered across the thickness of the piece. Make the cut. Clamp the second piece in the jig with its marked side out, and cut it as well.

10 The mirror and the backing are contained in a stepped rabbet that's cut in the pediment and frame sides. To make these cuts, set up a 3/4"-wide (19mm) dado along with a rabbet fence. Set the height of the blade to 3/4" (19mm) and adjust the fence to expose slightly more than 1/8" (3mm) of the blade. Mark the table at the front and the back of the blade so you can see where to start (or stop) the cut. Mark the front side of each pediment piece 9" (23cm) from the mitered end to show where the rabbets stop.

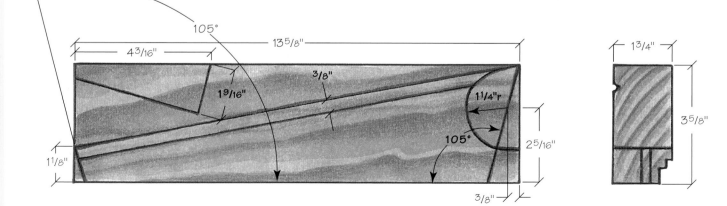

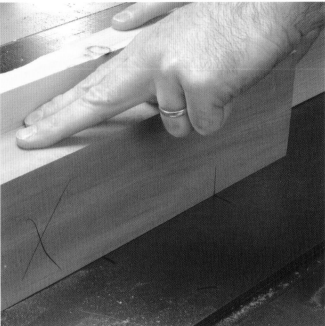

11 For one of the pediment pieces, you'll need to pivot the piece onto the spinning blade. Lower the blade beneath the table. Position the piece with the mark aligned with the mark towards the rear of the table. Clamp a stop block behind the piece to prevent kickback. Raise the blade to its original height. Hold the piece against the fence above the blade. Start the saw and slowly pivot the piece down into the cut. When the piece is down on the table, push it past the blade to complete the cut.

12 For the second piece, cut as you would normally but stop when the line on the piece reaches the line toward the front of the table. Also cut rabbets along the inside edges of the frame sides. These cuts should stop 2½" (63mm) from the upper ends of the pieces. Reset the fence and the blade height to make a second rabbet. This one should be ½" (13mm) wide (blade height) and ¼" (6mm) deep [the exposed blade width should be slightly more than ⅜" (9mm)]. Re-mark the table and make the second rabbets in all the pieces.

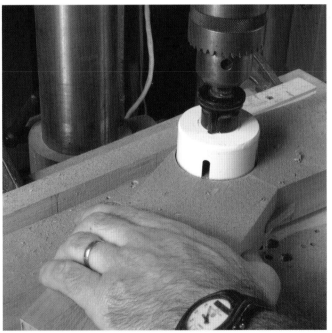

13 Cut notches in the top edges of the pediment pieces. Cut a spline to fit into the slots you just cut into the ends of the pieces—the grain in the spline should run perpendicular to the glue line. Apply glue to the joint and clamp the pieces together.

14 Chuck a 2½" (63mm) Forstner bit (or a hole saw) in your drill press. Carefully locate the center of the circular cutout and drill the pediment assembly. Sand the inside of the cutout to clean it up.

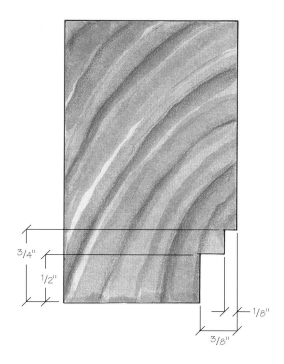

15 Lay out the taper along the top edge of both sides of the pediment. Place the pediment on a carrier board so that one of the layout lines is aligned with the edge of the carrier board. Screw a fence to the carrier board to hold the pediment in this position. Position the rip fence so the blade runs along the edge of the carrier board. Hold the pediment in place and run the carrier board along the fence to make the cut. Flip the pediment over to cut the second side.

16 Put the molding head back on the saw with the V-cutter. Make a V-cut along the top edge of the pediment. Place the cut into the circular cutout on each side.

17 Cut off the ends of the pediment at 86°.

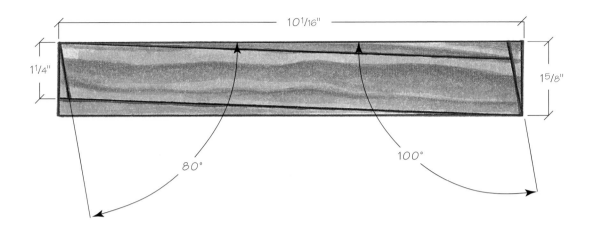

$10^1/_{16}$"

$1^1/_4$"

$1^5/_8$"

80°

100°

18 Cut the pieces for the frame bottom to the size listed. Crosscut one end of each piece at 79° and slot the pieces for a spline as you did for the pediment pieces. Be sure to mark the outside faces so you can keep track of them. Lay out the tapers on the pieces and cut them with the aid of a carrier board as you did before. Note: This time you're tapering the pieces before gluing them together.

19 To chamfer the top outside corner of the frame bottom pieces, tilt the blade at a 45° angle. Position one of the pieces against the fence with its outside face toward the blade, its bottom side down and its narrower end toward the blade. Adjust the fence so the blade just nicks the upper corner of the piece. Note: On a saw that tilts to the left, the fence should be to the left of the blade. Push the piece through the cut. The chamfer should go from next to nothing at the narrow end to about ½" (13mm) wide at the wide end. Repeat with the second piece, this time running the wide end first.

20 Cut off the narrow ends of the pieces at an 80° angle. Glue wedge-shaped clamping blocks to the undersides of the pieces. Insert the spline and glue the pieces together. Once the glue dries, cut off the wedges.

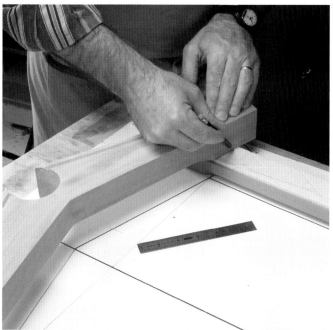

21 Set up the frame side pieces on your full-size drawing, carefully aligning them with the layout. Place the pediment on top of the sides. Even if it doesn't quite agree with the drawing, be sure to position it "square" to the center line. Mark the frame sides where the pediment crosses. Repeat the process with the frame bottom.

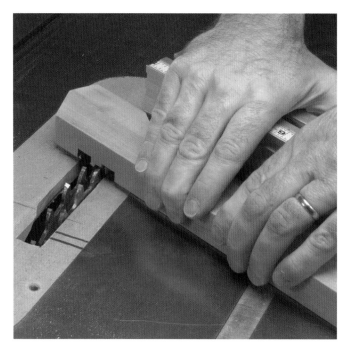

22 Set up a ½"-wide (13mm) dado blade and set it to make a ½"-deep (13mm) cut. Cut notches which will receive the pediment and bottom across the frame sides. You'll need to reset the angle on the miter gauge to accommodate the taper of the pieces.

23 Assemble the frame on the drawing, with the pieces set firmly in their notches. Flip over the frame to mark the bottom and pediment for their notches. Reset the height of the dado blade to match the remaining side thickness. Cut the notches in the bottom and pediment.

24 Slip the frame bottom into its notches in the side pieces. Mark the rabbets on the bottom. Set up a wide dado and make repeated passes to cut away a place for the mirror and its backing to run past.

25 Apply a coat of finish to seal the surface and keep the paint from wicking into places it shouldn't go. Paint the lines with artists' acrylic paint. The blue in the photo is a mix of ultramarine blue and phthalocyanine green. Cut the mirror backing to size and paint its bottom edge with the same color.

26 Glue the frame together. Square the rabbets with a chisel where the pediment meets the sides. Cut a piece of hardboard to serve as a pattern for the mirror. Take the pattern to the glass shop and have them cut a piece of ¼" (6mm) mirror to match. Have them grind the bottom edges as they will be exposed.

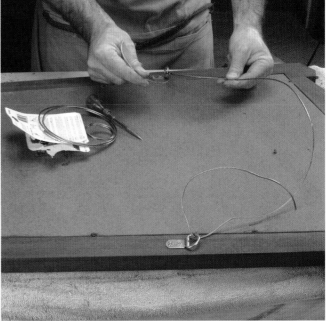

27 Sand and finish the frame. Note: Be sure to clean up and finish rabbets that will be in contact with the glass—you'll be able to see them in the mirror. Set the mirror in place along with the backing. Screw the backing to the frame every 8" (20cm) or so. Also install screw eyes and a heavy-duty wire for hanging.

Two Frames

BY CHRISTOPHER SCHWARZ

If you're new to woodworking or to Arts & Crafts furniture, you should try your hand at building a frame for a picture or mirror first. You'll learn how to cut a mortise-and-tenon joint without the fear of blowing an entire morris chair. You'll learn how to peg this joint to make it even more durable. And you'll get a feel for working with white oak and get to experiment with finishes.

The picture frame featured here was built to hold a photo in a mat that measures 16" × 20", which is a standard size. It's a simple matter to adjust the measurements of the stiles and rails if your photo or painting is bigger. I built this frame after a visit to the Gamble House in Pasadena, California, which was designed by the Greene brothers. On the tour of the house it became evident that one of the keys to their designs was that everything be in threes: three rails, three cutouts, three inlays. So with that in mind, I designed this traditional Arts & Crafts frame.

The second piece is a mirror frame designed to hold a standard 24" × 24" mirror, which is available at most home center stores. This design was taken from an actual mirror that was featured at an auction held by Treadway Gallery of Cincinnati, Ohio. Construction of both frames is similar, but because they use different thicknesses of wood, I'll cover each one separately.

Picture Frame

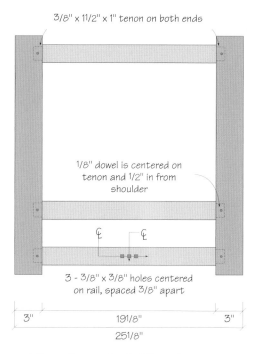

3/8" x 11/2" x 1" tenon on both ends

1/8" dowel is centered on tenon and 1/2" in from shoulder

3 - 3/8" x 3/8" holes centered on rail, spaced 3/8" apart

3"   191/8"   3"

251/8"

3/4"

1/4"   1/2"

1/4"

Mirror Frame Corbel Detail

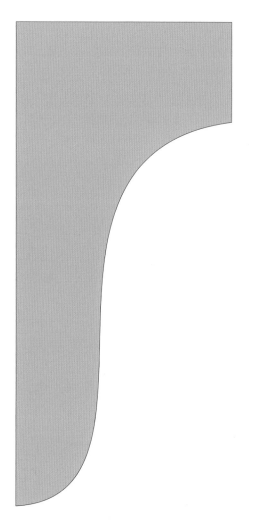

Mirror Frame

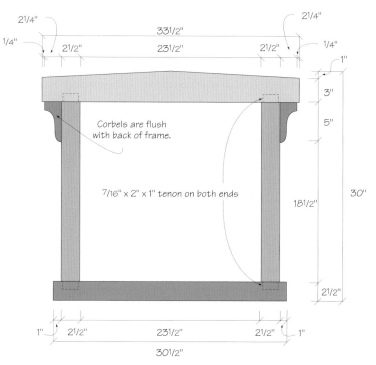

21/4"   331/2"   21/4"

1/4"   21/2"   231/2"   21/2"   1/4"

1"

3"

5"

Corbels are flush with back of frame.

30"

7/16" x 2" x 1" tenon on both ends

181/2"

21/2"

1"   21/2"   231/2"   21/2"   1"

301/2"

REFERENCE	QUANTITY	PART	STOCK	THICKNESS	(mm)	WIDTH	(mm)	LENGTH	(mm)	COMMENTS
PICTURE FRAME										
A	2	stiles		¾	(19)	3	(76)	26⅛	(664)	
B	3	rails		¾	(19)	2	(51)	21⅛	(537)	1" tenon both ends
C	6	dowels		⅛ dia.	(3)			¾	(19)	
MIRROR FRAME										
D	1	top rail		⅞	(22)	4	(102)	33½	(851)	
E	1	bottom rail		⅞	(22)	2½	(64)	30½	(775)	
F	2	stiles		⅞	(22)	2½	(64)	25½	(648)	1" tenon both ends
G	2	corbels		¾	(19)	2¼	(57)	5	(127)	
H	4	dowels		⅛ dia.	(3)			¾	(19)	

Picture Frame

The first step is to choose your wood. With picture frames you have to remember that you've got only a few sticks of wood so you want to show the best grain possible. However, that being said, you also don't want the grain to be so wild that it competes with or outshines the artwork it's supposed to display. So look for ray flake that is somewhere in the middle.

Cut all your pieces to size and get ready to cut your mortise-and-tenon joints. The rule of thumb is to cut your tenons to be half as thick as your wood. So if your wood is ¾" thick, your tenons should be ⅜" thick. For wood this narrow, you should cut ¼" shoulders on the edges. I usually make all my tenons 1" long. So the tenons on the rails B should measure ⅜" thick, 1½" wide and 1" long. I like to cut my tenons using a dado stack in a table saw.

Now, cut your mortises. You want your mortises to be a little deeper than your tenons so the tenon won't bottom out in your mortise. So your mortises should measure ⅜" thick, 1½" wide and 1 1/16" long. I like to use a hollow chisel mortiser, but it's not necessary. If you own a drill press, you can cut these mortises using a ⅜" Forstner bit and a fence clamped to your drill press's table. Then square the corners using a chisel.

While you're set up for mortising, make the three square cutouts on the bottom rail.

Now, cut the ¼"-deep by ½"-wide rabbet on the backs of the stiles A and rails B to hold the picture in place. You'll have to stop the rabbet in the stiles, but this is a simple thing to do with a rabbeting bit in a router table.

Now, test the fit of everything and clamp your frame without glue to make sure everything fits and closes tightly. When you're satisfied, put glue in the mortises and clamp your picture frame. Make sure your frame is square by measuring the frame's diagonals (from corner to corner). If the diagonal measurements are not identical, place a clamp across the two corners that were longer. Apply a slight bit of pressure and check your diagonals again.

When the glue is dry, remove the frame from the clamps. Now, peg your tenons for additional strength. I like to use ¼" oak dowels C. The size of store-bought dowels is rarely consistent, so first cut some holes in scrap pieces of wood to test how your dowels fit. I like to use a drill press for this operation. When you've found the perfect bit, drill the holes about ⅝" deep into your frame. The holes don't need to go all the way through. Put a little glue into the hole and hammer the dowel home. Cut any excess flush to the stiles.

Now finish-sand the frame. Start with 100 grit, then move up to 120 and finish with 150. This frame is finished with a simple mahogany gel stain. After your stain dries, cover it with three coats of a clear finish. Install the glass, photo and mat, and hold them in the rabbet using mirror clips, which screw to the back side of your frame.

Mirror Frame

This frame is a little more work, but the operations are all the same. After you cut your pieces to size, cut your tenons on the ends of the stiles F. Because this stock is ⅞" thick, you'll need to make your tenons 7/16" thick. So your tenons should measure 7/16" thick, 2" wide and 1" long. Your mortises should be 7/16" thick, 2" wide and 1 1/16" long. Once you've got your joints cut, turn your attention to the top rail D.

The top rail D slopes from 4" high in the middle to 3" on the ends. Mark this on the rail and make the cut on a band saw. Clean up the cut on your jointer.

Now, cut the rabbet on the back of the pieces to hold the mirror in place. I cut a ⅛"-deep by ¼"-wide rabbet using a rabbeting bit in a router table.

Test the fit of all joints and then glue up the frame. When the glue is dry, peg the joints. Cut out the two corbels G according to the pattern in the diagram and finish-sand all your parts. Glue the corbels G in place and finish the frame.

I combined two dyes to get this dark color — a brown dye and a deep red dye. Then I followed it with three coats of a clear finish.

Three-tier Keepsake Chest

BY KERRY PIERCE

The three tiers of this chest are all assembled at the same time from the same four pieces of wood. The tiers are then sawn apart on the table saw. This results in tiers that — in the finished piece — align perfectly.

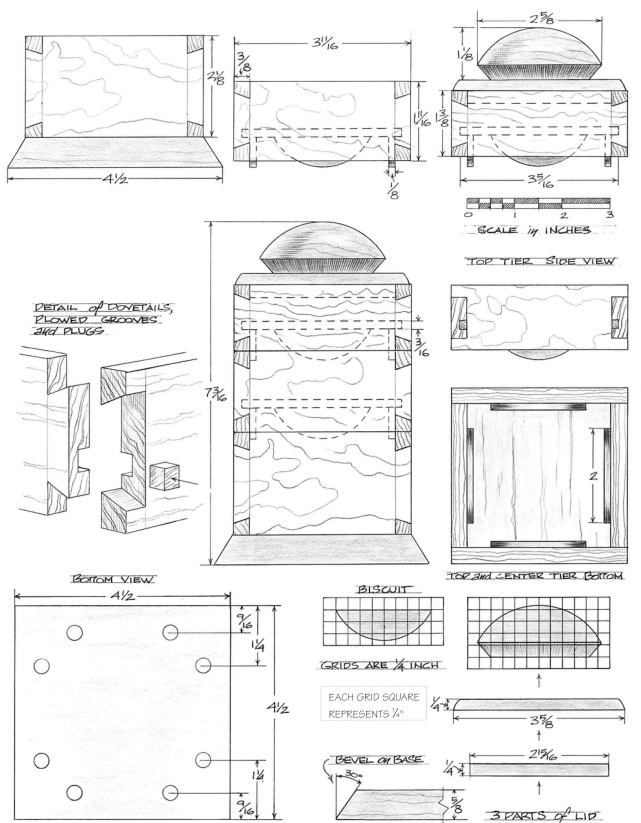

BOTTOM TIER

CENTER TIER

TOP TIER with LID

2⁵⁄₈

1¹⁄₈

2¹⁄₈

3¹¹⁄₁₆

3⁄₈

1¹¹⁄₁₆

1³⁄₈

4½

1⁄₈

3⁵⁄₁₆

0   1   2   3

SCALE in INCHES

TOP TIER SIDE VIEW

DETAIL of DOVETAILS, PLOWED GROOVES and PLUGS

7³⁄₁₆

3⁄₁₆

2

TOP and CENTER TIER BOTTOM

BOTTOM VIEW

4½

9⁄₁₆

1¼

4½

1¼

9⁄₁₆

BISCUIT

GRIDS ARE ¼ INCH

EACH GRID SQUARE REPRESENTS ¼"

BEVEL on BASE

30°

⁵⁄₈

¼

3⁵⁄₈

¼

2¹⁵⁄₁₆

3 PARTS of LID

THREE-TIER KEEPSAKE CHEST ■ INCHES (MILLIMETERS)

REFERENCE	QUANTITY	PART	STOCK	THICKNESS	(mm)	WIDTH	(mm)	LENGTH	(mm)	COMMENTS
A	4	sides	hardwood	$3/8$	(10)	$5^3/4$	(146)	$3^{11}/16$	(94)	
B	2	tier bottoms	hardwood	$3/16$	(5)	$3^5/16$	(84)	$3^5/16$	(84)	
C	1	lid bottom	hardwood	$1/4$	(6)	$3^1/8$	(79)	$3^1/8$	(79)	
D	1	lid top	hardwood	$1/4$	(6)	$3^5/8$	(92)	$3^5/8$	(92)	
E	1	lid pull	hardwood	$1^1/8$D	(29)			$2^5/8$	(67)	
F	8	dovetail plugs	hardwood	$3/16$	(5)	$3/16$	(5)	$3/16$	(5)	
G	1	base	hardwood	$5/8$	(16)	$4^1/2$	(114)	$4^1/2$	(114)	
H	8	biscuits		$1/8$	(3)	$5/8$	(16)	2	(51)	
J	8	screws	steel	No.8				$1^1/4$	(32)	
		brads								

* This includes $9/16$" (14mm) of width to allow for the box's three tiers to be cut apart.

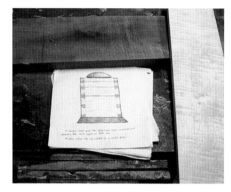

1 I originally intended to create four tiers, however, when I got into the shop, I realized there simply wasn't enough height for a fourth tier without making significant changes to the chest's proportions. The curly maple and the planed walnut are both cutoffs. The rough-looking walnut was taken from a load of discards.

2 Here you see the material planed to its finished thicknesses. Notice the sections of the walnut board in the front are planed to three different thicknesses. The thickest piece on the left was cut off once I'd reached the required thickness for the base. I cut out the section closest to the vise once I'd reached the thickness of the tier bottoms. The remainder of this board was planed to the $1/8$" thickness of the tiny arcs that align the tiers.

3 Rip to width and cut to length the four sides of the case from which the tiers will be cut. Score lines around each end of the four pieces. These lines should be placed a distance from the ends that is $1/32$" greater than the thickness of the sides; this gives you material to sand away after the chest is assembled in order to remove the end-grain saw marks. Most woodworkers use a marking gauge to create these scorings, but I just mark the distance with a pencil and use a knife to score along the blade of my combination square.

4 This detail shows the scoring, running across the width and the edge of one of the side panels.

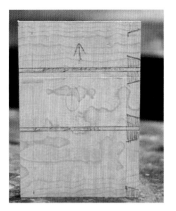

5 Before you plow the grooves for the tier bottoms, lay out the location of the dovetails and the table saw cuts that will ultimately separate the tiers. The scribbles along the ends of this panel indicate the waste to be removed between the dovetails. (Remember: Only two of the four side panels will have dovetails. The other two panels will have pins that will fit between those dovetails.) The scribbles between the horizontal lines indicate the waste that will be removed when cutting the tiers apart. After you establish these features, locate the grooves to plow on the inside face of each side and end panel.

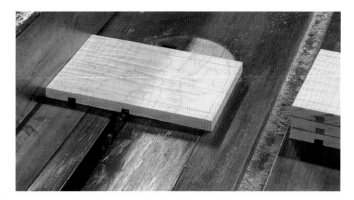

6 Plow the grooves with rabbet cutters on your table saw or a 1/4" bit on your router table. The table saw guard has been removed for the purpose of illustration. Never operate a table saw without a blade guard.

7 With a fine-tooth backsaw, cut the sides of each dovetail down to the scored line. Remember to keep the saw cut on the waste side of the line.

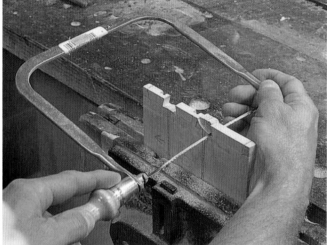

8 Use a coping saw to hog out the waste between the tails. Keep the coping saw well above the scored line.

9 Rotate the side panel 90° in the vise. Use the backsaw to cut away the waste on one end of the dovetails. Then rotate the panel 180° and cut the waste on the other end.

10 Remove the panel from your vise and clamp it to your bench top on a piece of scrap. Then, with a paring chisel, clean up the areas between the dovetails. To do this, locate the tip of the chisel in the scored line and cut an oblique angle. Then on your next pass, make a cut that is closer to the perpendicular.

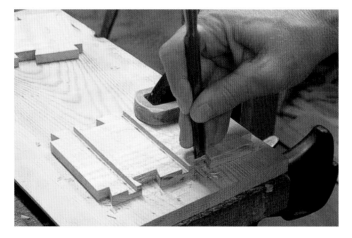

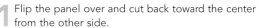

11 Flip the panel over and cut back toward the center from the other side.

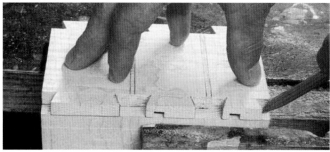

12 Once you've cut all four sets of dovetails (one on each end of the two side panels), lay out the first set of pins. Begin by positioning one of the end panels in your vise so the edge just peeks up above the level of the bench top. Place one set of tails on the end-grain edge so the bottom of the waste areas between the tails just meets the inside edge of the end panel. With a sharp pencil, mark the sides of each tail on the end grain of the end panel.

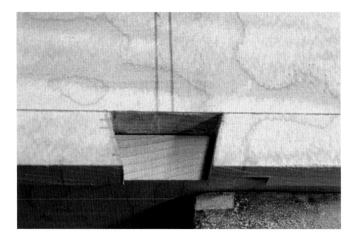

13 This detail shows the proper relationship between the dovetail and the pin stock when marking pins.

14 Raise the end panel a couple of inches in your vise. Then with your combination square, connect the marks you just made on the end-grain surface of the end panel with the end panel's scored line. Again, the scribbling indicates waste.

15 Cut the sides of each pin with your backsaw. Remember: Your saw cut must be on the waste side of the line.

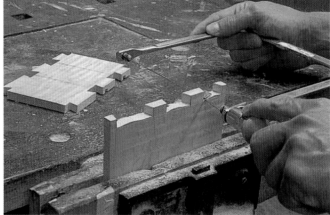

16 Use a coping saw to hog out the waste between pins.

17 Pare down the waste areas between pins from each side toward the center just as you did when cleaning up between the tails.

18 Test fit the tails and pins without fully seating the joint. If you seat the joint fully, you may not be able to get it apart again. Here, the pins and tails fit together without any fine-tuning, but in many cases a little fitting is necessary. Tweak the joint by paring very fine shavings from the sides of the tight pins until a successful fit is accomplished.

19 Before gluing up the case, use your block plane to put a slight bevel on all four sides of the tier bottoms to help ease the bottoms into their grooves during assembly.

20 Before beginning any gluing operation, do a practice run to help you avoid panic situations. Above you can see my preparations for a dry run: all the parts, glue in a paper cup, a glue-spreading stick, the C-clamp to bring the sides together and a bucket of water for cleanup of glue squeeze-out.

21 Apply glue to all the areas that will abut in the finished dovetail joint. Then assemble the case around the two bottom panels, which will fit unglued into their grooves.

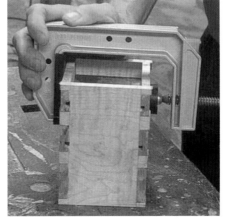

22 Use the C-clamp to squeeze the tails into position between pins. Do this in increments, working your way up and down the case. Too much pressure too quickly at a single location will crack a side panel.

23 After you've washed away any glue squeeze-out, it's time to fill the gaps where the grooves run through the end panels. Plane a length of wood to the same width and thickness as the grooves. Then put a dab of glue on the end of the stick, tap the stick gently into a gap, cut it off and move on to the next gap.

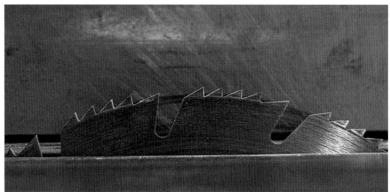

24 I dislike the noise and dust generated by a belt sander, but for this particular operation — grinding flush the ends of the pins and tails — it can be persuaded to perform well. If you do use a belt sander, be cautious: This aggressive tool can remove too much material very quickly at a single location. You can substitute a sharp block plane or a rasp, as demonstrated in chapter nine.

25 Separate the three tiers by sawing them apart on your table saw. I used a hollow-ground planer blade because it leaves shallower saw marks.

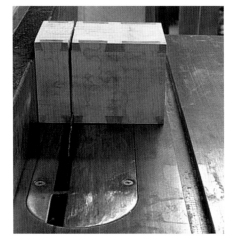

26 Carefully push the box past the saw blade. Again, the table saw guard has been removed only for illustration. Never operate a table saw without a blade guard.

27 Clean up the saw marks with a block plane.

28 When laying out the base allow enough material for the removal of saw marks on the beveled edges.

29 With your saw blade set at a 30° angle, rip the base to width.

30 Using the miter gauge to guide the stock past the blade, cut the base to width.

31 Align the bottom tier on the base. Then mark around that base. These lines will identify the material that must be removed with your block plane in order to establish a good fit.

32 Carefully plane the bevels to the correct size.

33 Drill the countersunk and through holes for the No. 8 × 1¼" screws you will use to fasten the base to the bottom tier.

34 Tape the base to the bottom tier. Then clamp the bottom tier in your vise and attach the base.

36 I didn't have any brads short enough for this particular application, so I snipped ¼" from each with a pair of wire cutters.

35 To attach the alignment biscuits, predrill the holes in which you will drive brads.

39 Slather glue on the top of the lid bottom and bottom of the lid top. Notice that the lid top has been ripped and cut to length at the same 30° angle as the base.

37 Lay some scrap material into the top tier so that the material reaches to within ³⁄₁₆" of the top of the tier sides.

38 Place the lid bottom on top of that scrap material. Notice that the lid bottom completely fills the tier. Notice also that it sticks up ¹⁄₁₆" above the top of the tier sides.

40 Align these two parts. Then bring them together by clamping them to the top tier.

41 Attach the lid-pull blank to a piece of scrap with a bit of newspaper in between. I glued up two blanks in case I ran into a problem with the first blank.

42 Attach the scrap to a faceplate with three screws.

43 Turn the faceplate onto the drive center of your lathe.

44 With a fingernail gouge, shape the top of the pull.

45 With your skew standing on edge, relieve the underside of the pull.

Tip

When you're cutting a set of dovetails, assign a letter to each corner of the case. These letters will help you ensure that you're marking the correct set of pins from the correct set of tails.

47 Scrape away the glue and newspaper from the bottom of the pull.

46 With a paring chisel, separate the pull from the scrap. The bit of newspaper you glued between these two parts will allow a clean separation.

48 Align the pull onto the lid. Glue it in place and clamp.

49 Turn a No. 8 × 1¼" wood screw up through three layers of the lid.

Almost in the Round

BY JIM STACK

Band-sawn boxes are made from a chunk of wood. The idea is that the box already exists in the block and you just remove material to reveal it. So find a block of wood you like or glue a few pieces of wood together to make a block.

I thought it would be interesting to make a box that is similar in shape to a bentwood Shaker box but made primarily using the band saw. The techniques used to make this box can be used to make any shape or size box. You could make this box without the drawer, an easier project. Then, with the block you have left, you could make another smaller box.

When making a band-sawn box, you need to think inside the box and plan your cuts carefully. This project teaches you to visualize how the parts (lid, bottom, outside, drawer) relate to each other. Before you cut any wood, study the drawing and see where each part is located. Then you'll start to see it's not as complicated as it might seem at first glance.

You can fill this box with scented potpourri or jewelry.

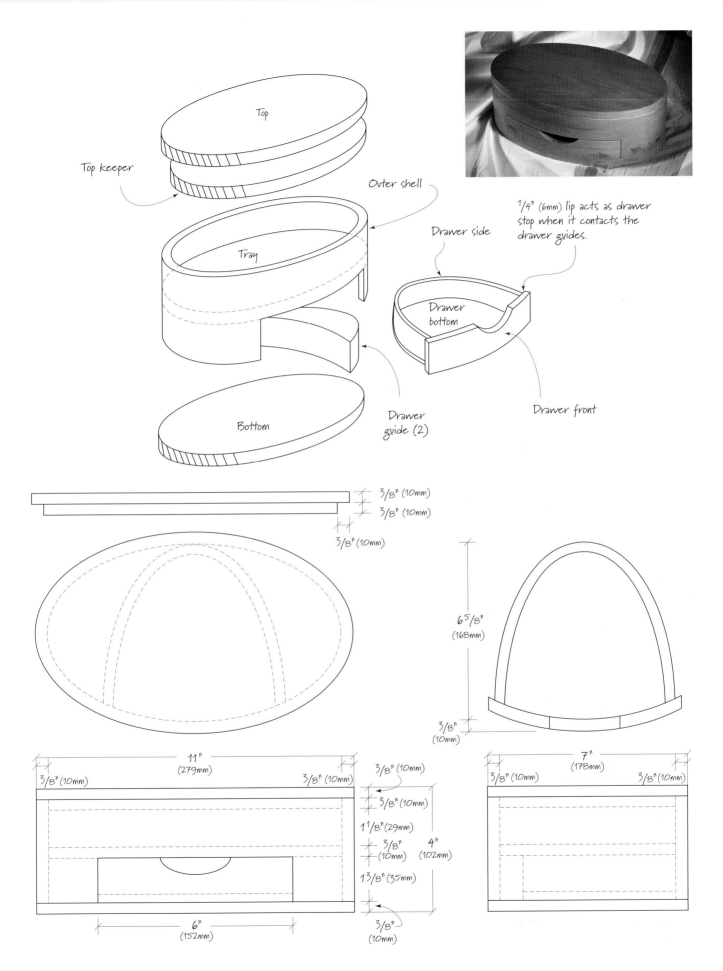

Top

Top keeper

Outer shell

Tray

Drawer side

1/4" (6mm) lip acts as drawer stop when it contacts the drawer guides.

Drawer bottom

Bottom

Drawer guide (2)

Drawer front

3/8" (10mm)
3/8" (10mm)
3/8" (10mm)

6 5/8" (168mm)

3/8" (10mm)

11" (279mm)

3/8" (10mm)
3/8" (10mm)

3/8" (10mm)
3/8" (10mm)

1 1/8" (29mm)

3/8" (10mm)

4" (102mm)

1 3/8" (35mm)

6" (152mm)

3/8" (10mm)

7" (178mm)

3/8" (10mm)
3/8" (10mm)

REFERENCE	QUANTITY	PART	STOCK	THICKNESS	(mm)	WIDTH	(mm)	LENGTH	(mm)	COMMENTS
A	1	block of wood	cherry	4	(102)	7½	(191)	11	(279)	

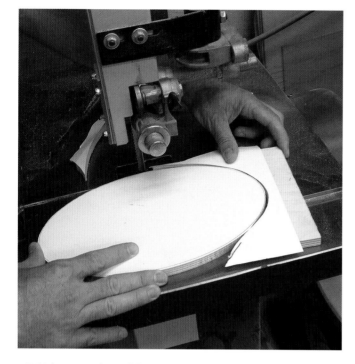

1 Make a template of the box shape. Plywood or MDF is the best material for making templates because it won't change shape with the seasons.

2 Take your time and make the pattern the exact shape you'd like your finished box to be. You can use a stationary sander or hold the template in a vise and shape it with a sanding block.

Cutting Order for Band-sawn Box

1. Cut ellipse from box block.
2. Cut bottom from ellipse block.
3. Cut top from ellipse block.
4. Cut inner block from ellipse, leaving outer shell.
5. Cut lid keeper from top of inner block.
6. Cut tray from inner block.
7. Cut drawer block from remaining inner block.
8. Cut drawer bottom from drawer block.
9. Cut drawer side from drawer block, leaving inner drawer block.
10. Cut drawer front from outer box shell.

3 Using another piece of plywood, make a guide for the template. Cut a curve on one edge and cut a notch to fit around the band saw blade. Clamp the guide to the band saw table so the curved edge of the guide is flush to the outside of the band saw blade.

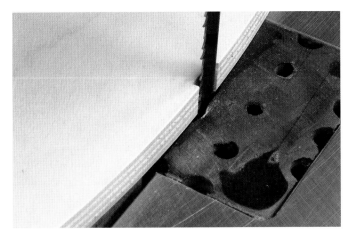

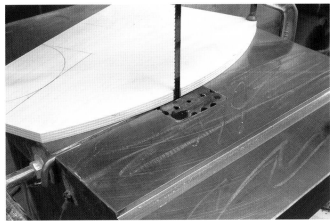

4 This photo shows how the guide should be set in relation to the band saw blade. The box template will ride against the edge of the guide as the saw blade cuts the box block to shape.

5 I use a small wax candle to reduce the friction on the band saw table. Products that come in a spray can are also excellent for keeping your saw's table slick. Check your local hardware store.

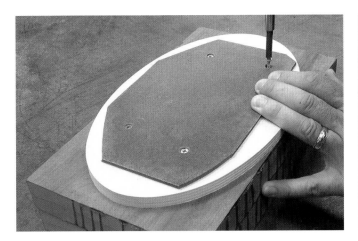

6 Attach the box template to the bottom of your box blank. Add a ⅛"-thick (3mm) spacer to the bottom of the template. This spacer makes sure the box blank clears the guide on the saw table.

7 Before making any cuts, write down each cutting step in the order they're to be done. (See sidebar, "Cutting Order for Band-sawn Box".) If you don't do this, you could easily get the order mixed up and that's frustrating, because it means you've ruined your box blank and you'll need to start over!

8 Hold the box template against the guide. Then cut the box blank to shape. I recommend you practice with scrap material until you're comfortable. Then go for it.

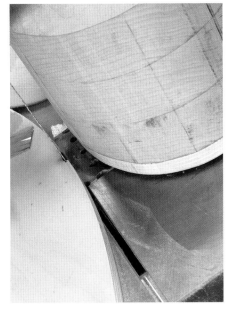

9 This is another view of the setup. You can copy any shape you like using this setup on your band saw. The key is a sharp blade and a slow, steady feed of the material past the saw blade.

10 Sand the box blank smooth before making more saw cuts.

11 Set the saw's fence and cut the lid and bottom from the box blank.

Put pencil mark here on the fence behind the blade.

12 Cut the outside of the box from the blank. Make the entrance cut parallel to the wood's grain direction, then make the cut using the saw's fence as your guide. I find it helpful to make a pencil mark that lines up with the saw blade on the saw's fence. Keep pressure at this point on the fence with the box blank. Again, practice this technique using scrap material until you're comfortable with the process.

13 Slice the remaining box blank material to the thickness of the drawer. Trace the shape of the drawer on this blank. The drawer may be square or oval, as I've chosen. I used one end of the box lid as a template. Cut the drawer from this blank.

14 Reset the band saw fence and, using the same technique you used in step 12, cut the drawer bottom from the blank. Then cut the drawer side from the drawer blank. Glue the drawer side to the drawer bottom, and glue the entrance cut on the box together.

15 Use the two blocks leftover from the drawer blank as drawer guides. Place them inside the box side and mark the location of the drawer.

16 Transfer the marks to the front of the drawer side. Make sure the drawer front is ¼" longer than between the marks. Cut the drawer front from the box's side. I found it helpful to clamp a straightedge to guide the saw. Start this cut on the outside of the box side and cut through the side. After you've cut through the side, plunge the saw through the cut and cut cleanly to each edge of the drawer front.

17 Here's a closer look at the start of the plunge cut. Note the triangle pencil mark showing which end is up on the side.

18 I used the box tray to hold the shape of the box side while I finished cutting the drawer front.

19 Glue the drawer guide blanks to the tray and box's side

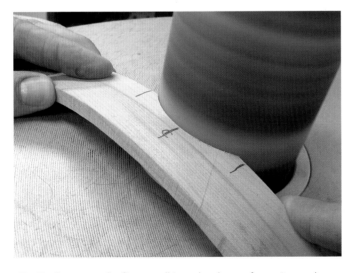

20 Cut or sand a finger pull into the drawer front. As an alternative, you could add a drawer pull to the drawer front.

21 Glue the drawer front to the drawer. Use spacers inside the box to take up the space between the tray and the lid keeper. Set the lid keeper in the box on top of the spacers, add glue to the top of the lid keeper and set the lid on top of it. Use clamps to hold the lid in place until the glue dries. Sand the box with the lid and drawer in place. Finish-sand using 220-grit sandpaper.

Inlaid Bible Box

BY GLEN HUEY

From the minute I brought this lidded box into the *Popular Woodworking* office, debate began. I called it a Bible box, but some wondered where that term originated. Is it a name coined by those interested in building an interest in these boxes so they could sell them for a profit? Or is that term what the original owner used in 1730?

You can call it a Bible box, a lidded box or whatever you like. I'm going to call it a great project that is an introduction to, or a chance to practice and improve upon, many woodworking techniques, from lathe work to shop-made herringbone inlay to half-blind dovetails. And it's a project that I've had on my "to build" list for many years.

INLAID BOX ■ INCHES (MILLIMETERS)

REFERENCE	QUANTITY	PART	STOCK	THICKNESS	(mm)	WIDTH	(mm)	LENGTH	(mm)
A	2	box sides	walnut	5/8	(16)	5⁵/₁₆	(135)	22¹/₂	(572)
B	1	box ends	walnut	5/8	(16)	5⁵/₁₆	(135)	12³/₄	(324)
C	2	bottom	walnut	3/4	(19)	13¹/₈	(333)	22¹/₂	(572)
D	1	feet	walnut	1⁷/₈	(48)	1⁷/₈	(48)	2⁵/₈	(666)
E	2	top	walnut	3/4	(19)	13⁵/₈	(346)	23¹/₂	(597)
F	2	No. 1 inlay	cherry	3/4	(19)	7/16	(11)	12	(305)
G	4	No. 2 inlay	maple	3/4	(19)	7/16	(11)	12	(305)
H	4	stringing	maple	3/4	(19)	3	(76)	12	(305)
J	2	wedges	oak	3/4	(19)	1/8	(3)	5/8	(16)

Supplies

Rockler
800-279-4441 or rockler.com
1 pr. fixed pin hinges, #57108
Whitechapel Ltd.
800-468-5534 or whitechapel-ltd.com
1 lock, #176LBC2
1 escutcheon, #182E11A

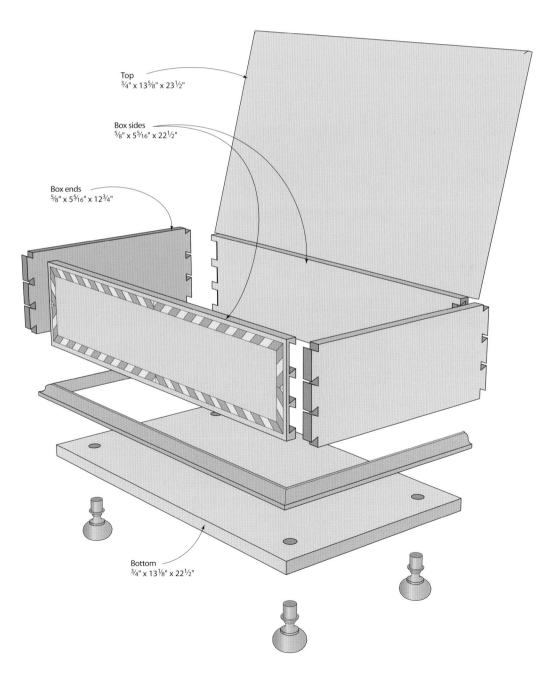

Top
³/₄" x 13⁵/₈" x 23¹/₂"

Box sides
⁵/₈" x 5⁵/₁₆" x 22¹/₂"

Box ends
⁵/₈" x 5⁵/₁₆" x 12³/₄"

Bottom
³/₄" x 13¹/₈" x 22¹/₂"

Four Dovetailed Corners

This box is assembled with half-blind dovetails at both the front and rear. Half-blind dovetails are required on the front, because you need an un-interrupted surface for the inlay. You could join the rear corners of the box with through-dovetails as was done on the original, but I chose to keep the joinery the same at both front and back so I could choose the best-looking joints for the front of my box after it was assembled.

Whether it's pins first or tails first for you, the pin boards should be the front and rear box pieces. Cut your tails in the end pieces. I set the marking gauge to leave ⅛" thickness between the pins and the face of the boards. As I worked on the dovetails, I had no troubles. Later, however, as the grooves were cut for the inlay, I found that this thin area was rather delicate and weak. So when I build another box, I'll mark the thickness at around ³⁄₁₆" (if you leave it too thick, the tails begin to lose their holding power, especially if you're using a 1:6 dovetail ratio — I use a 12° dovetail angle).

If you're new to dovetails, there's tons of information available, scads of articles written and more than a few videos that will walk you through the dovetail process. So as not to be redundant (and for brevity), I'll relate just a couple dovetail pointers that I find helpful.

First, do the layout work on your box pieces. To this day, I saw lines that are drawn on the workpieces and extend the saw cuts beyond the baseline on the face of the pin board — hold to the lines on the pin board ends.

Second, as you begin to remove that waste, take small cuts at the corners of the dovetail area and work slowly. As your chisel displaces the waste, it drives the material upward against the pin – any damage is there forever. If you work slowly and in small steps, the chisel drives the waste upward and along the beveled edge of the pin; this process keeps the pins intact. Work both corners of the waste, then remove the center portion as you progress to the scribe line.

Thin, but not too. With ⅝" material, you'll want to leave an area beyond the dovetails that's thick, but anything extra is pulled from the dovetails and that causes tedious work at the joints.

Go past the line. Over-cut lines are found on many, if not most, of the antique pieces we hold in the highest esteem. The extra sawing pays dividends as you remove the waste material to form the pins.

Tweak the corners. Work carefully as you remove the waste to create the pins. If the edge becomes damaged, it shows forever.

Pinpoint accuracy. Lip the marking gauge cutter just past the end of the tail socket to ensure the tails are the correct length.

Perfectly matched. Make sure your tail board is matched to the pin board as you transfer the layout. Any variations affect your joint fit.

Another tip for half-blind dovetails deals with how you set your marking gauge when establishing the baseline for your tails. It's best to set the gauge wheel or cutter just past the previously scribed baseline of the pin board as shown in the photo at left. This ensures the resulting tails are the exact length needed to fill the area without any small gaps in the fit.

Scribe your box end pieces on both faces, then position the pin board to transfer the layout to your tail board. It's helpful to find a way to hold the pin board vertical so you can slip the tail board into position (just at the scribe line) while you keep your hands free from a balancing act as the layout is transferred.

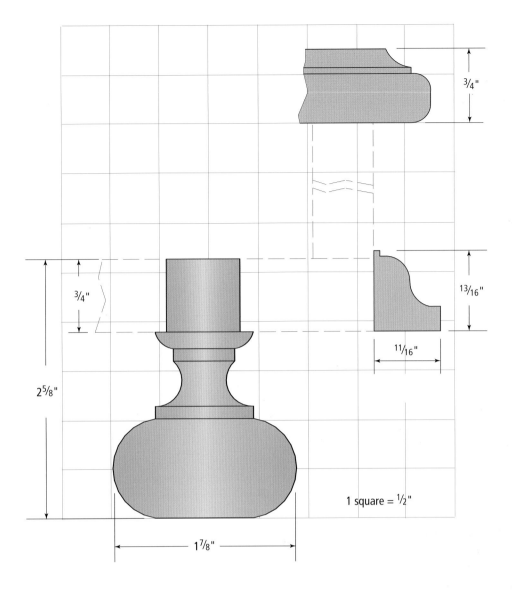

3/4"

13/16"

3/4"

2⁵⁄₈"

11/16"

1 square = ½"

1⁷⁄₈"

foot & moulding details

Complete and test-fit your joints, but don't glue up any of the corners yet. There is still work to do to prepare for the herringbone inlay.

Bottoms Up

With final dimensions available from the completed box, we can size the box bottom and turn and install the ball feet.

The ball feet in this project are a great introduction to turning. The sizes are small, but the turning is detailed. Chuck your stock into the lathe and turn four feet to profile, keeping these thoughts in mind as you turn: The four feet are positioned at the corners of the box, set away from each other. In fact, each foot

is located away from the corner, as well, presenting a shadowy overhang that covers a portion of the foot. Also, the feet are 1⁷⁄₈" tall, so it's all-but-impossible to see more than two of the feet at any one time as the box sits.

What I'm driving at is that you should turn the feet as close to the provided profile as you can, but please don't get caught up in the idea that each foot should be perfect. Don't get bogged down in the process and become discouraged. The feet aren't the focus of the piece. Just get them turned as nicely as you can then move on.

That said, there is one part of the turning that should be accurate — the

tenon that's used to attach the feet to the box bottom. The tenons need to be properly sized so you can drill a hole (¾"), slide the feet into the bottom and have a snug fit. A trick I like when sizing turnings to a specific measurement is to use an open-ended wrench as a gauge. Turn the tenon area to an approximate size, then continually check the size with a wrench that matches the specific measurement you're after.

Mill your box bottom to size (based on your joined box) and to thickness. This is a place to use lesser-quality lumber. My box bottom contains several areas of sapwood that I would never use in a "show" position.

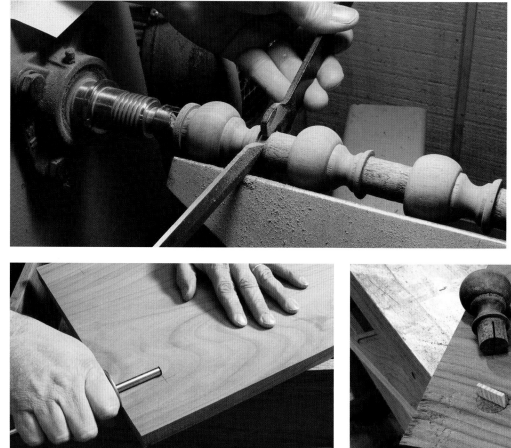

Wrenched to size. Feet tenons need to fit tight, so an easy measurement setter is an open-ended wrench. Work slowly; as the wrench slides over the tenon, the tenon is the right size.

Marked for boring. A marking gauge easily sets the location for the feet tenons. Mark from each corner to find the hole's center.

Tight fit becomes tighter. The fit of the foot tenons to their holes should be snug, but add a wedge in each saw cut and the fit is locked in place. Cut the wedge flush after installation.

Set your marking gauge to 1¾" then find the location for each of the four feet as shown below. After the lines are set, the holes need to be bored completely through the bottom. If a drill press is your tool of choice, there are no worries. But if you're into hand tools and plan to use a brace and bit, make sure the hole is bored at 90º to the face. The foot has to fit square to the bottom to keep the look right.

Slide each foot tenon into its hole then cut the length of the tenons to match the thickness of the bottom. Each tenon is wedged after it is installed through the box bottom. (I made the wedges from a scrap of oak I had in the shop, but any wood does the job.) Make a single cut across the grain of the foot for the wedge. Placing the cut across the growth rings allows the tenon to expand and tighten to the hole as the wedge is inserted without the possibility that the foot could split as the wedge is driven — as might be the case if the cut was parallel to the growth rings.

Slide the tenon into the hole ensuring that the foot is tight to the underside of the bottom, add a small amount of glue on the wedge then drive the piece into the tenon. Complete the installation of all four feet, trim the extra wedge length from each wedge then set the assembly aside.

Inlay Preparation

The grooves for the inlay are cut at a router table with a drop-cut action. The process is not difficult, but does require accuracy in set-up. You may wish to make the grooves with a plunge router — if you're more comfortable using that tool, go for it.

Step one is to position the router table fence after a bit is installed. The groove is ½" wide and ³⁄₃₂" deep and any straight ½"-diameter router bit works. Position the fence with a ¼" between the blade and the fence. Use a scrap to test and adjust the fence setting; the final position is important.

Next mark lines on your fence to indicate the exact cut of the router bit — one mark on each side of the bit. To find the lines, slide a square end of an offcut to just touch the router bit cutting edge (with the tool unplugged, of course). Rotate the bit until the cut-off stops being pushed away from the bit. Mark that location on your fence. Repeat the same process on the other side of the bit.

There is some layout work on the front piece to establish the start and stop

Define the cut. It's important to establish the router bits start and stop cut lines to accurately create the inlay grooves. Rotate the bit to determine the edge of the cut then mark both locations on an auxiliary fence that's locked in position.

Plunge cut at the start. Layout lines on the rear of the box front are matched to the layout lines on the fence in order to accurately cut the inlay groove. The start of the cut is shown here.

Move with slow and steady hands. As the trailing line aligns with the second fence line, the groove is complete. It's better to stay short of the lines and finish the groove with a chisel.

lines of the router cut. With the distance between the fence and the router bit set at ¼" (that leaves a ¼" of box front before the inlay begins), you need to match that distance with the start and stop lines. Pull in a ¼" from each corner and make a pencil line on the backside of the box front.

The idea is to drop-cut the workpiece onto the router bit with the start line aligned with the proper line on the router table fence. Continue through the cut until the stop line aligns with

the opposite fence line, then remove the workpiece from the cut.

I've found that it's best to stay shy of the fence lines whether you are at the start or the stop end of the cut. That way you won't cut away too much wood, and you can clean up and straighten the grooves with your chisels. You'll need to square each corner by hand anyway.

The grooves for the long sides of the box front are easy to rout. It's the short ends that are a bit trickier — it's harder to keep the box front square and tight to

the router fence as you work. Work these two cuts with care. After the grooves are complete, straighten any lines and square the corners.

Shop-made Herringbone
Most of us have scrap piled high in our shops. The inlay used on the front of this box puts some of that scrap to work. The process is simple. You add a personal touch to the box and you'll save money because you don't have to purchase the inlay.

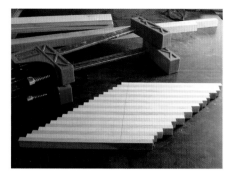

Scraps of design. There's nothing more satisfying than to use shop scraps. Here you see the beginning of the shop-made inlay. Positioning the pieces at a 45° angle as assembled increases the yield of inlay.

For starters, select a couple woods that complement your box. I like cherry and maple for inlay into a walnut box, but the original piece only had white cedar as the inlay. Whether you use hardwood or softwood, the creative steps are the same.

Begin with 10 strips of each color that are ¾" thick and ⁷⁄₁₆" wide; wider strips begin to look too bulky in the completed inlay. Alternate the species then assemble the pieces into a plank. To save material (even scraps are valuable!), glue the pieces at or near a 45° angle as shown at left.

After the glue-up dries, flatten both faces parallel to one another, keeping the panel as thick as possible. Cut the assembly at 45° to create an edge to take small rips off of. Next, slice the ⅜"-thick pieces from the panel. Why ⅜"? You need to work the inlay to fit into the ½" groove cut in the box front, so with the herringbone at ⅜" you can add a ¹⁄₁₆" piece of string to both sides to arrive at the ½" size.

To make the ¹⁄₁₆" stringing pieces, rip pieces from wide stock at your table saw. Mill and square a piece of stock then just cut the stock at the table saw so as to clean up the second edge — note the fence setting. Next, slide the fence toward the blade enough to compensate for the blade thickness and provide a

Not a random rip. Sizing the pieces of assembled scraps is important to the overall task. All the parts of the inlay add up to match the width of your groove.

Thin is in. String pieces border the herringbone strips. Set your fence to leave the string pieces as cutoffs – that's the safest method to produce multiple thin pieces.

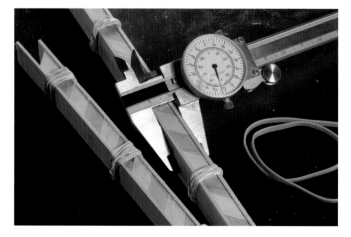

It's good to be strong. Inlay pieces assembled with glue and clamped with rubber bands are slightly wider than the groove size.

The last step. Strips of herringbone inlay are ripped at a band saw to produce the final pieces. Plane the faces before work at the band saw commences and keep the pieces thicker than the groove is deep.

Check the fit. The key to fitting the inlay is to use sandpaper to work the edges so the fit is tight and to begin at the corners to establish the color matches.

$\frac{1}{16}$" strip — stay on the thick side more than thin. It's better to have the assembled strip a wee bit stronger than $\frac{1}{2}$". Repeat the steps to produce the second string strip.

Now it's time to assemble the pieces. Add glue to both faces of the herringbone pieces, position a $\frac{1}{16}$" strip on each side and add clamps. For this type of work, my favorite clamps are ordinary rubber bands. Twist the bands around the glue-up a number of times until tight, then slide the band along the inlay so there are no small gaps when complete.

After the glue is dry, clean up the faces with your hand plane then, using a band saw, cut pieces that are slightly thicker than the grooves are deep ($\frac{3}{32}$"). Clean up the face after each cut. You'll need five or six pieces of finished inlay to complete the box front. Each group should yield three or four pieces, so assemble at least two.

Inlay Installation

With the pieces of inlay in hand, you'll need to fit the pieces into the grooves of the box front. This step is pretty self-explanatory, but here are a couple hints to smooth out any small bumps.

With the inlay matched closely to the groove width, there should be little

It's a quick trim. With the inlay design at 45°, the fit at the corners is easy. Use a square block end to guide your saw as you make the initial cut.

work to do on the pieces to get them to fit. A piece of 120-grit sandpaper adjusts the inlay where needed on the edges. Work carefully and check the fit as you progress.

As the pieces are fit, the corners need to be trimmed. A square end of a block is a big help to get the cuts just right. Mark where you wish to cut the inlay, position the block, add a bit of downward pressure on the block to hold everything in place then make the cut

keeping your saw tight against the block. The worst that could happen is you tilt away from the block as you make the cut and that would cause the inlay to have the slightest bevel. That's great when fitting two pieces of inlay together, but don't overdo it. This allows the top edges of the inlay to meet for tight seams.

A block works great when you need to trim the inlay with a chisel as well.

Take a close look at the photo below. The inlay reverses at the middle of each

Fine-tune for looks. That same square block end acts as a guide for your chisel when fine-tuning the fit of the corners. If you undercut the end just a bit, the fit at the top of the inlay is sure to be tight.

There's a method to the madness. The inlay is not randomly added to the front. Notice each corner has two opposing colors matched and that each run is split at the center with the half-runs being mirrored images.

run. This was common practice when the box was built. Fit the inlay to the corner first. Find the center point of the run then trim the piece with a square cut. If you match opposing hardwoods at the corners, the center meeting point should be mirrored images.

After the inlay is fit to the box, remove the pieces, apply glue to the grooves and to the back face of the inlay, then place the strips back in position. Add a piece of waxed paper over the inlay to stop potential glue transfer, position another similar-sized piece on top then apply a few clamps to hold everything while the glue dries.

As the front comes out of the clamps, it's a great time to prep for the installation of the lock and the escutcheon. Of course, you can do that after the box is assembled, but the area is more confined and the work requires a bit more patience.

Wrap Up Construction
So far, all the work has been on individual pieces. It's time now to assemble the box. Add glue to the dovetail joints (remember those, from a few pages back?) and slip the joints together. Use a square to check the box, or measure the diagonals, then set the box aside.

As the box dries, mill the material for the top according to the schedule. Use your favorite router bit profile on the ends and front edge. I used a cove and bead bit on the top edge and a small roundover bit on the bottom edge to complete the profile.

After the glue has dried, attach the bottom/feet to the box. Nails are the answer for this job because the nails allow for some seasonal movement. Drill pilot holes for the fine finish nails then drive the nails through the bottom into the box. Set the nails just below the surface.

Sand the assembled box through #180-grit making sure to level the inlay and to true up the bottom edges to the box on all four sides.

After the sanding is complete, it's time to make and install your bottom mouldings. Profile the edges of a wider piece of stock with a small-diameter Roman ogee router bit, then rip the moulding off that stock. The moulding wraps three sides of the box and is attached with glue and brads. Notice that the moulding is taller than the thickness of the box bottom. The extra $\frac{1}{16}$" makes sure the joint between the box and bottom is hidden.

The top is a snap. Mill the top according to the schedule — or size it to your box so that there is a $\frac{1}{2}$" of overhang on the front and ends. Next, profile those same three edges. I used a cove-and-bead bit on the top edge of the piece and a $\frac{3}{16}$" roundover bit to shape the bottom edge, leaving a bullnose profile behind.

After the work is complete and the top is sanded, mount the hinges that join the top to the box. I like to waste away as much of the area as possible then finish the work with hand tools. Set the hinges to the top first then position the top to the box and transfer the hinge location. Fit the lid tight to the box, but without any binding.

Finishing the Box

Stain or dye is not a wise choice in my opinion. These would color the inlay and that's not a good thing. A natural finish is best. I chose shellac as a topcoat after a single coat of boiled linseed oil. A few coats, either brushed, ragged or sprayed on, and you're done. Sand the surface between coats to keep things smooth and use No. 0000 steel wool to knock the high sheen off the box when the application is complete. There is no finish on the inside of the box.

This box is a great place to store the family Bible — but if you're not a member of the "Bible box" crowd, it's still a fun piece to build and an excellent test of one's woodworking skills.

Nail, don't glue. The bottom of the box is attached with nails. The nails hold tight, but allow for seasonal movements in the cross-grain application.

The finish is as easy as the box. There's no need for stain or dyes that would color the inlay. Boiled linseed oil (one coat) and shellac makes the walnut sing and the inlay stand at attention.

Bungalow Mailbox

BY DAVID THIEL

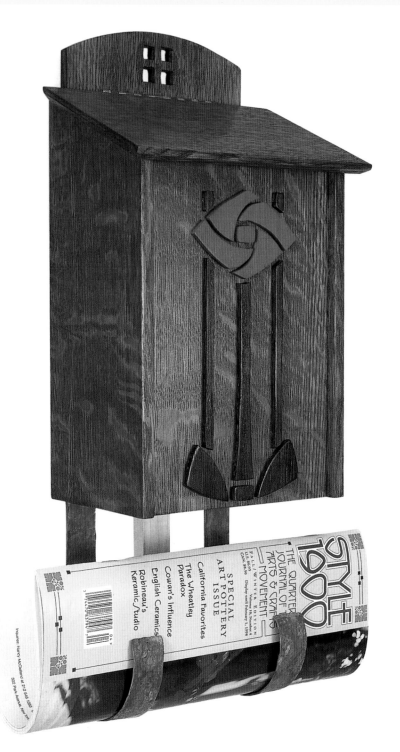

This project was by request. As I live in the 'burbs and have to walk to the curb to pick up my bills, a mailbox mounted next to my front door would be purely decorative. But a friend lucky enough to have postal delivery right to his door asked if I could come up with an appropriate design for his Arts & Crafts–style bungalow home.

After a little research I settled on a design reminiscent of the work of Charles Rennie Mackintosh. Arguably Scotland's greatest 20th-century architect and designer, Mackintosh inspired much of the European Arts & Crafts movement during the early 1900s. A stylized flower motif is found on many of his pieces.

BUNGALOW MAILBOX ■ INCHES (MILLIMETERS)

REFERENCE	QUANTITY	PART	STOCK	THICKNESS	(mm)	WIDTH	(mm)	LENGTH	(mm)	COMMENTS
A	2	sides	white oak	$\frac{3}{8}$	(10)	$4\frac{1}{2}$	(114)	11	(279)	
B	1	front	white oak	$\frac{3}{8}$	(10)	6	(152)	9	(229)	
C	1	back	white oak	$\frac{3}{8}$	(10)	$5\frac{1}{4}$	(133)	13	(330)	
D	1	bottom	white oak	$\frac{3}{8}$	(10)	$3\frac{11}{16}$	(94)	$5\frac{7}{8}$	(149)	
E	1	lid	white oak	$\frac{3}{8}$	(10)	5	(127)	$7\frac{3}{4}$	(197)	
F	1	applied detail	white oak	$\frac{1}{8}$	(10)	6	(152)	9	(229)	
G	2	magazine detail	copper pipe	$\frac{3}{4}$D	(19)			14	(356)	
		continuous hinge	cut to fit							

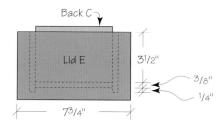

Back C

Lid E

$3\frac{1}{2}$"

$\frac{3}{8}$"

$\frac{1}{4}$"

$7\frac{3}{4}$"

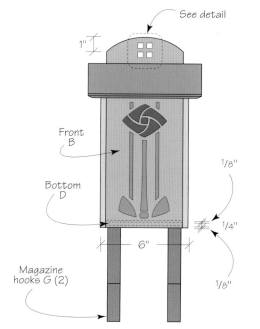

See detail

1"

Front B

Bottom D

6"

Magazine hooks G (2)

$\frac{1}{8}$"

$\frac{1}{4}$"

$\frac{1}{8}$"

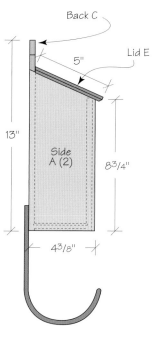

Back C

Lid E

5"

13"

Side A (2)

$8\frac{3}{4}$"

$4\frac{3}{8}$"

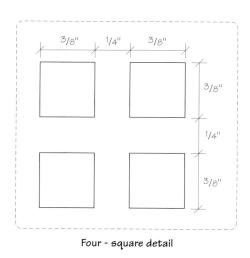

$\frac{3}{8}$" $\frac{1}{4}$" $\frac{3}{8}$"

$\frac{3}{8}$"

$\frac{1}{4}$"

$\frac{3}{8}$"

Four - square detail

Mostly Glue

The joinery for the box is primarily glue and butt joints, utilizing the long-grain-to-long-grain orientation of the sides, back and front. The bottom, however, sits in a tongue-and-groove joint between the front and back pieces to allow the wood to move.

After cutting the pieces according to the materials list, cut a ¼" × ⅛" rabbet on the underside of the two long edges of the bottom D. Then, cut the dadoes on the inside bottom of the front B and back C by setting the rip fence for ½" and the blade height to ³⁄₁₆".

Adding the Angles

Now, cut the sides A of the mailbox on an angle so you can attach the mailbox to your house without cramming a tool inside the box. The sides A slope at a 25° angle with the front edge measuring 9" tall and the back edge 11" tall.

Now, cut the chamfer on the underside of the lid E. The front B and two sides A are chamfered at a 45° angle on the table saw, leaving a ³⁄₁₆" flat edge to the top of the lid E. The back edge of the lid is cut at a 25° angle to mate with the box's back.

Detailing the Back

To add another Mackintosh feature, I cut a four-square pattern centered in the top of the curved back C.

First, mark the location of the four-square pattern as shown on the diagram. Use a ⅜" drill bit to remove most of the waste from the squares. Then use a chisel and a triangular file to clean up the cuts. To make the curve, draw a 6" radius along the top edge of the back C and cut to the mark on the band saw.

After sanding, you're ready to glue up the box. The front B is set back ¼" on the sides A, while the back C is flush to the back edge. The bottom D is left loose in the assembly.

Now, using the full-size pattern, cut out the applied detail F from ⅛" stock on the scroll saw.

Finishing Touches

Before gluing the flower to the box, stain the box a rustic-looking gray-brown by applying a black aniline dye wash. The wash was made by diluting the dye eight-to-one with denatured alcohol. I then colored the flower and stem pieces with undiluted aniline dye. Attach the flower pieces using cyanoacrylate glue. To finish, use a coat of spar urethane for outdoor protection.

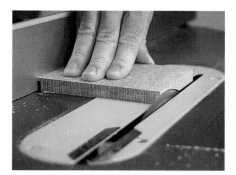

The bottom fits into the front and back pieces using a tongue-and-groove method. The sides are not attached to the bottom, and in fact, the bottom is cut to allow a ¹⁄₁₆" gap on either side. Should water happen to get into the mailbox, these gaps will allow it to escape rather than pool up in the bottom.

The top is chamfered on three edges and angle-cut on the back edge. By moving my rip fence to the left of the blade, my right-tilt saw is able to make the cuts safely, allowing the waste to fall away from the blade.

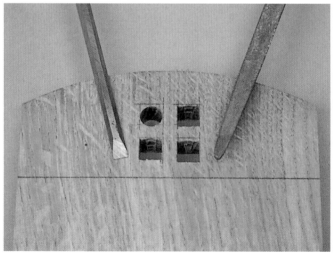

After drilling the holes, use a ⅛" chisel and a triangular file to clean up the hole. The top left hole is shown after drilling, while the two lower holes have been completed.

FULL-SIZE PATTERN OF THE ROSE/STEM/LEAF

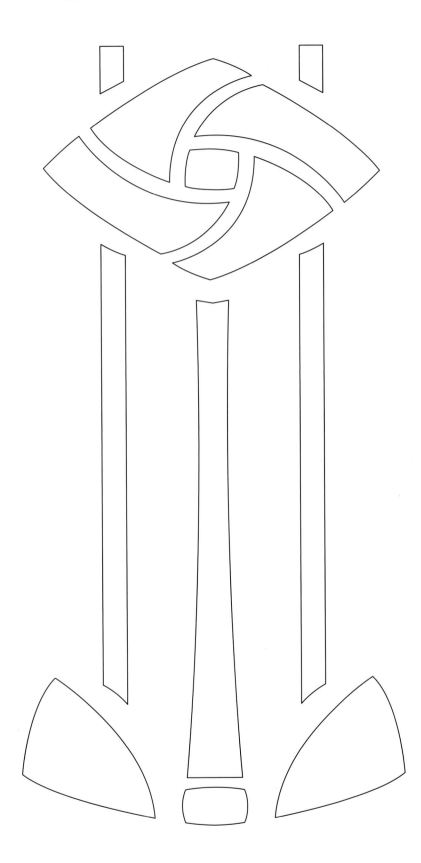

Flower Basket

BY KERRY PIERCE

This basket can be made from just two pieces of wood: one a section of ¼" material 7" wide and 14" long, and the other a ³⁄₁₆" rip 1¼" wide and 45" long. I used an ash rip for the handle because ash bends very nicely, but white oak could also be used here, and virtually any wood could be used for the dovetailed body of the basket.

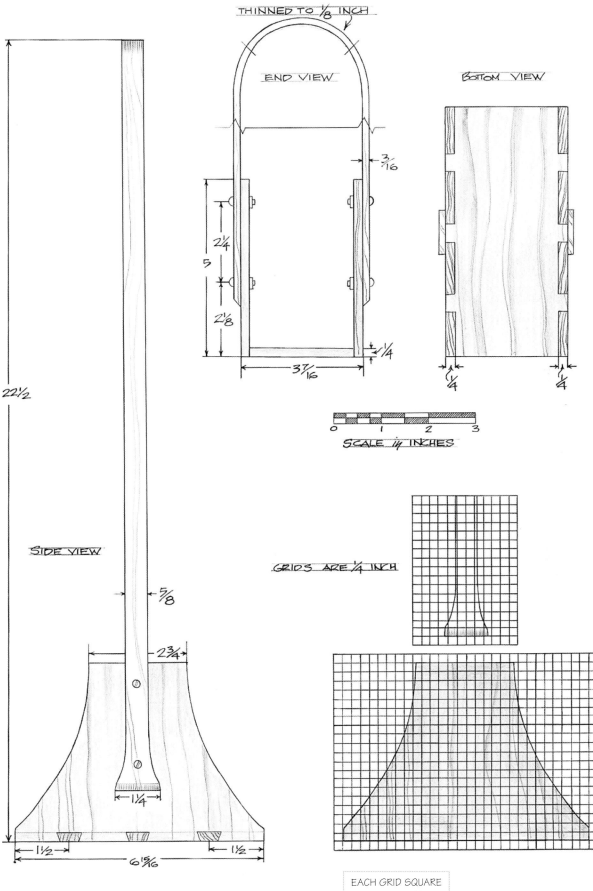

THINNED TO 1/8 INCH

END VIEW

BOTTOM VIEW

3/16

2 1/4

5

2 1/8

1/4

3 7/16

1/4   1/4

0   1   2   3

SCALE in INCHES

GRIDS ARE 1/4 INCH

22 1/2

SIDE VIEW

5/8

2 3/4

1 1/4

1 1/2   1 1/2

6 15/16

EACH GRID SQUARE
REPRESENTS 1/4"

REFERENCE	QUANTITY	PART	STOCK	THICKNESS	(mm)	WIDTH	(mm)	LENGTH	(mm)	COMMENTS
A	2	sides	cherry	1/4	(6)	5	(127)	6^{15}/16	(176)	
B	2	sides	cherry	1/4	(6)	12	(305)	6^{15}/16	(176)	
C	1	back	cherry	3/16	(5)	1 1/4	(32)	44 1/8	(1121)	

Brass machine screws and nuts

Allow an extra 1/32 (.8mm) of length to dovetailed parts so you can clean up end-grain saw marks.

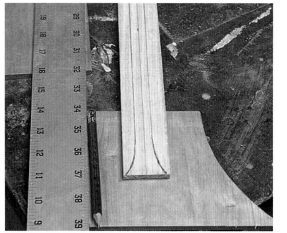

1 Although the photos are presented in a single sequence with the handle being built first, I actually worked on the handle and body simultaneously. The photo above shows the shape relationship I tried to achieve between the profile of the basket body and the profiles at the ends of the handle.

2 After planing and cutting out the band-sawn profiles of the handle, the edges must be dressed. However, the profiles at the ends of the handle won't allow these edges to be passed over the jointer. To dress these long edges, clamp the handle between two pieces of wood in your vise so the band-sawn edge peeks up over the pieces of wood. Then work this edge with a block plane.

3 The very ends of the handle should be worked with a rasp.

4 Cut a bevel on the end of the handle with a paring chisel.

5 The pencil mark on the edge of the handle marks the halfway point along the handle's length. Scrape away ¹⁄₁₆" of thickness 4" each way from that halfway point. This is the section of the handle that will be bent. The extra thinness makes the bend easier to create.

6 My steamer cost me $15. I heat water in a garage-sale deep-fat fryer to generate steam, which is then conducted, through an opening cut in the fryer's lid, into a length of PVC. The ladder is simply there to stabilize this awkward construction. Although it looks pretty crude, I've successfully steamed the slats and back posts for hundreds of post-and-rung chairs in this device.

7 This close-up of the top of the steamer with the lid cocked open shows the steady flow of steam that is conducted over any part inside the section of PVC.

8 After you've steamed the handle, take it immediately to the bending form and fix it into place. The form, which you'll prepare in advance, is just a length of scrap band-sawn to the bend of the finished handle.

9 The body of the basket can be made from a single piece of wood cut into three sections, or it could be made from three different pieces of wood.

10 Trace the curve onto one of the end pieces. After cutting the curve, use it as a guide to mark the others.

11 Before you begin to cut a set of dovetails by hand, you need to establish depth lines across the width of all the parts to be dovetailed. These lines should be scored with a knife, rather than drawn with a pencil, because knife scorings later give you positive locations in which you can register the tip of your chisel when you're paring down to the mark. In this case, I set the marks a bit less than $5/16$" from the end of the piece. That allows the pins and tails to protrude a bit more than the $1/4$" thickness of the parts. Most woodworkers use a marking gauge for this task, but since I don't have one I just measure and score.

12 Lay out the tails on the bottoms of the two end pieces. Sketch the approximate angles you'll be cutting, but don't worry if the angle you cut is a little different from the one you've drawn; no one will know. The scribbles identify the waste between the tails. Because the material is very thin, you can use your fine-toothed backsaw to cut the tails in both end pieces at the same time.

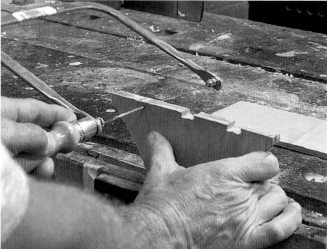

13 With a coping saw, remove the bulk of the waste between the tails. Don't worry about precision. You'll clean the bottoms of each cut with your paring chisel.

14 Locate the tip of your paring chisel in the knife scoring and begin to remove the waste. Work at this gradually in several passes. The first pass should be at an oblique angle. Each successive pass should come closer and closer to the perpendicular.

15 Before you cut all the way to the perpendicular on one side, flip the end panel over and begin to pare from the back. Your cuts should meet in approximately the middle of the end's thickness.

16 Place the bottom panel in your vise so that one end-grain edge just peeks up above the surface of the bench top. Then place the fresh-cut tails onto this end grain. The tails should be aligned so that the knife scoring on the bottom side just meets the bench-side edge of the bottom panel. With a sharp pencil point, mark the pins (those parts of a dovetail joint that fit between the tails) on the end-grain surface of the bottom panel.

17 Reposition the bottom panel so it sticks up a couple of inches from the top of the vise. Then with a combination square connect the ends of the lines you just made on the end grain with the scored line on the bottom of the bottom panel.

18 This photo shows the relationship between the pins you've just marked and the tails from which you marked them. Again, the scribbles indicate waste.

19 Use your fine-toothed backsaw to cut the sides of each pin. Be sure to keep your saw on the *waste* side of each line.

Fixing Gaps with Cherry Dust

STEP ONE Unfortunately, once I had filed away the protruding ends of the pins I saw gaps at two locations above the pins. To remedy this, I created a little cherry dust by running a belt sander over a piece of cherry clamped to my bench.

STEP TWO I mixed a thick paste of cherry dust and glue which I then worked into place in those gaps.

20 Use a coping saw to hog out the waste between the pins.

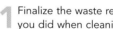

21 Finalize the waste removal with your paring chisel just as you did when cleaning up the waste between the tails.

22 Coat with glue all surfaces that will abut in the finished joint.

23 Squeeze the joint together with clamps. It will be necessary to move the clamps back and forth across the width of the basket parts bringing them together gradually. Too much force, too quickly applied at a single location, will bend and then crack one of the end panels.

Take Time to Think About the Work in Progress

This photograph illustrates something I think is often overlooked in the woodshop; taking time to think about the work in progress.

At this point in the construction of the basket I'm trying to decide where the handle should be attached. I spring-clamp it into place at several different heights, stepping back each time to assess the placement.

It's true that no real work is being done. Nevertheless, I think it's essential that we remember to include this passive activity as part of our woodshop regimen. In some instances, a little time spent thinking can prevent problems from occurring, and when things have taken a bad turn a few minutes of thought can keep us from transforming a simple problem into a disaster.

I will also mention that when I looked at this photo several days after taking it, I realized it illustrated another, entirely unrelated, woodshop problem: the complete lack of fashion sense some woodworkers exhibit in their shops. Notice the missing belt and the brown corduroys paired with a gray T-shirt. I'm just glad you can't see the shoes I'm wearing.

24 After the glue has cured overnight, use a wood file to bring the protruding ends of the pins level with the surfaces of the tails.

25 Use a spring clamp to hold the handle temporarily in place while you drill holes for the bolts that will hold the handle permanently in place. Notice the backup strip I'm holding on the back side of the end panel. This will keep the drill bit from splintering the material when it pierces the back side.

Game Box

BY KEN BURTON

The first project in my beginning woodworking classes is often a box—but not a generic box. I require students to design a box that holds something specific, such as this one. I designed it as a wedding present for some of my colleagues. It has special compartments to hold two decks of cards, a set of six dice, a score pad and pen (advertising my shop, Windy Ridge Woodworks, of course), and two other card games my family and I particularly enjoy (Skipbo and Split). The dice are for a game I learned several years ago that I know simply as "Dice." I include the rules in the box with the rest of the game supplies and have reproduced them on page 207 for you to enjoy as well. Of course, you should feel free to customize the box and include your favorite games in place of mine.

Building the box is pretty straightforward. The corners of both the main box and the tray are joined with finger joints. The box and the tray bottoms are trapped in grooves cut in the box and tray sides. The lid is a frame and panel assembly joined with slip joints at the corners. The lid's panel is a little unusual, as it overlaps the front of the frame. I made my box from luan (Philippine mahogany) that I had leftover from another project, but almost any hardwood is suitable.

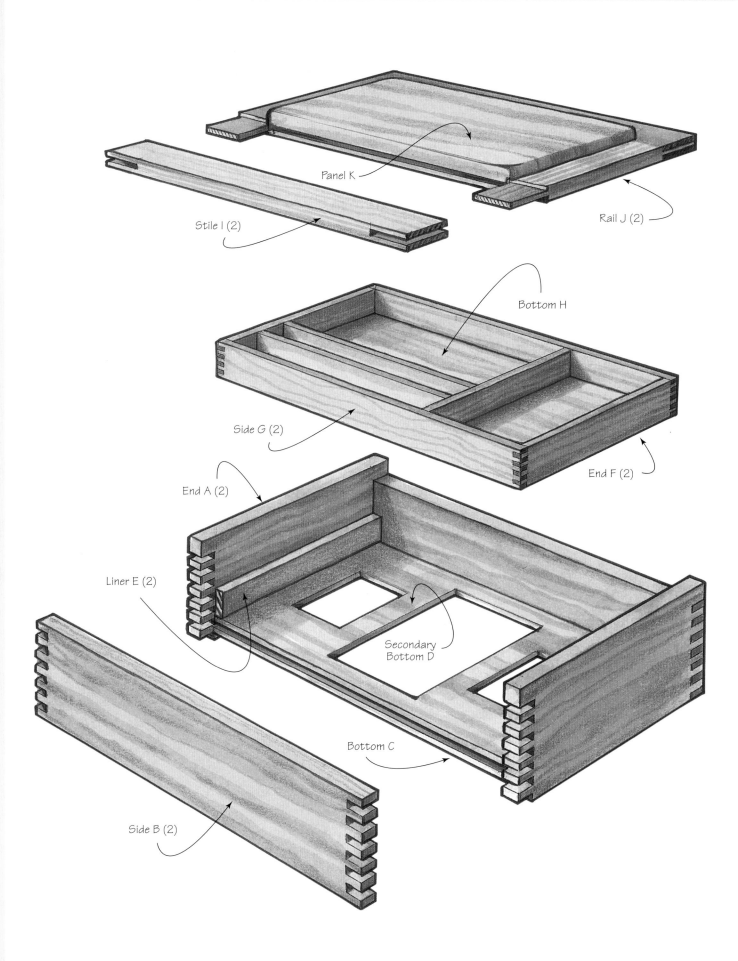

Panel K

Stile I (2)

Rail J (2)

Bottom H

Side G (2)

End F (2)

End A (2)

Liner E (2)

Secondary
Bottom D

Bottom C

Side B (2)

REFERENCE	QUANTITY	PART	STOCK	THICKNESS	(mm)	WIDTH	(mm)	LENGTH	(mm)	COMMENTS
A	2	ends	hardwood	7/16	(11)	3 3/4	(95)	7 5/8	(194)	
B	2	sides	hardwood	7/16	(11)	3 1/4	(82)	13 1/8	(333)	
C	1	bottom	hardwood	3/16	(5)	7	(178)	12 1/2	(317)	Can use 1/8" (3mm) plywood.
D	1	secondary bottom	hardwood	3/16	(5)	7	(178)	12 1/2	(317)	Can use 1/8" (3mm) plywood.
E	2	liners	hardwood	1/4	(6)					
TRAY										
F	2	ends	hardwood	7/16	(11)	3 3/4	(95)	7 5/8	(194)	
G	2	sides	hardwood	7/16	(11)	3 1/4	(82)	13 1/8	(333)	
H	1	bottom	hardwood	3/16	(5)	7	(178)	12 1/2	(317)	Can use 1/8" (3mm) plywood.
LID										
I	2	stiles	hardwood	1/2	(13)	1 3/8	(35)	7 5/8	(194)	
J	2	rails	hardwood	1/2	(13)	1 3/8	(35)	12 1/4	(311)	
K	1	panel	hardwood	1/2	(13)	5 5/8	(136)	10 1/4	(260)	

Supplies

1 pair   1 3/4" × 1 1/2" (19mm × 38mm)

12   No.4 × 3/8" (9mm) brass screws

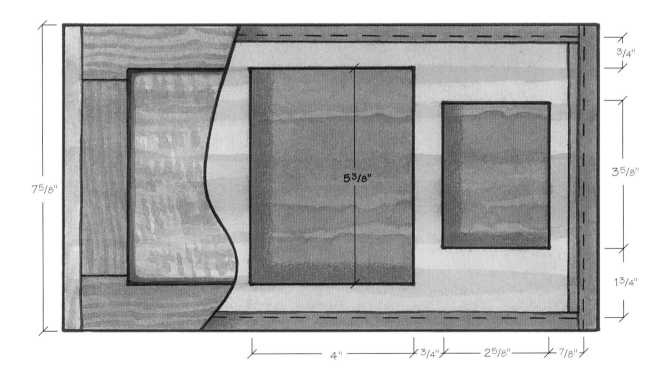

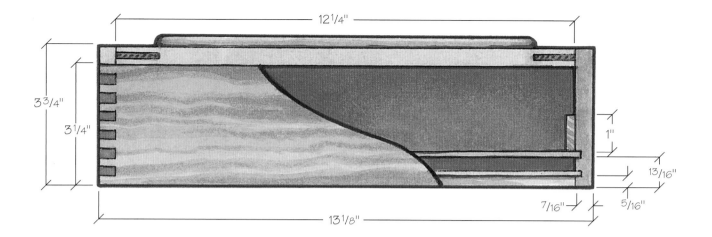

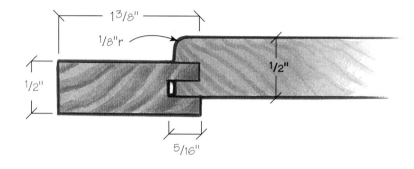

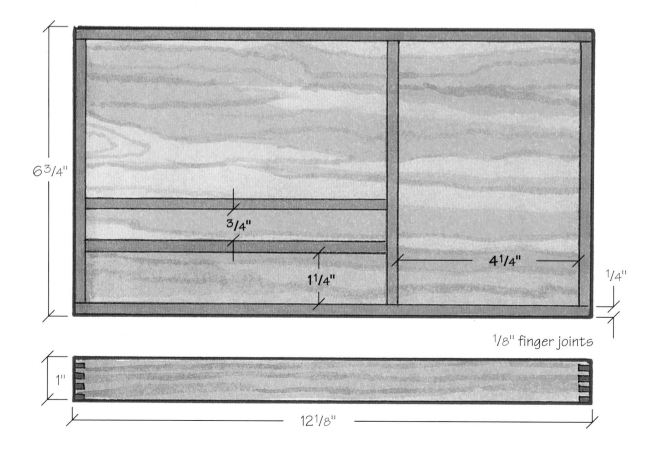

1/8" finger joints

1 Cut the pieces for the box and tray to the sizes specified in the materials list. Rip the pieces to width first, then cut them to length. I always cut one end of each piece square and stack the pieces with the square ends facing away from me on the saw table. Then I set up a stop and saw the other ends square, cutting the pieces to length in the process.

2 Cut the corner joints for the box. Cut the ends first, starting with their bottom edges against the jig's key. Stop the cuts when you get to ½" (13mm) of the top edge. Repeat the process with the side pieces, starting these pieces with a cut rather than a finger.

3 Swap the finger joint setup for a rip blade and cut the grooves for the two bottoms in the end and side pieces. This process creates notches in the ends of the sides that will be visible in the finished piece. Rather than trying to make a stopped cut, I simply fill these notches with small pieces of wood after assembly.

4 If you use hardwood for the bottom panels, you'll probably have to rabbet the edges so they fit in their grooves. Cut these rabbets by running the pieces vertically past the blade. Be sure to hold the pieces as flat as possible as they run along the fence so the resulting tongue has a consistent thickness.

5 There are a few things the table saw doesn't do well. Making the cutouts for the games is one of them. Instead, make these cuts with a ¼" (6mm) straight bit in a router table. Lay out the openings to suit the games you intend to include. Make the cuts by first tipping the piece onto the running bit, then running the piece along the fence from right to left. Reposition the fence as necessary to make the required cutouts.

6 Sand the two bottoms and the inside surfaces of the sides and ends. Prefinish the bottoms (at least one coat). Put the box together after spreading glue on all the mating surfaces of the fingers. Clamping is a lot easier if you make a set of box clamps.

7 It's important that you cut the pieces for the tray to fit snugly inside the box—by the time you fit the joints and sand everything, you'll create a little clearance. Cut finger joints to join the corners of the tray. If possible, use a rip blade to make the cuts as it leaves a square cornered kerf. Note: I made a separate jig to cut ⅛"-wide (3mm) fingers, but you could easily use the same jig you have for ¼" (6mm) fingers. Just flip the fences upside down and make a new slot and key for the narrower blade. The advantage to having two separate jigs is that once you have them adjusted, they stay that way.

8 Like the box bottom, the tray's bottom is captured in a groove that's cut in the tray's sides. Try hard to position the fence so the groove aligns with the fingers. If you're off by more than a hair, you'll have to patch both the sides and ends of the tray after glue-up.

9 Glue the tray together. When the glue dries, cut small square plugs to fill the bottom grooves and glue them in place. Cut pieces for the dividers. Size the dividers and the openings in the tray to suit your purposes. Position the dividers within the tray. Drill ⅛" (3mm) holes into the ends of the dividers and dowel them in place. You may find it helpful to cut spacers to go in between the dividers to maintain the proper spacing.

10 Cut the stiles and rails for the lid frame to size (cut a few extras just in case). Arrange the four best pieces the way you want the frame to go together. Mark the pieces with triangular marks as shown, with the open sides of the marks toward the inside of the frame.

Reference Surfaces

Occasions will arise when you'll want to make a cut that is centered on your workpiece. An example is the groove for the panel in the Game Box lid. The temptation is to make one cut, with one side of the piece against the fence, then turn the piece around and run it a second time with the opposite side against the fence. This will work, but if your workpieces vary at all in thickness, the resulting grooves won't be consistent.

My preference is to set the fence for the first cut. Cut all the pieces. Then reset the fence and make the second cut, running the same side of the workpiece against the fence. By using the same side of the workpiece as a reference surface for all cuts, your results will be consistent even if the dimensions of your workpieces are not.

11 Cut the groove for the lid's panel in two passes. Start with the fence ³⁄₁₆" (5mm) away from the blade and the blade raised about ⁵⁄₁₆" (8mm) above the table. Cut the pieces with their marked side away from the fence. After making the first cut in all of the pieces, bump the fence away from the blade, widening the cut to ³⁄₁₆" (5mm). Be sure to cut grooves in your test pieces as well.

12 The corners of the lid frame are joined with a slip joint (also called a bridle joint or an open mortise and tenon). In this joint, tongues cut on the ends of the rails fit into slots cut in the ends of the stiles. Start by cutting the slots in the stiles. Use a rip blade, if possible, as it will leave a square-bottomed kerf. Set the blade height equal to the width of the rails less slightly more than the depth of the groove.

13 Clamp a stile in the simple tenoning jig with the marked side facing away from the jig and the groove facing the blade. Adjust the rip fence so the blade cuts along the fence side of the groove. Cut all the pieces with the marked side facing out. Then readjust the fence so the blade cuts along the opposite side of the groove, creating a slot ³/₁₆" (5mm) wide. Make the second cut in all the pieces. Note: I rarely make test-cuts for the stiles, as I'll be cutting the rails to fit whatever size slot I end up with.

14 To cut the tongues on the rails, raise the blade height to slightly less than the width of the stiles. Because the cuts required are slightly wider than the width of the blade, you'll need to make them with two passes. The first pass, on the outside of the pieces, simply removes the excess material. Clamp a test rail into the jig and adjust the fence so the blade cuts along the face of the jig—don't worry if you actually cut into the jig a little. Turn the piece around in the jig (no need to worry about precision yet) and cut the waste away from the second side. Repeat the process on the other ends of the rails.

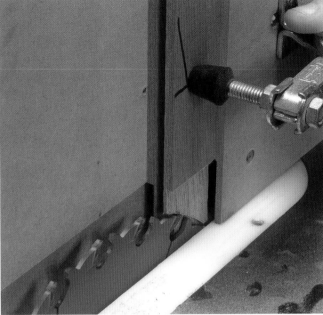

15 With the waste out of the way, you can concentrate on making the precision cuts. Clamp the test rails in the jig with the marked side out and the groove facing the blade. Adjust the fence so the blade just kisses the edge of the groove. Make the cut. Ideally you will leave a hair-thin bit of wood alongside the groove. Take the test piece out of the jig and compare it to one of the stiles. Make adjustments, if necessary, and make the first precision cut on all the pieces. Note: Be sure to load the pieces into the jig with the marked side out.

16 Reposition the fence to make the second precision cut. Again, your aim is to leave a hair-thin bit of wood alongside the groove. Cut the test piece and check the fit of the tongue in the slot. The pieces should go together with firm hand pressure. Adjust as needed, then cut all the pieces.

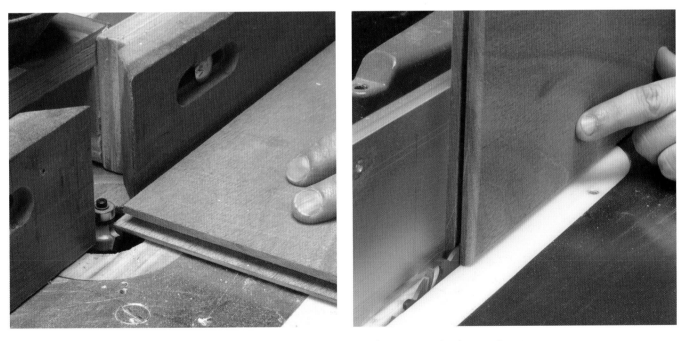

17 Assemble the lid frame without glue to check the fit of the joints and to measure for the panel. Cut the piece for the panel ¾" (19mm) larger than the frame opening in both width and length. Cut a ⅛" (3mm) roundover on the edges of the panel. If you have the right cutters, you can do this with a molding head on the table saw. You can also use a roundover bit on a router table.

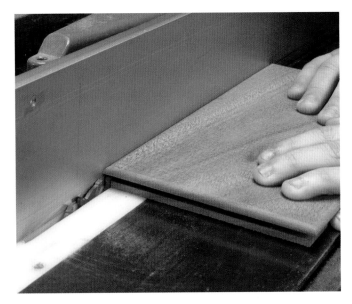

18 While the panel laps the top of the frame by ⅜" (9mm), the tongue that engages the grooves only projects about ¼" (6mm) to allow the panel room for expansion. To cut the tongue down to size, reset the blade height to a hair more than ³⁄₁₆" (5mm). Position the fence ¹⁄₃₂" (less than 1 mm) from the blade. Cut the tongue down on all four sides of the panel by running the panel along the fence.

19 Sand all the pieces, then glue the lid assembly together. When I glue up slip joints, I like to apply clamping pressure in all three directions.

20 While the glue dries, make sure you can still move the panel within the frame. The whole idea behind frame and panel assembly is that the panel is free to move with changes in humidity. After you remove the clamps, center the panel. Drill two ⅛" (3mm) holes through the frame and into the edge of the panel. Place the holes in the center of each stile about ³⁄₁₆" (5mm) in from the edge. Glue short pieces of ⅛" (3mm) dowel in the holes to keep the panel from shifting. By pinning the panel along its center line, you keep it from rattling around while still allowing it to expand to either side.

21 After pinning the panel in place, trim the lid to fit and hinge it to the back of the box. You can cut the mortises for the hinges by hand, or you can make up a C-shaped template to use with a handheld router equipped with a guide bushing and a ¼" (6mm) straight bit. As an option, you might want to carve a finger recess along the front of the box to make it easier to open. Finish the box with your favorite wood finish. I gave the box in the photo several coats of Watco oil.

Dice

Dice is played with six dice. During each turn a player rolls all six dice and scores depending upon the combination of dots that appear. The first player to accumulate exactly 10,000 points wins.

Scoring is as follows:
Ones count as 100
Fives count as 50

The rest of the numbers don't count unless rolled in these combinations:
3 twos count as 200
3 threes count as 300
3 fours count as 400
3 sixes count as 600

In addition,
3 fives count as 500
3 ones count as 1000
3 pairs count as 1000
A straight (1, 2, 3, 4, 5, 6) also counts as 1000

During a turn, you roll all six dice. Set aside any that score. At this point you can either stop and collect your points or roll any non-scoring dice to try for more points. To qualify for a combination, all the scoring dice must have been thrown in a single roll. For example, if on your first roll, you get 3 fives, they would score 500. However, if you get 2 fives on your first roll and 1 five on your second roll, your total would be only 150.

If you choose to roll more than once, you can roll only non-scoring dice the second time. The exception to this is if all of the dice score on the first roll. Then you can roll them all again (if you dare) for more points. If you roll the dice and none of them score, you forfeit any points earned that turn and your turn ends.

To begin the game and get on the scoreboard, you need to earn a minimum of 500 points in one turn. Keep score by simply maintaining a running total for each player. To win, you need to score exactly 10,000 points. If you go over, your score goes back to whatever it was at the end of your previous turn.

CLASSIC STYLING MASKS THE FUNCTIONALITY OF THIS TABLETOP KEEPSAKE.

Jewelry Armoire

BY DAVID THIEL

Though I'm very much aware I never will be able to make a jewelry box large enough to satisfy my wife's ambitions, I think I've finally made one attractive enough to keep her content.

This jewelry armoire uses clean, art deco styling and highly figured curly maple, accented with black lacquer. The most important aspect of this project is selecting a finely figured wood to serve as the focal point.

REFERENCE	QUANTITY	PART	STOCK	THICKNESS	(mm)	WIDTH	(mm)	LENGTH	(mm)	COMMENTS
A	2	top & bottom	poplar	3/4	(13)	6⁵/₈	(168)	13³/₄	(349)	
B	2	interior sides	maple	5/8	(16)	4³/₈	(112)	13¹/₂	(343)	
C	2	door sides	maple	5/8	(16)	5	(127)	13³/₈	(340)	
D	2	door fronts	maple	5/8	(16)	2	(51)	13³/₈	(340)	
E	2	door backs (hinged)	maple	5/8	(16)	1	(25)	12¹/₈	(308)	
F	4	door tops & bottoms	maple	5/8	(16)	1	(25)	5	(127)	
G	3	drawer fronts	maple	5/8	(16)	2	(51)	8¹/₂	(216)	
H	1	drawer front	maple	5/8	(16)	2¹/₄	(57)	8¹/₂	(216)	
J	1	drawer front	maple	5/8	(16)	2¹/₂	(57)	8¹/₂	(216)	
K	1	drawer front	maple	5/8	(16)	2⁵/₈	(64)	8¹/₂	(216)	
L	6	drawer box sides	plywood	1/4	(6)	1⁵/₈	(64)	4	(102)	
M	6	drawer box fronts/backs	plywood	1/4	(6)	1⁵/₈	(64)	7³/₁₆	(183)	
N	2	drawer box sides	plywood	1/4	(6)	1⁷/₈	(48)	4	(102)	
P	2	drawer box front/back	plywood	1/4	(6)	1⁷/₈	(48)	7³/₁₆	(183)	
Q	2	drawer box sides	plywood	1/4	(6)	2¹/₈	(54)	4	(102)	
R	2	drawer box front/back	plywood	1/4	(6)	2¹/₈	(54)	7³/₁₆	(183)	
S	2	drawer box sides	plywood	1/4	(6)	2³/₈	(60)	4	(102)	
T	2	drawer box front/back	plywood	1/4	(6)	2³/₈	(60)	7³/₁₆	(183)	
U	5	drawer bottoms	plywood	1/4	(6)	4	(102)	7⁵/₈	(194)	
V	1	drawer bottom	plywood	1/4	(6)	4	(102)	7¹/₄	(184)	
W	1	armoire back	plywood	1/4	(6)	7⁷/₈	(200)	13¹/₂	(343)	
X	6	handles	poplar	1/4	(6)	1	(25)	2	(51)	

1 The case sides have ¼" dadoes cut on the insides to accept the drawer bottoms, which do double duty as drawer slides. Starting from the bottom edge of the sides, cut the dadoes at 2⁷/₈", 5³/₈", 7⁵/₈", 9⁵/₈" and 11⁵/₈". Also cut a ¼" x ¼" rabbet on the inside rear edges to receive the back.

Select Your Wood

To achieve the most dramatic effect from the wood, I chose a single piece of curly maple that measured 8½" across. This allowed me not only to cut all the drawer fronts from one piece, but also I was able to match the grain so it carried around the side of the door to the front. Construction is actually very simple. First cut all the parts as shown in the cutting list, marking the door and drawer parts to retain grain orientation. Then make the side dado cuts as shown in photo 1.

The door backs require a clearance cut to receive the mortise hinges, as detailed in photo 2. The drawer fronts receive similar cuts for the drawer pulls to fit flush with the top edge. Center these cuts and make them ⅛" deep. Then cut the drawer pulls from a strip of poplar on the table saw, making a lip at the front of the pulls (see diagram detail).

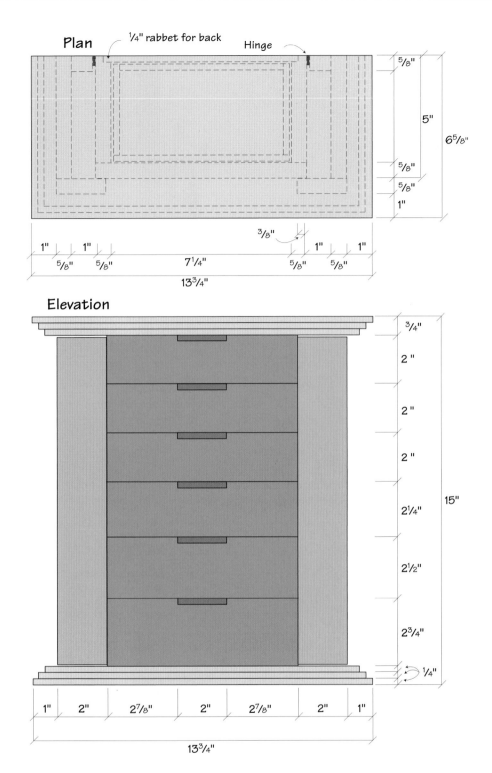

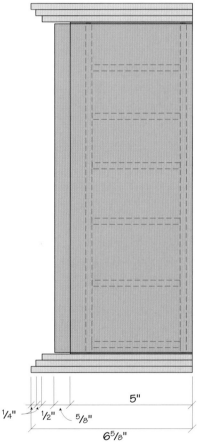

The detail on the top and bottom of the armoire comes next (see photos 3 and 4).

Make the Doors

First sand all the interior surfaces of the door pieces, then glue the pieces of the doors together. Start with the door fronts and sides. Do each of these steps individually, because if you try to glue all the pieces in place at one time, you may end up with a horrible, sticky mess.

Spread the Glue

Once the door fronts are in place and the glue dries, glue the top and bottom pieces in place using the back pieces to gauge the spacing at the rear of the door. The final step is to glue the back pieces in place.

Drawer Assembly

Next, assemble the drawer boxes using finger, or box, joints. I used Baltic 5-ply plywood for the drawer sides. This material works well for strength, and it adds an attractive detail to the finger joints. After cutting the pieces, assemble as shown in photos 5 and 6.

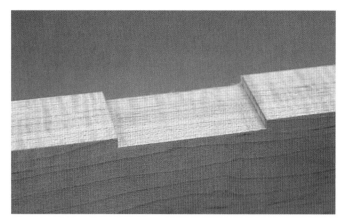

2 I mortised the door back pieces for the three ⅛"-thick hinges used on each door. The hinges you use may be different, so I won't bother giving you their cutting locations. To mill the relief cuts, I made repeat passes over the saw blade using my slot miter gauge to guide the work.

3 Create the step detail on the top and bottom pieces using four saw setups. The first two cuts (on edge) define the horizontal face of the steps.

4 The last two cuts define the depth of the steps. The cleaner these cuts are, the better. Otherwise some serious sanding will be necessary to make them look good under the black finish.

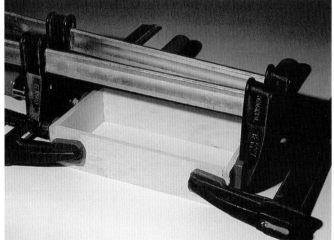

5 The construction of the drawers is the next step. After cutting the finger joints, glue and clamp the drawer sides, fronts and backs. Again, sand the interior faces of the drawers before you start gluing.

6 With all the drawer boxes assembled, tack the bottoms in place. Make sure the boxes are equally spaced to square and define the tongues of the drawer bottom guides.

7 Once assembled, the drawers determine proper spacing of the interior sides in relation to the top and bottom. After determining the drawer spacing, drill clearance holes in the bottom and screw it to the sides (pilot drill into the sides). Use dowels and glue to attach the top from its underside only to hide the joinery, leaving a flawless top.

8 Before attaching the drawer fronts, use shims to equally space them. Work down from the top drawer. Drill clearance holes in the drawer box fronts, and use double-sided tape to temporarily secure the front while screwing the fronts to the drawer boxes. Remove the cabinet back to make it easier to push the drawers out without changing the front's spacing before finally securing it.

9 Finishing touches include lining the bottoms of the drawers with felt to protect the jewelry. Use small hooks attached to the inside of the doors to hang necklaces and bracelets. Felt pads attached to the underside of the bottom protect the surface of the dresser.

Drawer Pulls

Finish all parts prior to assembly. Put masking tape on the drawer pull bottoms to leave bare wood for a better glue bond to the drawer front.

Armoire Assembly

Begin assembling the armoire by locating the sides on the top and bottom (photo 7). Use the back to square up the case, but don't nail the back in yet. Attach the top with dowels and glue.

You'll find a tight fit when screwing on the fronts. To solve this, mark a pilot hole while the front is "stuck" to the drawer box, then remove and pilot drill the fronts. An L-shaped screwdriver, ratchet screwdriver or long-shanked screwdriver held at an angle will ease this step. Next, drill and insert a small magnetic catch at the top of each door prior to hanging. Remember to pilot drill for all the brass screws, or you'll end up with a bunch of twisted-off screw

heads. Once the doors are hung, locate the proper spot for the catch plate on the cabinet side.

Finishing Touches

To make the armoire jewelry-friendly, add felt as shown in photo 9. After that, it's up to the box's new owner to arrange all her jewelry — just watch that you aren't talked into buying more.

Let's Eat

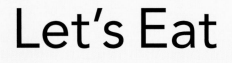

BY JIM STACK

Hey, when do we eat?

Get the table set, then we can eat...

You won't keep your everyday flatware in this box but it is the right place for the good stuff. This box keeps the silver safe and ready to use when the need arises.

This project involves a lot of hand-work, along with power tools. But like everything else in woodworking, this project is built following a series of steps that in and of themselves are not complicated.

This project will show you how to match and lay up burl veneers. You'll also get to cut some dovetails using hand tools. The scrollwork on the lid and bottom is an exercise in cutting curves and routing along those curves. It's fun!

The final finish on this project becomes an aerobic workout when completing the finish.

Then it will definitely be time to eat!

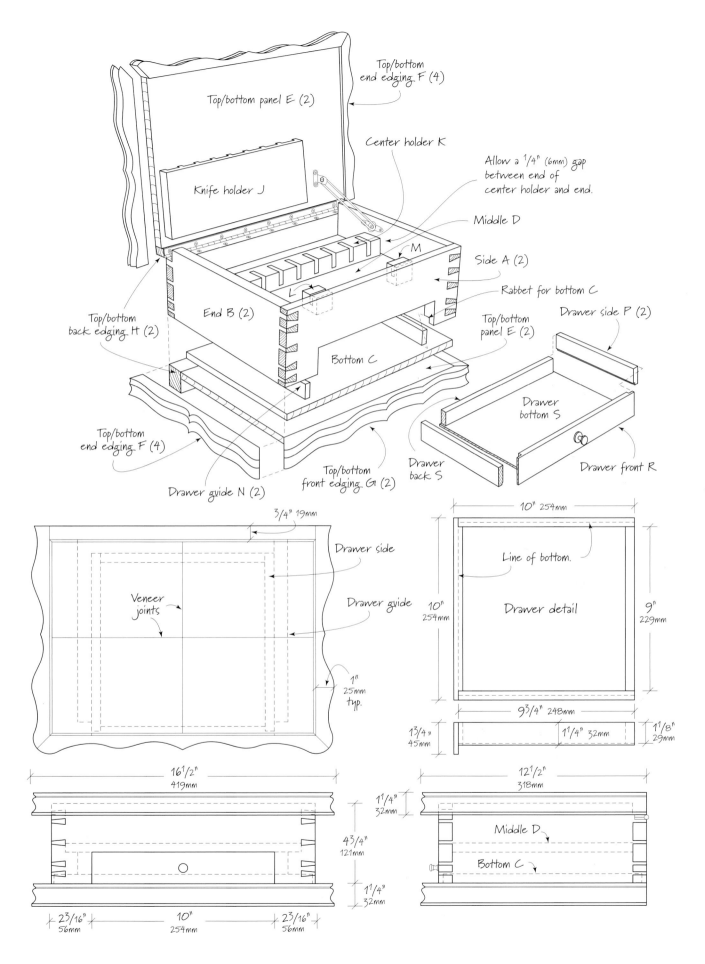

Top/bottom panel E (2)

Top/bottom end edging F (4)

Center holder K

Allow a 1/4" (6mm) gap between end of center holder and end.

Knife holder J

Middle D

M

Side A (2)

L

Rabbet for bottom C

Top/bottom back edging H (2)

End B (2)

Bottom C

Top/bottom panel E (2)

Drawer side P (2)

Top/bottom end edging F (4)

Drawer guide N (2)

Top/bottom front edging G (2)

Drawer bottom S

Drawer back S

Drawer front R

3/4" 19mm

Drawer side

Veneer joints

Drawer guide

1" 25mm typ.

10" 254mm

Line of bottom.

10" 254mm

Drawer detail

9" 229mm

9 3/4" 248mm

1 3/4" 45mm

1 1/4" 32mm

1 1/8" 29mm

16 1/2" 419mm

1 1/4" 32mm

4 3/4" 121mm

1 1/4" 32mm

2 3/16" 56mm

10" 254mm

2 3/16" 56mm

12 1/2" 318mm

Middle D

Bottom C

REFERENCE	QUANTITY	PART	STOCK	THICKNESS	(mm)	WIDTH	(mm)	LENGTH	(mm)	COMMENTS
A	2	sides	mahogany	3/4	(19)	4 3/4	(121)	14 3/8	(365)	
B	2	ends	mahogany	3/4	(19)	4 3/4	(121)	11 1/2	(292)	
C	1	bottom	plywood	1/2	(13)	11	(279)	14 1/8	(359)	
D	1	middle	plywood	1/2	(13)	10	(254)	12 7/8	(327)	
E	2	top/bottom panels	plywood	1/2	(13)	10 13/16	(275)	14 1/2	(368)	veneer top panel
F	4	top/bottom end edging	mahogany	1	(25)	1 1/4	(32)	12 1/2	(318)	
G	2	top/bottom front edging	mahogany	1	(25)	1 1/4	(32)	16 1/2	(419)	
H	2	top/bottom back edging	mahogany	3/4	(19)	1 1/4	(32)	14 1/2	(368)	
J	1	knife holder	plywood	1/2	(13)	4	(102)	11	(279)	
K	1	center holder	poplar	1 1/4	(32)	1 1/2	(38)	12 5/8	(321)	
L	1	long front holder	poplar	1 1/4	(32)	1 1/2	(38)	2 5/8	(67)	
M	1	short front holder	poplar	1 1/4	(32)	1 1/2	(38)	2	(51)	
N	2	drawer guides	poplar	3/4	(19)	1 1/4	(32)	10	(254)	
P	2	drawer sides	mahogany	1/2	(13)	1 1/4	(32)	9 3/4	(248)	
Q	1	drawer back	mahogany	1/2	(13)	1 1/8	(29)	9	(229)	
R	1	drawer front	mahogany	1/2	(13)	1 3/4	(44)	10	(254)	
S	1	drawer bottom	plywood	1/4	(6)	9 1/2	(241)	9 3/4	(248)	
T		inlay strip		1/16	(2)	1/4	(6)	54	(1372)	running inches

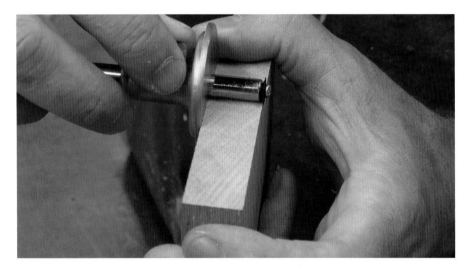

Supplies

1   14 3/8" (365mm) continuous hinge
1   lid stay
1   1/2" (13mm) brass knob
spray or wipe-on lacquer

1 After cutting the sides and ends to dimensions, set your marking gauge to the thickness of the parts.

2 Score a line on the ends of the end parts. This scored line is where you'll stop the dovetail pin cuts.

3 Lay out the pins using your sliding T-bevel and a ruler. It's traditional to make the pins narrow. Space them however you like. I put the two outside pins closer together. Cut on the outside of the lines that mark the pins and cut down to your scored line. Be sure to mark the waste material between the pins.

4 It's easier for me to make all the cuts on the same side of each pin, then make the cuts on the other side of each pin. That way, I only change the angle of the saw two times.

5 Remove the material between the pins. Clamp the part to a scrap board and start chiseling. Some woodworkers like to use a coping saw or band saw to remove the bulk of the material, then clean up using a chisel. I never trusted myself doing it that way, so I stick with the mallet and chisel. Try it both ways and see what you like the best. There's no magic bullet to this process. Keep practicing using your chisel and mallet and you'll soon get a feel for it.

6 Use the pins as a template and, using a sharp pencil, mark the tails on the sides. Note the numbers on each part. Each set of pins is probably a little different (because they're hand-cut), so be sure to mark each set of pins and matching tails.

7 Cut the tails down to the scored line. Cut on the outside of the tail marks. Again, remember to mark the waste between the tails. After you've cut the tails, remove the material between them as you did for the pins.

8 Hopefully the joints fit together. You may need to trim the inside of the tails just a little to get a snug fit. What's a snug fit? It varies with the density of the wood you're using. For mahogany, the joint can be a little snug and still go together because the wood is soft and will give a little. If you're using maple, however, the joints need to be cut precisely. Maple will not forgive imperfections. (That's why I like softer woods for making hand-cut dovetails.) Once you're a pro, use all the maple you want.

Flattening Veneer

STEP ONE If veneer has been stored in a dry place and/or has been around for awhile, it has a tendency to dry out. When this happens with burl veneer, it becomes like the Appalachian Mountains — lots of hills and valleys. If you were to put this into a press, the veneer would scream for mercy and crack up. I use a spray bottle with water in it to spritz a mist over the veneer. Do this with each sheet of veneer that you're going to use.

STEP TWO When all the veneer sheets are damp, layer them in your press with three or four sheets of newspaper between each sheet of veneer. The newspaper will absorb the excess water and help disperse the moisture evenly throughout the sheets of veneer. Apply enough pressure on the press to squeeze the veneers flat and leave the press alone for at least 24 hours. Then release the clamps and check the veneer. If it is still quite damp, replace yesterday's damp newspaper with today's news. Retighten the clamps and give it another 24 hours, then check again. You want the newspaper and veneer to be almost dry or, at most, slightly moist. The veneer will feel cool to the touch. This means the veneer is happy and you've been successful in rehydrating it. It will gladly bend, not crack or break.

9 Glue the box sides and ends together. Let the glue dry, then rout the bottom panel. I used a rabbeting bit, which is made especially for this kind of cut. It won't tear or splinter the wood.

10 What is this, cutting in the middle of the front? Yup. I wanted the drawer front to match the piece from which it's cut, and this handsaw has a small kerf that ensures the drawer front will fit nicely in the cutout. This is called a plunge cut because you start the cut on the surface of the wood and work your way down.

11 Make the vertical cuts squarely to the edge of the front using a combination square.

12 I left the rounded corners in the rabbets and fitted the bottom to the cut. Glue the bottom in place. Then cut the drawer guides and glue them inside the box. The edges of the guides should be flush with the ends of the drawer-front cutout and square to the front of the box.

13 Cut the drawer parts to length and slightly wider than shown in the cutting list. Then fit the sides to the drawer opening so they slide in and out smoothly. Cut the back to the same width as the sides minus the thickness of the bottom. Cut a rabbet in the bottom inside of the drawer front so it fits over the front edge of the box's bottom. This rabbet needs to include the thickness of the drawer bottom. Cut rabbets in the drawer sides for the drawer bottom. Cut the drawer bottom and glue the drawer together.

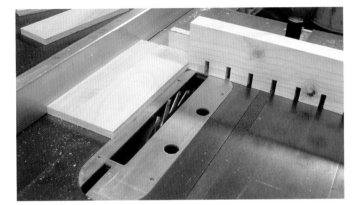

14 Cut the notches in the center holder using a dado head in your table saw. If you don't have a dado cutter, use your router table with a straight router bit. I used different sized spacers to locate the notches. Or, you could simply move the saw's fence after making the cuts at each end of the part. Move it the same distance each time and you're good to go. Make the two front holders from a long piece of wood, cut the notches, then cut the parts to length.

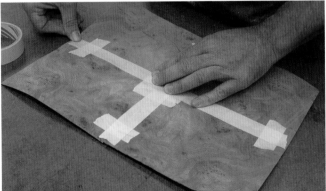

15 Cut the grooves in the knife holder using a table saw or, as shown here, a router table. I chose the router table because it cuts plywood cleanly.

16 If necessary, flatten the burl veneers (see sidebar, "Flattening Veneer" on the previous page). Cut four consecutive pieces of veneer to one-quarter the size of the top panel. Joint two adjacent edges to exactly 90°. Flip two veneers over (like opening a book), then flip up a single veneer from each set like you're opening a briefcase. This is a four-way book-match. The 90° corners should all come together perfectly; unless you're dead accurate, you'll need to do a little tweaking of the joints. That's OK. A hair's-width removal of material won't be noticed. Tape the joints together and glue the edges at the taped joints. This adds strength to these joints and keeps them from shifting in the veneer press.

17 Remove the tape from the veneer joints after the glue has dried. Prepare another veneer layer (I used mahogany) for the inside of the top panel. Apply an even layer of yellow glue to both sides of the top plywood panel. Put the mahogany veneer down first, put the glued panel on top of it, then put the burl veneer on top of the panel. Then clamp the whole mess in your and lay up the top panel in your benchtop veneer press.

18 When the panel has been in the press for 24 hours, remove it. From the middle of the panel, where the joints converge, measure half the length and width of the finished dimensions of the panel and draw a mark. Do this both ways on the panel and cut the panel to your marks. This is the surefire way to get the veneers centered on the panel.

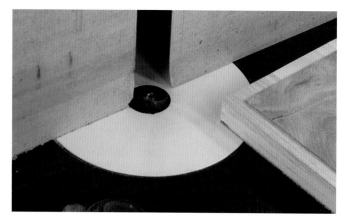

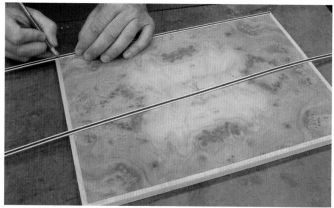

19 Use a straight bit and your router table to cut the rabbet for the inlay strips. Make the rabbets slightly less deep than the thickness of the inlay. After the inlay is glued in place, it will be easy to level it to the veneer.

20 Mark each inlay strip to length using the panel as your guide.

21 Miter cut the ends of the inlay strips.

22 Tape each strip in place and fit the next one to it. Then remove the tape, add glue to the rabbet and tape the strips back in place. Place the panel in your veneer press for 1 hour. Then remove the panel from the press, remove the tape and carefully hand sand the inlay strips level with the veneer.

23 Mill the edging to size, miter the ends and glue them to the top and bottom panels. Attach the back edging (not shown in the photo) first, then the front edging, then cut and fit the end edgings. Hold the edgings as close to flush as possible to the surface of the veneer or just slightly proud of the veneer. Do not let the top of the edgings get below the surface of the veneer. You'll end up sanding through the veneer trying to level the edging to the veneer. I've found that using blocks cut to precise thickness and placed under the panel is an easy way to keep the edging level to the panel.

24 Gently clamp the edging to the panel. No undue clamping pressure is necessary — ever. If you have to apply excessive clamping pressure, you need to check and fix your joinery. No amount of pressure will make it right — you'll end up ruining your clamps and your work.

25 Make a full-scale layout of the scalloping on the top and bottom panels' edges. Then apply the patterns with spray adhesive. Cut the patterns using a band saw or jigsaw. Sand the scalloping to final shape, removing any saw blade marks.

26 Cutting this profile is easily done using your router table and a router bit. I recommend you purchase a router bit that has the profile you like so you can perform this operation in one step. You will find many uses for this router bit in future projects.

27 Using your table saw, cut a ¹³⁄₁₆"-deep (21mm) by ⅞"-high (22mm) rabbet in the top back of the box. The dimensions of this rabbet are determined by the thickness and height (add the thickness of the continuous hinge to the height) of the top back edging. Adding ¹⁄₁₆" (2mm) to the depth of the rabbet gives clearance for the lid to be closed.

28 Cutting the rabbet in step 27 makes it possible for the back of the lid to be flush with the back of the box and the back of the bottom. It also makes it possible for the lid to close around the top of the box, creating a mild seal which helps to slow down the tarnishing of the silver flatware. Finish with 4 to 6 coats of clear lacquer.

Step One – Wet Sanding, Not Sanding Wet

The first time I ever wet sanded a project, I was confused. Wasn't lacquer allergic to water? And here I was using water to wet sand a freshly lacquered tabletop. (Actually the lacquer had been curing for a week.)

That's the first thing to remember — let the lacquer cure for at least a week, even more if you have time. Lacquer will shrink in its first few days of being in the world. Then it settles down to live life one day at a time. If you're planning on wet sanding, you should have 10 to 15 good, even coats of lacquer on the surface. Lacquer blends with itself, so every time you apply another coat, it essentially becomes one thicker coat. And so it goes coat after coat.

The reason for wet sanding is to level the little hills and valleys in the lacquer. Use 600-grit wet/dry sandpaper to do the trick. I use water and a few drops of liquid dishwashing soap. The soap helps the sandpaper glide better. The water keeps the sandpaper lubricated and clean so it can cut through the surface of the lacquer. Dip the sandpaper in the water and drip some water on the surface to be sanded. Start sanding, occasionally adding water so the surface stays wet.

As you're sanding, the surface of the lacquer will start to dull. These are the hills being leveled. There

will be places where it stays shiny. Those are the valleys. You want to keep sanding until the whole surface becomes dull. This means you're done.

Check your progress frequently so you don't sand through the lacquer! If you do sand through, you'll need to stop sanding and reapply more coats of lacquer. If you sand through the lacquer on veneer, it's possible the veneer could absorb the water and buckle. Trust me, it's happened. So avoid sanding through the lacquer!

Step Two – The Rub Out

When you've successfully wet sanded your project to a wonderfully smooth lacquer finish, you're ready to rub it with No. 0000 steel wool. Unroll the steel wool bale and make it fit your hand. Rub completely from one end of the surface to the other.

Be careful not to get the lacquer too warm or it will start to melt. Take it easy and pay attention to the warmth of your hand. Also, take care at the edges and sharp corners. These areas don't have much lacquer on them, so you could rub through. How do I know about all these mistakes? I've made them, so hopefully you won't!

When the surface is shiny and even, you're done. As the final finishing touch, apply some paste or liquid wax to the surface. Let the wax dry a little, then rub it shiny. Wow, I can see myself!

Media Storage Rack

BY CHRIS GLEASON

CDs and DVDs pile up pretty quickly around my place, and I'm fairly

certain I'm not alone. Here's a smart, simple storage unit that comes together in very little time — an hour or so. Twenty-eight CDs fit into a 12" space, so count them up and plan accordingly.

This two-tiered 30" rack holds up to 170 CDs — I use the negative space in the middle to display knickknacks, but you can fill it with CDs and gain even more storage capacity.

You can use plywood as I did, or reasonably substitute medium-density overlay (MDO), medium-density fiberboard (MDF), or even solid wood.

project drawing top, front, elevation

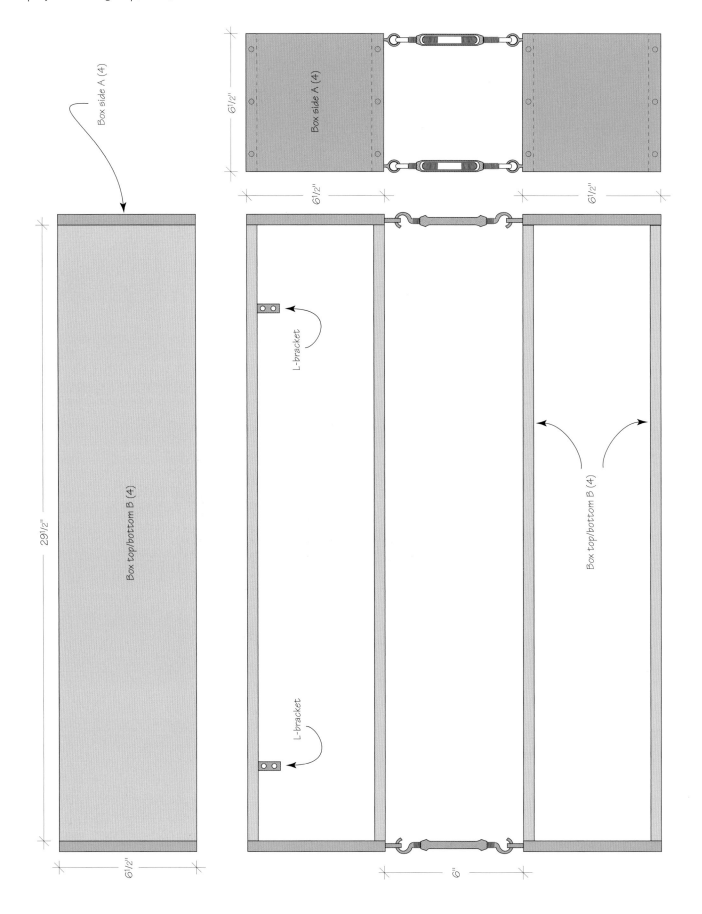

Box side A (4)

Box side A (4)

6¹/₂"

6¹/₂"

6¹/₂"

29¹/₂"

Box top/bottom B (4)

Box top/bottom B (4)

L-bracket

L-bracket

6¹/₂"

6"

REFERENCE	QUANTITY	PART	STOCK	THICKNESS	(mm)	WIDTH	(mm)	LENGTH	(mm)
A	4	box sides	birch veneer plywood	3/4	(19)	6½	(165)	6½	(165)
B	4	box tops & bottoms	birch veneer plywood	3/4	(19)	6½	(165)	29½	(749)

Supplies

4 - eye screws

4 - screw-in hooks

4 - 4" (150mm) turnbuckles

2 - 2½"- (65mm) long L-brackets

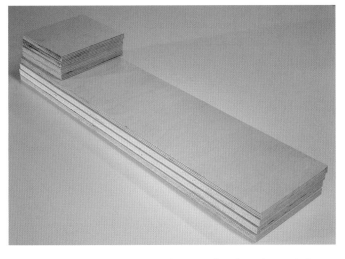

1 The storage rack is comprised principally of two four-sided boxes that are held together by turnbuckles and eye screws. Cut out the parts for the boxes. You'll need four sides, four tops and bottoms.

2 I used countersunk screws to assemble the rack. Put a countersinking bit into your drill and drill a series of holes along the top and bottom edges of the sides. Three screws per edge provides plenty of strength.

3 I used a water-based stain to color the sides of the boxes. It's relatively simple to apply prior to assembly. Stain the sides after drilling the countersunk holes for the screw heads — this way, the stain will cover up any tear-out that may occur.

4 With a clamp at the ready, lay out a thin bead of glue and put the boxes together one joint at a time. Use a wet paper towel or rag to wipe up any glue that squeezes out.

5 To ensure that the parts are flush along the front edge, use a sander and 80-grit paper. This is also a good way to clean up any stain that may have dripped onto the edges during step 3.

6 The upper box gets fastened to the wall with L brackets. The brackets are screwed onto the underside of the box's top. My trick here is to put the brackets in place and mark where the rear screw will go in. Then spin the bracket out of the way and drive the screw in tightly with the drill. With some effort, you should be able to spin the bracket back into place so it sits flush against the wall. Then insert the other screw in the bracket.

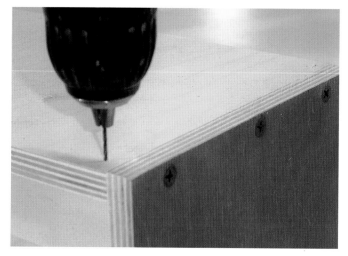

7 Drill a hole into each of the four corners of the top side of the lower box and also into the four corners of the bottom side of the upper box.

8 The eye screws are too hard to turn by hand, but with a long bolt or something similar, you can twist them in easily. The lower box gets the four eye screws, and the upper box gets the hooks. To screw in the hooks, use a pair of needle-nose pliers.

9 To install the unit, simply screw the upper box into the wall (be sure to either hit studs with your screws or use an appropriate anchor of your choice). Once the upper box is in place, hang the turnbuckles from the hooks and suspend the lower box from the turnbuckles. The inherent adjustability of the turnbuckles allows you to level out the lower box.

A SIMPLE PROJECT THAT IS WORTHY OF THE QUILTS IT WILL HOLD.

Quilt Rack

BY DANNY PROULX

I don't know a great deal about making quilts, but I can appreciate how beautiful they are and how much work is lovingly done to create them. They should be on display, and this quilt rack can proudly show off three of your best.

I understand, based on my research, that these quilt racks were a common furniture item in bedrooms at one time. Before we had the luxury of central heat, it was often necessary to add a quilt or two to the bed to keep folks warm during cold winter nights. The quilts were stored on racks near the bed. They were more of a practical item in those days, but many people continue to use them as accent pieces in their homes.

If you are lucky enough to have a home with Colonial or rustic furniture, or any other appropriate decorative theme, this quilt rack will be a perfect fit. This rack was built for my mother-in-law, who is an avid quilter.

I was surprised to learn how popular quilting has become. There seems to be a club in every town and a great deal of activity about the hobby on the Internet. A simple Internet search yielded over 100,000 hits on the words quilts and quilting. PBS television produced a 60-minute documentary on the subject, describing the program as "selections from the 100 most acclaimed quilts of the 20th century." They traveled across America to meet the quilters in their homes and studios to discover the stories behind the creation of these magnificent treasures. It's a popular hobby with a long history, so you can see why this project will be a hit for your favorite quilter.

The quilt shown in the photograph is one of many, lovingly crafted by Elsie Lawrence of Prescott, Ontario. The care and attention to detail in her work is obvious.

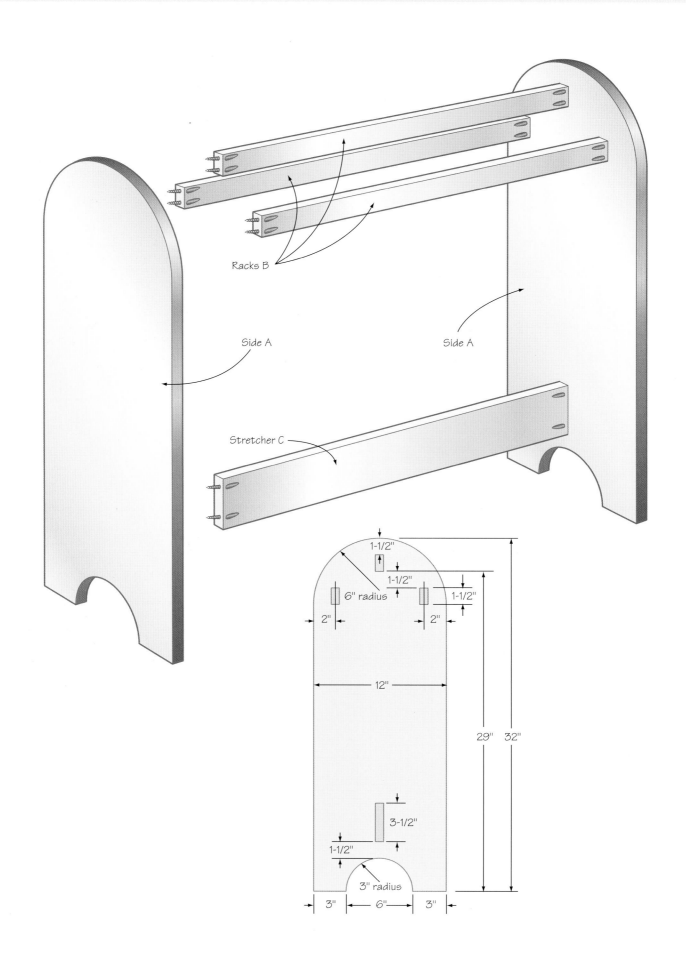

Racks B

Side A

Side A

Stretcher C

1-1/2"

1-1/2"

6" radius

1-1/2"

2"

2"

12"

29" 32"

3-1/2"

1-1/2"

3" radius

3" 6" 3"

QUILT RACK ▪ INCHES (MILLIMETERS)

REFERENCE	QUANTITY	PART	STOCK	THICKNESS	(mm)	WIDTH	(mm)	LENGTH	(mm)
A	2	sides	hardwood	¾	(19)	12	(305)	32	(813)
B	3	racks	hardwood	¾	(19)	1½	(38)	31	(787)
C	1	stretcher	hardwood	¾	(19)	3½	(89)	31	(787)

Supplies

Pocket hole screws: 1¼" (32mm)

Glue

Pocket hole plugs

1 Glue up enough boards to make the two rack sides A. I simply glue the edges and clamp the boards together until the adhesive sets. The edges can be prepared by cutting the boards on a well-tuned table saw, or, if you have a jointer, the edges can be dressed. If your table saw isn't accurate enough to rip the boards straight, or you don't own a jointer, your wood supplier will dress the edges for a small fee.

2 While the side panels are setting up, cut the three racks B and bottom stretcher C to the sizes indicated in the materials list. Drill two pocket holes on the ends of each board. These holes will be visible and filled with wood plugs, so space them equally on each board face.

3 Round over the four edges on the racks and stretcher boards, using a ¼"-radius router bit. Complete the sanding on these parts before assembly.

4 Clamp the two sides A together and draw a 6"-radius arc at one end (top) of the boards. Use a jigsaw to cut the arc. Keep the boards tightly clamped after cutting and sand both so the arcs are identical.

5 Draw a 3"-radius arc at the bottom center on each side panel. Cut the arc with a jigsaw and sand smooth. To complete the machine work on each side, round over all the edges, with the exception of the straight portion on the feet, using a ¼"-radius roundover bit.

6 Attach the three racks and one stretcher board to the sides with glue and 1¼" pocket hole screws. The racks are centered on the 2", 6" and 10" marks from the front edge of each side, as shown on the illustration. To align the racks, clamp a straight 1½"-wide board, with its top edge 29" from the bottom edge of the side. The center rack is aligned on top of the marker board, and the two outside racks are aligned on their marks below the marker board. The stretcher board is attached 1½" above the center of the lower arc on each side panel.

Shop Tip

I discovered that screws buried a little deeper leave more room for the wood plugs. Set the stop collar on your bit about ⅛" higher than normal to achieve the extra hole depth.

Shop Tip

A certain amount of tear is normal when drilling pocket holes. Often, the filler plugs have small gaps between them and the hole lines. To hide the damage, rub colored paste filler that matches your final finish into the edge where the wood plug meets the hole lines.

Once the colored filler paste dries, sand the area until the joint between the plug and hole outline is smooth and almost invisible. I discovered that a random-orbit sander was the best tool to sand the filled pocket holes.

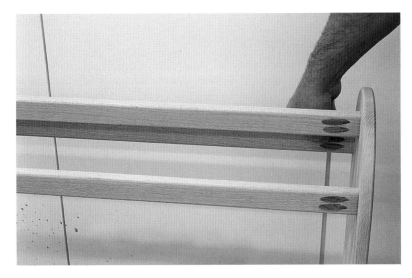

7 Install the pocket hole wood plugs, using glue. Once the adhesive is cured, sand the plugs smooth. Now you can apply your favorite finish to the rack.

Construction Notes

The choice of wood to use in this project is up to you. I encourage you to experiment with a few design changes and wood types.

As I was finishing this project, I realized that I missed using a design feature that would have added interest to the project. I could have joined the side boards with pocket holes and contrasting filler plugs, much like the rack and stretcher boards. If I had carefully cut my boards for the sides, taking into account the offset position of the pocket holes, I could have centered four plugs down the outside face of each panel.

I would have to place the pocket holes outside the waste area of each arc, but with a little planning, it would have been a nice-looking feature on my rack. I'll build the next rack with that technique.

Spice Cabinet

BY DAVID THIEL

Though members of your family aren't likely to store spices in a cabinet like this, you can bet that it will be an oft-requested item for you to build. So you might want to think about making more than one cabinet when you begin.

First, cut the sides, top and bottom to size, noting the top and bottom are ½" narrower to accommodate the applied hanger and back. Then cut ½" finger joints on the ends of each piece. Next cut ¼" × ½"-wide dadoes on the sides and ends as located on the diagrams. Also cut a ¼" × ½"-wide rabbet on the back edge of each side for the back.

Next, cut the two dividers and center to size, and with the case dry-clamped together, check the dimensions of the dividers against your case. Trim them to fit, then cut ½"-wide bridle joints to fit the dividers together. Glue up the case, holding the dividers' front edges flush to the case front. When dry, sand the joints flush to the outside surfaces.

Now cut the hanger to shape from the diagrams, then glue and nail the hanger in place at the back of the cabinet. Cut the back to size and nail it in place.

Next cut the drawer box pieces to size. Then cut ⅛" × ¼"-wide rabbets on the ends of the sides and cut ⅛" × ¼"-deep grooves for the bottoms on the ends and sides, starting ⅛" up from the bottom edge. To assemble, glue and nail the drawer boxes together.

Cut the drawer fronts to size, then make the knobs. Cut a ⅜" × 1" × 8" strip of cherry, beveling the sides at a 25° angle. Then cut the knobs off at 1" intervals, again beveling the sides at 25°. Use either a band saw to cut the knobs to shape, or sand them to shape after separating. Attach the knobs to the drawer fronts with No. 4 flathead screws and glue. Then glue the fronts to the drawer boxes.

Before finishing the piece, distress the cabinet with keys, screwdrivers and a hammer. I then applied brown mahogany gel stain; when the stain was dry, I then applied a coat of wax.

SPICE CABINET ▪ INCHES (MILLIMETERS)

REFERENCE	QUANTITY	PART	STOCK	THICKNESS	(mm)	WIDTH	(mm)	LENGTH	(mm)	COMMENTS
A	2	sides	cherry	$1/2$	(13)	5	(127)	12	(305)	
B	1	bottom	cherry	$1/2$	(13)	$4^1/2$	(114)	8	(203)	
C	1	top	cherry	$1/2$	(13)	$4^1/2$	(114)	8	(203)	
D	1	center	cherry	$1/2$	(13)	$4^1/2$	(114)	$11^1/2$	(292)	
E	2	dividers	cherry	$1/2$	(13)	$4^1/2$	(114)	$7^1/2$	(191)	
F	4	hanger	cherry	$1/2$	(13)	8	(203)	$3^1/2$	(89)	
G	4	back	plywood	$1/4$	(6)	$7^1/2$	(191)	11	(279)	
H	4	drawer fronts	cherry	$1/4$	(6)	$3^1/4$	(83)	$3^5/16$	(84)	
J	4	drawer sides	plywood	$1/4$	(6)	$3^3/16$	(81)	$4^1/8$	(105)	
K	4	drawer ends	plywood	$1/4$	(6)	$3^3/16$	(81)	3	(76)	
L	4	drawer bottoms	plywood	$1/4$	(6)	$2^{15}/16$	(75)	$3^7/8$	(98)	
M	4	drawer knobs	cherry	$3/8$	(10)	1	(25)	1	(25)	

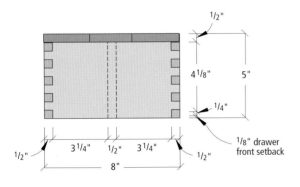

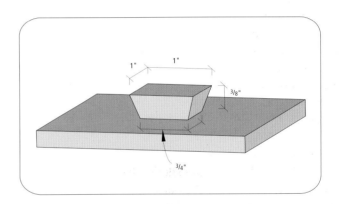

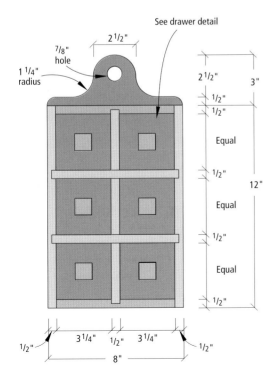

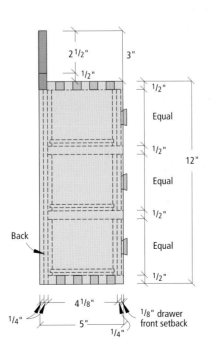

Tabletop Desk

BY KERRY PIERCE

We live in an age of highly specialized home furnishings. We have tables on which we prepare food, other tables at which we eat it, still others from which we serve it. We have desks at which we do our writing and figuring, other desks at which we work at our computers. In eighteenth- and nineteenth-century American homes, in which there was often less space available for specialized pieces and in which there was often less disposable income for their purchase, furniture often served multiple functions.

A nightstand might double as a washstand. Food might be prepared at a table that was later used for dining. In some cases, cleverly designed accessories were necessary to make this flexibility possible. The tabletop desk shown here is one example.

Created to be placed upon a table that might otherwise be used for dining, food preparation, or holding a wash basin — the desk-described by John Kassay in The Book of Shaker Furniture — is a completely equipped writing station, with a tiny inkwell drawer, a till for pens and pencils, and a large drawer for stationery.

After the material has been dimensioned, edge-joint and glue the boards that will make up the desktop.

Plough a ⅛" × ¼" groove on the inside faces of the desk sides, front, and back. This groove will later receive the bottom of the materials compartment. Then, cut openings in the sides for the inkwell and stationery drawers.

Next, cut the angles on the desk sides on the band saw, after which the four sides of the case are dovetailed. The case is dry-assembled, and the bevels on the top edge of the front and back are marked from the angles on the sides. Form these bevels with a hand plane, and glue-up the four walls of the case around the bottom of the materials compartment.

Before installing the bottom, glue and brad into place the cock bead that frames the stationery drawer. Also at this time, glue the two fill strips that will guide the stationery drawer in position. Then, tack the bottom into place using small finishing nails. Nails are perhaps better than screws for this particular application because they are flexible enough to allow for seasonal expansion and contraction of the bottom across its width. Screws-unless they pass through oversized holes which would be very difficult to achieve in such thin stock-could lock the material so that cracking would occur in connection with this expansion and contraction.

The inkwell drawer is next. The unusually shaped long drawer side does two things. First, it is a drawer guide, and second, it prevents the drawer (with its bottle of ink) from being completely withdrawn from the case, a circumstance that could easily have had messy results.

After forming the drawer parts, glue and tack them together. Then, fit the drawer to its opening and screw the wooden bracket that acts as its guide and keeper to the inside face of the desk back.

Assemble the stationery drawer with through dovetails at the front and half-blind dovetails at the back.

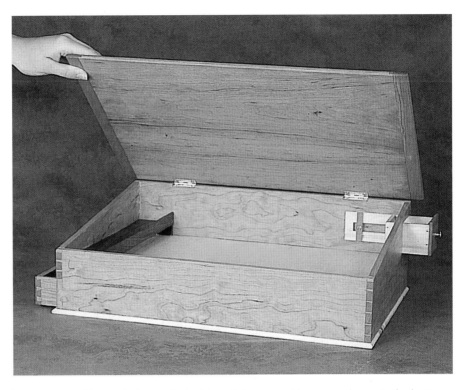

The opened tabletop desk reveals the ink well drawer and the paper drawer in the bottom.

The till rests on a pair of ⅛"-thick supports which are glued to the inside faces of the desk front and back. After installing these supports, glue the till-with its side already glued to the bottom-into place atop the supports. Fasten it also to the desk side with a thin line of glue.

The top panel is removed from the clamps and planed to a thickness of ⁵⁄₁₆". Then, cut ⅛" × ⅛" grooves in both ends of the top panel to receive the tongues on the breadboard ends. Form and fit the tongues to the grooves.

Hold each breadboard end in place with a dab of glue on the tongue at the middle of the tongue's length. The remainder of the tongue floats on the groove, allowing for seasonal expansion and contraction of the top.

Hinges are problems because of the top's extreme thinness. My dad, who built this particular piece, struggled to find screws that could get a good enough bite in the top to hold it in place. After trying and discarding several brass screws, he settled on deep-threaded ⁵⁄₈" no. 6 steel screws from which he'd ground away the tips so that they

wouldn't penetrate the upper surface of the top.

After fitting the hinges, remove the hardware, and give the desk a final sanding.

Kiln-dried or air-dried

Reference books inevitably cite the necessity of using kiln-dried material for furniture construction.

I think that's misleading.

Of the thousands of board feet of lumber I've turned into chairs and into casework, less than a quarter was kiln-dried. The remainder was air-dried outdoors and finish-dried in my shop. Nevertheless, I can remember only two occasions when pieces I built experienced wood failure.

Once, I built a Hepplewhite huntboard from air-dried cherry. The top (which didn't fail) was fastened to cleats fixed with slotted screw holes. But one of the end panels, which I had triple-tenoned into the posts, split after sitting in our living room through a couple of cold, dry Ohio winters. In looking back on the construction of the huntboard, I remember hurrying to finish it before Christmas since it was a present for my wife.

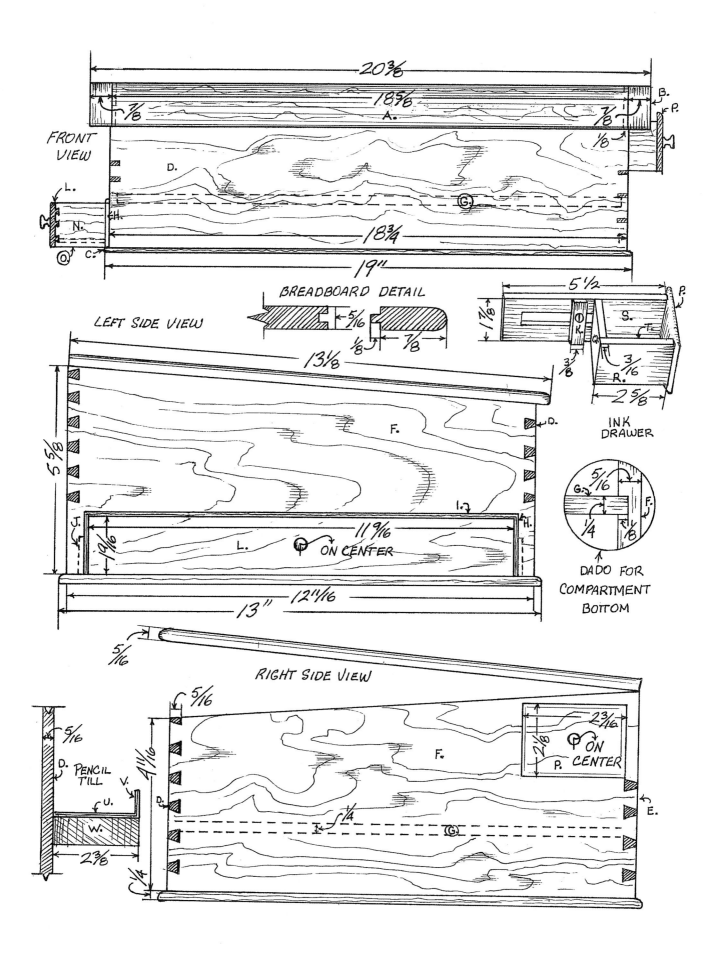

FRONT VIEW

20⅜

18⅝

⅞

A.

B.

P.

⅞

⅛

D.

L.

H.

N.

G.

O.

C.

18¾

19"

LEFT SIDE VIEW

BREADBOARD DETAIL

5/16

⅛

⅞

5½

⅞

P.

S.

T.

13⅛

⅜

D.

5⅝

F.

3/16

3/8

2⅝

INK DRAWER

J.

9/16

L.

ON CENTER

11 9/16

I.

H.

13"

12 11/16

5/16

⅛

¼

F.

G.

DADO FOR COMPARTMENT BOTTOM

RIGHT SIDE VIEW

5/16

5/16

5/16

¼

D. PENCIL T'ILL

V.

U.

W.

2⅜

4 1/16

D.

¼

F.

I.

G.

2 3/16

2⅛

P. ON CENTER

P.

E.

REFERENCE	QUANTITY	PART	STOCK	THICKNESS	(mm)	WIDTH	(mm)	LENGTH	(mm)	COMMENTS
DESK										
A	1	top	cherry	$5/16$	(8)	$13^1/8$	(333)	$18^5/8$	(473)	
B	2	breadboard ends	cherry	$5/16$	(8)	1	(25)	$13^1/8$	(333)	
C	1	bottom	cherry	$1/4$	(6)	13	(330)	1	(25)	
D	1	front	cherry	$5/16$	(8)	$4^{11}/16$	(119)	$18^3/4$	(476)	
E	1	back	cherry	$5/16$	(8)	$5^5/8$	(143)	$18^3/4$	(476)	
F	2	sides	cherry	$5/16$	(8)	$5^5/8$	(143)	$12^{11}/16$	(322)	
G	1	compartment bottom	cherry	$1/4$	(6)	$12^5/16$	(313)	$18^3/8$	(467)	
H	2	short cock beads	cherry	$1/8$	(3)	$1/2$	(13)	$1^7/8$	(48)	
I	2	long cock beads	cherry	$1/8$	(3)	$1/2$	(13)	$11^7/8$	(302)	
J	2	drawer filler strips	cherry	$1/8$	(3)	1	(25)	$16^1/4$	(413)	
K	1	ink-drawer stop	cherry	$3/8$	(10)	$3/8$	(10)	$1^7/8$	(48)	
STATIONARY DRAWER										
L	1	front	cherry	$5/16$	(8)	$1^9/16$	(40)	$11^9/16$	(294)	
M	1	back	cherry	$1/4$	(6)	$1^9/16$	(40)	$11^9/16$	(294)	
N	2	sides	cherry	$1/8$	(3)	$1^9/16$	(40)	18	(457)	
O	1	bottom	cherry	$1/8$	(3)	$11^5/16$	(287)	$18^1/4$	(464)	
INK DRAWER										
P	1	front	cherry	$5/16$	(8)	$2^1/8$	(54)	$2^{11}/16$	(68)	
Q	1	back	cherry	$3/16$	(5)	$1^7/8$	(48)	$2^3/32$	(53)	
R	1	short side	cherry	$3/16$	(5)	$1^7/8$	(48)	$2^5/8$	(67)	
S	1	long side	cherry	$3/16$	(5)	$1^7/8$	(48)	$5^1/2$	(140)	
T	1	bottom	cherry	$3/16$	(5)	$2^{11}/16$	(68)	$2^1/2$	(64)	
PENCIL TILL										
U	1	bottom	cherry	$1/8$	(3)	$2^1/4$	(57)	$12^1/16$	(306)	
V	1	side	cherry	$1/8$	(3)	$3/4$	(19)	$12^1/16$	(306)	
W	2	supports	cherry	$1/8$	(3)	$3/4$	(19)	$2^3/8$	(60)	
HARDWARE										
X	2	hinges	brass	$1^1/2$	(38)	$7/8$	(22)			
Y	2	pulls	brass	$1/2$	(13)	$1/2$	(13)			
Z		screws	various							

When I glued up the end panels, I remember noticing, as I slathered glue on the middle tenon, that I hadn't cut the top and bottom tenons back to allow the end panel to shrink. Each tenon completely filled its mortise. But the glue was already on the middle tenon and in its mortise.

To cut the other tenons back, I would have to wash away the glue, find my paring chisel, pare the tenons, and reglue. Or risk having the aliphatic resin glue set before the joint was assembled. I remember thinking it wasn't worth the effort. I remember thinking I could get away with it.

The end panel failed because I built it to fail.

I think that if allowances are made during design for the inevitable movement of wood, carefully air-dried material is every bit as good as kiln-dried. In fact, I think that careful air-drying is preferable to the kind of rushed kiln drying practiced by some commercial driers. At least in humid Ohio, air-drying is a gradual process during which wood surrenders its moisture so slowly that surface checking is almost unheard of. And it's worth mentioning that, just like air-dried stock, kiln-dried stock, when exposed to humid, July conditions, quickly takes on enough moisture to reach 11, 12 or even 13 percent.

The answer to the problem of wood movement isn't laboring to make wood inert; it is, I think, to accept movement as an inevitable component of solid-wood construction and to design to accommodate that inevitability.

There's No Point

BY JIM STACK

This one is called "There's No Point" because the top doesn't come to a point. Maybe it should be called "Pyramid Power" or "Why Didn't You Just Make the Box Square So the Drawers Would Be Easier to Make?"

This drawer box has lots of room for jewelry, birthday cards or a prized set of socket drivers. (It would make a conversation-starting toolbox!)

The body is veneered, and the veneer wraps itself around the box in one continuous grain pattern. You'll use your biscuit joiner to make this box. Also, you'll learn to make fitted drawers (drawers that are fitted to the opening of the cabinet — no hardware needed) that use the drawer bottoms as runners. The drawer style isn't new, but it is easy to make (well, it's easy to make when the drawers are square). You can use the techniques to make a larger cabinet or toolbox with drawers — the cool part being you don't have to buy, or deal with, mechanical drawer glides.

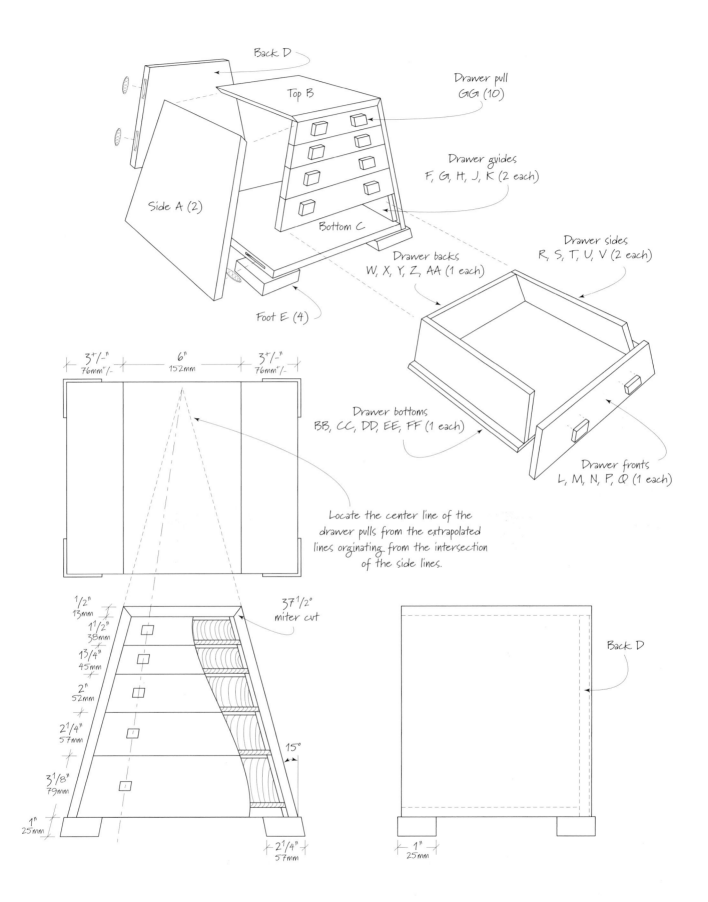

Back D

Top B

Drawer pull
GG (10)

Drawer guides
F, G, H, J, K (2 each)

Side A (2)

Bottom C

Drawer backs
W, X, Y, Z, AA (1 each)

Drawer sides
R, S, T, U, V (2 each)

Foot E (4)

Drawer bottoms
BB, CC, DD, EE, FF (1 each)

Drawer fronts
L, M, N, P, Q (1 each)

3⁺/−" 76mm⁺/−   6" 152mm   3⁺/−" 76mm⁺/−

Locate the center line of the
drawer pulls from the extrapolated
lines orginating from the intersection
of the side lines.

1/2" 13mm

1 1/2" 38mm

1 3/4" 45mm

2" 52mm

2 1/4" 57mm

3 1/8" 79mm

1" 25mm

37 1/2° miter cut

15°

2 1/4" 57mm

Back D

1" 25mm

REFERENCE	QUANTITY	PART	STOCK	THICKNESS	(mm)	WIDTH	(mm)	LENGTH	(mm)	COMMENTS
A	2	sides	veneered ply	½	(13)	10	(254)	11½	(292)	length includes miters
B	1	top	veneered ply	½	(13)	10	(254)	6	(152)	length includes miters
C	1	bottom	plywood	½	(13)	9⅛	(232)	11 +/-	(279)	
D	1	back	veneered ply	½	(13)	10⅝ H	(270)	11 +/-	(279)	veneer grain runs horizontally
E	4	feet	maple	1	(25)	2¼	(57)	2¼	(57)	
F	2	drawer guides	plywood	¼	(6)	2½	(64)	9⅛	(232)	15° bevel on two long edges
G	2	drawer guides	plywood	¼	(6)	2⅛	(54)	9⅛	(232)	15° bevel on two long edges
H	2	drawer guides	plywood	¼	(6)	1⅞	(48)	9⅛	(232)	15° bevel on two long edges
J	2	drawer guides	plywood	¼	(6)	1⅝	(41)	9⅛	(232)	15° bevel on two long edges
K	2	drawer guides	plywood	¼	(6)	1⅜	(35)	9⅛	(232)	15° bevel on two long edges
L	2	drawer fronts	veneered ply	½	(13)	3	(76)	9	(229)	15° miter on both ends
M	2	drawer fronts	veneered ply	½	(13)	2¼	(57)	9	(229)	15° miter on both ends
N	2	drawer fronts	veneered ply	½	(13)	1¹⁵⁄₁₆	(49)	9	(229)	15° miter on both ends
P	2	drawer fronts	veneered ply	½	(13)	1¹¹⁄₁₆	(43)	9	(229)	15° miter on both ends
Q	2	drawer fronts	veneered ply	½	(13)	1⁷⁄₁₆	(37)	9	(229)	15° miter on both ends
R	2	drawer sides	poplar	½	(13)	2⅜	(60)	9	(229)	15° bevel on two long edges
S	2	drawer sides	poplar	½	(13)	2	(51)	9	(229)	15° bevel on two long edges
T	2	drawer sides	poplar	½	(13)	1¾	(45)	9	(229)	15° bevel on two long edges
U	2	drawer sides	poplar	½	(13)	1⅜	(35)	9	(229)	15° bevel on two long edges
V	2	drawer sides	poplar	½	(13)	1¼	(32)	9	(229)	15° bevel on two long edges
W	1	drawer back	poplar	½	(13)	2⅜	(60)	9	(229)	15° bevel on both ends
X	1	drawer back	poplar	½	(13)	1¹⁵⁄₁₆	(49)	9	(229)	15° bevel on both ends
Y	1	drawer back	poplar	½	(13)	1¹¹⁄₁₆	(43)	9	(229)	15° bevel on both ends
Z	1	drawer back	poplar	½	(13)	1½	(38)	9	(229)	15° bevel on both ends
AA	1	drawer back	poplar	½	(13)	1¼	(32)	9	(229)	15° bevel on both ends
BB	1	drawer bottom	plywood	¼	(6)	10¹¹⁄₁₆	(271)	9	(229)	15° bevel on both edges
CC	1	drawer bottom	plywood	¼	(6)	10¹¹⁄₁₆	(271)	9	(229)	15° bevel on both edges
DD	1	drawer bottom	plywood	¼	(6)	10¹¹⁄₁₆	(271)	9	(229)	15° bevel on both edges
EE	1	drawer bottom	plywood	¼	(6)	10¹¹⁄₁₆	(271)	9	(229)	15° bevel on both edges
FF	1	drawer bottom	plywood	¼	(6)	10¹¹⁄₁₆	(271)	9	(229)	15° bevel on both edges
GG	10	drawer pulls	hardwood	½	(13)	½	(13)	1	(25)	15° miter on both ends

Supplies

spray or wipe-on lacquer

Note

This cutting list is as accurate as I could make it. I recommend cutting out the two sides, top, back and bottom parts first and assembling the box before cutting any other parts. Then use the box as your template for the exact angles. There's a possibility that your final box dimensions will differ slightly from what I've shown. That's the nature of making projects like this one. Use this cutting list as a guide for keeping track of all the parts.

Preparing Veneers for Layup

STEP ONE The joint between the veneer sheets becomes almost invisible if the edges of the sheets are straight and square. Using a jointer plane and a shooting board is the traditional method of straightening the veneer sheet's edges. Here I'm using a metal straight-edge to hold the sheets flat and secure.

STEP TWO The first step to laying up the veneer sheets is to secure them edge-to-edge with small pieces of masking tape.

STEP THREE Run a strip of masking tape the length of the veneer joint.

STEP FOUR I like to glue the edges of the veneer sheets together the same way you'd glue boards edge-to-edge. Using the tape on the joint as a hinge, open the joint and run a bead of glue along the edge of one veneer sheet.

STEP FIVE Fold the joint closed. The glue will squeeze out, letting you know that you've got the edge covered with glue.

STEP SIX Wipe away the glue squeeze-out with a damp cloth and let the glue dry. It helps to put the veneer between a couple of objects that will hold the joint tightly. (The tape is still on the other side.)

STEP SEVEN After the glue has dried on the veneer sheets, you can remove the masking tape. Apply a level coat of glue to the substrate only. If you're laying up more than one set of veneered panels, put waxed paper between the panels. Clamp them in your veneer press and let the glue dry for 24 hours. My veneer press includes two bench-top horses and two, 1½"-thick (38mm) particleboard plates. The horses hold the plates flat and allow room for the clamps under the plates.

1 Veneer panels for the top and two sides. If possible, have the grain wrap around the box. This adds a nice visual element. Also, veneer two panels: one for the back and one for the drawer fronts. Cut the top and two side panels to size. Cut some strips of the same veneer you used for the top and sides. Turn on your iron to its highest heat setting. Apply a layer of wood glue to the front edge of a side panel (level the glue so it covers the entire edge as shown in the photo). White, yellow or brown wood glue works for this procedure.

2 Place the veneer strip on the edge of the panel. Place the iron on the veneer and heat up the glue. You'll see some steam coming from the glue — that's the moisture leaving the glue. Move the iron steadily along the edge of the panel. When the steam stops, remove the iron. The glue should cure. If not, reheat until it does. Keep the iron moving so you don't scorch the veneer. Repeat this procedure to cover the front and back edges of the top and two side panels.

3 After you set down the iron, pick up one of your sanding blocks and use the back side of it to run back and forth on the veneered edge. This secures the veneer in place and speeds the cooling process.

4 Using a smooth-cut file, trim the excess veneer from the edge of the panel. Hold the file at a slight angle to the face of the panel as shown. You can smooth the edge veneer down to the face veneer without scratching the face veneer. Don't be too aggressive or you could cut into the face veneer. Use 150-grit sandpaper to sand the edges smooth.

5 Set your biscuit joiner to cut a slot ¼" (6mm) on center from the adjustable fence on the joiner. (Cut a No. 0 slot.) I've got an older biscuit joiner, so yours may not look like mine, but they all work the same way. Hold the joiner as shown to cut slots in the bottom inside of both of the side panels. Use the bevel on the bottom panel's edge as your angle guide.

6 Cut the slots in the ends of the bottom panel as shown. Register the biscuit joiner's fence on the bottom of the bottom. Note the bevel on the edge of the bottom. Don't let the face of the joiner register on this bevel.

7 Cut some biscuit slots in the edges of the back and the inside of the two side and top panels. The back is located 1/8" (3mm) in from the back edges of the top and two side panels, and covers the back edge of the bottom panel. Glue box together.

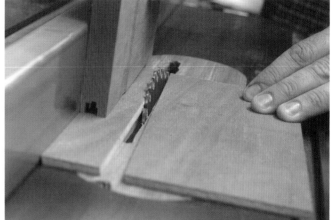

8 Cut some 1/4"-thick plywood (6mm) for the drawer guides. You'll need about 26" (660mm) running inches cut at 9 1/8" (232mm) wide. Then set your table saw blade to 15°. Start with the bottom drawer guides and work your way up the box.

9 Use some of the same plywood you'll use for the drawer bottoms as spacers for fitting the drawer guides. Each of the spacers represents the location of a drawer bottom.

10 Glue the drawer guides inside the box. Use a spring clamp to hold one end of the guide and use a finish nail to hold the other end. Push the nail into the back of the box just far enough to hold the nail in place as you wedge it against the drawer guide.

11 There obviously isn't enough room inside the box for you to swing a hammer (unless you know some little elves), so use a dowel with a hole as a pusher for the finish nails.

12 Here's what the drawer guide glue-up looks like when all the guides are held in place with spacers, clamps and nails. (Perhaps something ready to launch into space.)

13 Cut and fit the drawer bottoms before cutting any other drawer parts. It can take a little trial and error to get just the right fit. The bottoms should fit snugly but you should still be able to easily move them in and out of the box. Take your time with this operation as it will determine if the drawers work smoothly or if they stick or rattle.

14 Cut out the drawer sides next. Then cut out the drawer backs. I test-fitted each set of sides and back in the box before gluing anything together. The drawer sides and back should fit into their respective openings with about 1/64" (.4mm) total clearance. Now you can glue the sides to the backs.

15 Glue the drawer sides/back assemblies to their respective bottoms exactly on center with each other. The front ends of the sides are held flush with the drawer bottom. Note the temporary brace to keep the sides properly spaced during glueup.

16 This is the ideal fit for the drawers. There is a small space between the sides and the guides. More importantly, there is less space between the edges of the bottoms and the sides of the box. Remember that the bottoms also guide the drawers in and out of the box and hold the drawers at the proper spacing to one another.

17 Glue the drawer fronts to the front edges of the sides and bottom of each drawer. The bottoms of the fronts are held flush to the bottoms of the drawers. The one exception is the bottom drawer. This drawer front covers the front of the bottom panel of the box so its front is held 1/2" (13mm) below the bottom of the drawer. Got that?

18 You can make drawer pulls from any wood you choose. I chose bubinga because it matches the rosewood veneer on the outside of the box and it contrasts nicely with the curly maple veneer on the drawer fronts. Set your table saw or miter saw to 15° and cut a couple of blanks for the drawer pulls. Cut these blanks cross-grain. Then, when you cut the pulls from these blanks, the grain will run the length of each pull.

19 The drawer pulls run centered along a line that radiates from the focal point of the extrapolated lines of the sides. (See the illustration to understand what I just said.) Configuring the pulls like this enhances the angular shape of the box and feet. After you've applied the finish and rubbed it out, lay the box on its back with the drawers installed. Mark the locations for the drawer pulls.

20 Mix up some two-part epoxy and put a small drop at each pull location. Set the pulls in the epoxy, easing them down flush with the drawer front.

21 Double-check the alignment of the pulls by sighting down from the top of the box. Your eye will tell you better than a ruler whether they are aligned properly. Let the epoxy cure completely before moving the box.

A Case for Wine

BY DAVID THIEL

Once upon a time, I was a beer guy. Most woodworkers are, I suppose, and I still enjoy a good brew. But recently I've also learned to appreciate a glass of good wine. Usually a bottle or two of red wine in the house is adequate, but as my interest in wine has grown, so has my interest in having a selection of wines available. So I decided I needed a wine rack.

I don't have a lot of room in my house, so I turned to my computer-aided design program. After carefully measuring a variety of bottles (between sips) I calculated the best way to maximize my bottle storage in the smallest amount of space. The rack shown here is my best effort, with storage for 24 bottles (two cases) in a 20" × 20" × 14"-deep space.

This design allows for an efficient cutting list and an efficient use of space. I was able to design the rack using 11 pieces of wood in only four sizes. Maybe that's why I decided to complicate it by adding dovetails to the solid mahogany box. That, and the need for reliable strength — 24 bottles of wine are heavy.

The interior dividers are egg crate-joined Baltic birch with veneer tape applied to the front edges. Designed to hang on a wall with a hidden French cleat, the box could be easily be adapted for floor use with a simple base and maybe a drawer added above the box. It's a reasonable weekend project with some time left over to have a glass of wine and appreciate your work.

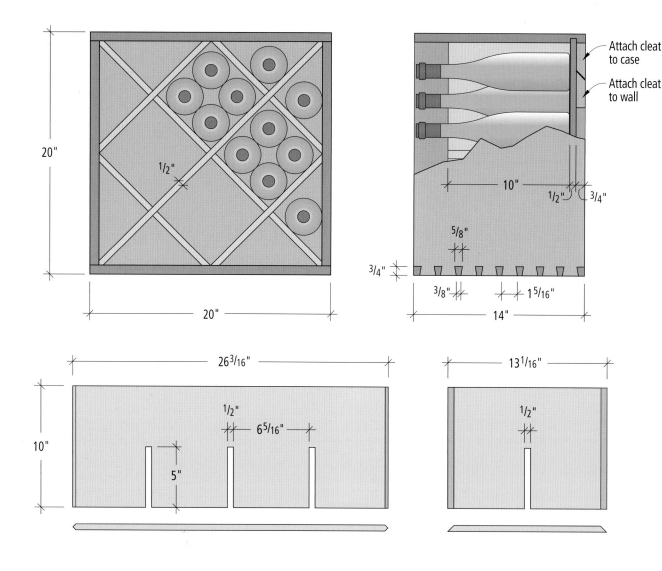

Building the Cabinet

Start construction with the outside of the case. The four pieces are exactly the same, 14" × 20", but because this is a simple piece, an attractive grain pattern can go a long way to make it more dramatic. I was lucky to have a slab of mahogany tucked away in the shop that was actually 14½" wide, which allowed me to avoid any glued-up panels.

After choosing the most attractive faces of the boards for the exterior, start laying out the dovetails. Everyone has their own method of making dovetails, and you may choose to cut yours by hand to get a more unique spacing pattern. I chose the easy plugged-in route and used a model 2200 Keller jig to cut the through-dovetails.

Keep On Groovin'

With the dovetails cut and fit, you will need to cut grooves for the back in all four pieces. Because I was hanging my rack on the wall, I allowed a ¾" setback from the rear of each piece and used a ½" router bit in my router table to make the ⅜"-deep grooves.

With the spacing I used on my dovetails, the grooves in the top and bottom pieces are able to run the entire length of the piece without interfering with the dovetail pattern. However, on the side pieces I had to use a stopped groove to avoid seeing the groove in the assembled box.

After running the stopped grooves, use a chisel to square out the ends. Next dry-assemble the box with the back in place to make sure everything fits well.

An Interlocking Complexity

The divided interior of the box is formed from just six pieces of ½" plywood, notched to interlock with one another.

Start by measuring from one inside corner of the box to the opposite corner. While a measurement for the length of these pieces is provided here, it's a good idea to double-check the dimensions against your project.

Your dimensions for the two long dividers should be the same, but if they're not, cut the pieces to the required lengths, then use your table saw to bevel both sides of each end at 45° to form a point on each. Cut them a little long at first, then fit the pieces so they slide snugly into the case.

When the pieces fit, slide one all the way in, then slide the other in against the

REFERENCE	QUANTITY	PART	STOCK	THICKNESS	(mm)	WIDTH	(mm)	LENGTH	(mm)	COMMENTS
A	4	sides	mahogany	$3/4$	(19)	14	(356)	20	(508)	
B	1	back	birch plywood	$1/2$	(13)	$19^{1}/4$	(489)	$19^{1}/4$	(489	
C	2	dividers	birch plywood	$1/2$	(13)	10	(254)	$26^{3}/16$	(665)	
D	4	dividers	birch plywood	$1/2$	(13)	10	(254)	$13^{1}/16$	(332)	
E	2	cleats	plywood	$3/4$	(19)	$2^{1}/2$	(64)	$18^{1}/2$	(470)	

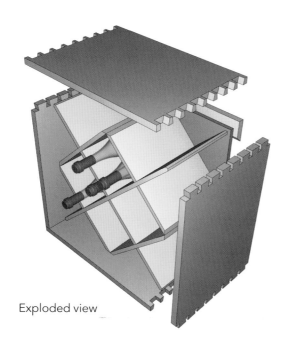

Exploded view

1 The box is dovetailed together. When laying out your dovetails, make sure the back groove falls between the tails and the pins on the sides so the groove won't show at the top. I had to run stopped-grooves on the sides to avoid the groove showing from the outside. All you have to do is stop the cut, then use a chisel to square out the end of the groove.

first. Mark both to indicate the intersecting spot, as shown in the photo at right.

Take the pieces out and use a try square and the intersection marks to lay out the 5" × ½" notches on each piece. Then head to the band saw and cut out the notches. Don't worry about being too neat, but cutting close to the inside of the lines allows for fine-tuning the fit. Test the two pieces in the case and move on to the last four dividers.

To locate the four smaller divider locations, start by marking the center line on each of the four sides. This mark is where the pieces will meet at 45° angles. Measure the necessary lengths of the four pieces (hopefully these lengths are the same) and then cut the four pieces to length, adding 45° bevels at all the ends.

Next, remove the front diagonal divider and fit two of the short dividers in place at the top left and bottom right corners of the rack, parallel with the remaining long divider. Place the front long divider back in its place, and again mark the notch locations on all the dividers.

The notches should be centered on the short dividers, but it's best to check the location against the actual pieces. Make your notches, then repeat the process with the short dividers for the bottom left and the top right corners. With everything fitting snugly in place, I added some birch veneer tape to the front edges of the dividers to hide the layered plywood.

Color and Character

Before gluing up the case, decide how you're going to finish it. I opted to

Marrying the Rack to a Wall

To hang the rack, I used a French cleat. This is so simple I'm surprised it doesn't get used more often. The cleat is made by cutting a 5"-wide piece of ¾" plywood to fit between the two box sides. Then simply set your table-saw blade to a 45° angle and rip the piece in half lengthwise.

By attaching the top half of the cleat (widest-width facing out) to the case and the lower half to your wall (use drywall anchors if that's not possible) you simply can slide the case down onto the wall cleat using the 45° angle and lock it tightly in place.

A Strong, Woody Finish

Remove the dividers one last time and finish the box as you see fit. A coat of clear lacquer on the dividers will protect against time (and unsightly red wine spills) and make it easier to slide the bottles in and out of the rack.

When the dividers are again reassembled in place, a couple of accurately placed nails through the back into the dividers will hold them firmly in place.

Seeing so many interesting opportunities for taste-bud titillation tastefully displayed in my house is almost as gratifying as the project itself.

2 To fit the interlocking dividers to one another, start with the two long dividers. First fit them between the corners of the box, then mark the overlapping locations of the two pieces. The egg crate notches are cut at the mark. Follow this same process to fit and notch the four smaller dividers.

leave the birch plywood pieces natural, but I used Moser's water-soluble Light Sheraton Mahogany aniline dye on the mahogany box. Because the back is birch plywood, I'd have trouble dying the box after assembly without coloring the back, too.

My solution was to give the back a few coats of a clear lacquer finish prior to assembly. Then, when the dye is applied to the mahogany, any errant dye that gets on the back simply can be wiped off the lacquer finish.

After sanding the interior of the project, it's time to move on to the glue-up stage. Make sure the dovetails are pulled up tight and the case is square. Measure from corner to corner in both directions and make any necessary adjustments.

After the glue is dry, take the case out of the clamps and flush up the pins and tails. This may require sanding or you may choose to use a low-angle block plane to flush the sides.

3 This is how the dividers all fit together. If you look closely at the right edge of the piece being dropped into place, you'll see a trick I had to use to fix a "too-loose" divider. By adding veneer tape to the beveled end I was able to fix the fit. Veneer tape added to the front of the divider after the fix made the fix virtually invisible.

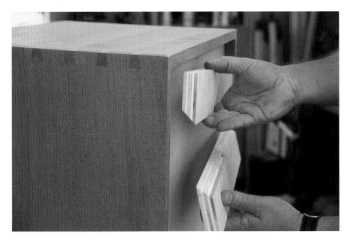

4 To hang the box on a wall I used a French cleat. The photo shows the two parts of the cleat pulled away from the recessed back of the box. Trés simple!

Storing Wine

So now you have this great wine storage box, but what do you need to know to properly store all of your wine? Well, wine is perishable, so you must keep it at a stable temperature and serve it at a temperature that best shows off its specific characteristics.

As you can tell, temperature is the most important factor when storing wine. The "golden temperature" for storing wine is 55° Fahrenheit, although a range of 45°-65°F is fine. But what hurts wine the most is fluctuation. If the temperature wavers, the cork gets pulled in and out, giving air a good chance of getting into the wine and ruining it.

A colder storage temperature will cause the aging process to slow down, preventing proper aging, while a warmer temperature can cause premature aging.

Also, don't just store a bottle of champagne in your refrigerator, waiting for the perfect day to drink it. When that day comes, the wine will be too cold to enjoy. You can temporarily store wine in the fridge to cool it off, but if you need it stored longer, keep it out of there.

Humidity fluctuations aren't nearly as bad, but they should be watched. A high humidity hurts the labels, while a low humidity dries out the cork, letting oxygen in, even if the bottle is properly stored on its side to keep the cork moist.

So throw out the old "refrigerate all whites, drink all reds at current room temperature" adage. According to wine.about.com, generally accepted wine-serving temperature guidelines are: vintage port (66°F), bordeaux and shiraz (64°F), burgundy and cabernet (63°F), pinot noir (61°F), chianti and zinfandel (59°F), beaujolais and rose (54°F), chardonnay (48°F), riesling (47°F), champagne (45°F).

Remember, though, the room temperature is usually higher than these "ideal" temperatures. A refrigerator can cool the wine, but to warm it, just hold it in your hands.

— MICHAEL A. RABKIN

SUPPLIERS

ADAMS & KENNEDY —
THE WOOD SOURCE
6178 Mitch Owen Rd.
P.O. Box 700
Manotick, ON
Canada K4M 1A6
613-822-6800
www.wood-source.com
Wood supply

B&Q
Portswood House
1 Hampshire Corporate Park
Chandlers Ford
Eastleigh
Hampshire, England SO53 3YX
0845 609 6688
www.diy.com
Woodworking tools, supplies
and hardware

BALL AND BALL
463 West Lincoln Hwyl.
Exton, PA 19341
800-257-3711
www.diy.com
Antique hardware reproductions
and restoration

BUSY BEE TOOLS
130 Great Gulf Dr.
Concord, ON
Canada L4K 5W1
1-800-461-2879
www.busybeetools.com
Woodworking tools and supplies

CONSTANTINE'S WOOD
CENTER OF FLORIDA
1040 E. Oakland Park Blvd.
Fort Lauderdale, FL 33334
800-443-9667
www.constantines.com
Tools, woods, veneers, hardware

DOVER DESIGNS, LLC
P.O. Box 3644
Hagerstown, MD 21742
301-733-0909
www.www.doverdesignsllc.com
Suppliers of fine inlay, borders,
wood lines and marquetry designs

FRANK PAXTON
LUMBER COMPANY
5701 W. 66th St.
Chicago, IL 60638
800-323-2203
www.paxtonwood.com
Wood, hardware, tools, books

HIGHLAND WOODWORKING
1045 North Highland Ave. NE
Atlanta, GA 30306
www.highlandwoodworking.com
Tools, woodworking supplies,
books

THE HOME DEPOT
2455 Paces Ferry Rd. NW
Atlanta, GA 30339
800-430-3376 (U.S.)
800-628-0525 (Canada)
www.homedepot.com
Woodworking tools, supplies
and hardware

HORTON BRASSES INC.
49 Nooks Hill Road
Cromwell, CT 06416
800-754-9127
www.horton-brasses.com
Fine reproduction brass and iron
hardware

KLINGSPOR ABRASIVES INC.
2555 Tate Blvd. SE
Hickory, N.C. 28602
800-645-5555
www.klingspor.com
Sandpaper of all kinds

LEE VALLEY TOOLS LTD.
P.O. Box 1780
Ogdensburg, NY 13669-6780
800-871-8158 (U.S.)
800-267-8767 (Canada)
www.leevalley.com
Woodworking tools and hardware

LONDONDERRY BRASSES LTD.
P.O. Box 415
Cochranville, PA 19330
610-593-6239
londonderry-brasses.com
Furniture hardware

LOWE'S COMPANIES, INC.
P.O. Box 1111
North Wilkesboro, NC 28656
800-445-6937
www.lowes.com
Woodworking tools, supplies
and hardware

ROCKLER WOODWORKING
AND HARDWARE
4365 Willow Dr.
Medina, MN 55340
800-279-4441
www.rockler.com
Woodworking tools, hardware
and books

TOOL TREND LTD.
140 Snow Blvd. Unit 1
Concord, ON
Canada L4K 4C1
416-663-8665
Woodworking tools and hardware

TREND MACHINERY &
CUTTING TOOLS LTD.
Odhams Trading Estate
St. Albans Rd.
Watford
Hertfordshire, U.K.
WD24 7TR
01923 224657
www.trendmachinery.co.uk
Woodworking tools and hardware

WATERLOX COATINGS
908 Meech Ave.
Cleveland, OH 44105
800-321-0377
www.waterlox.com
Finishing supplies

W.D. LOCKWOOD & CO., INC.
49 Walker St. 1st floor
New York, NY, 10013
866-293-8913
www.wdlockwood.com
Wood stains

WOODCRAFT SUPPLY LLC
1177 Rosemar Rd.
P.O. Box 1686
Parkersburg, WV 26102
800-535-4482
www.woodcraft.com
Woodworking hardware

WOODWORKER'S HARDWARE
P.O. Box 180
Sauk Rapids, MN 56379-0180
800-383-0130
www.wwhardware.com
Woodworking hardware

WOODWORKER'S SUPPLY
1108 N. Glenn Rd.
Casper, WY 82601
800-645-9292
http://woodworker.com
Woodworking tools and
accessories, finishing supplies,
books and plans

INDEX

Ideas. Instruction. Inspiration.

These and other great **Popular Woodworking** products are available at your local bookstore, woodworking store or online supplier.

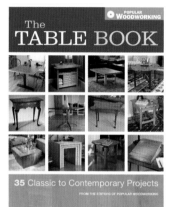

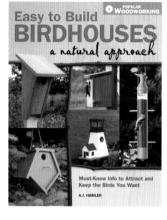

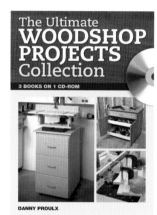

THE TABLE BOOK
FROM THE EDITORS OF POPULAR WOODWORKING
You'll find a table in every woodworking style to fit your needs and individual tastes. And, while building the projects, your woodworking skills will be challenged and improved!

ISBN 13: 978-1-4403-0427-9
paperback • 272 pages • Z7128

EASY TO BUILD BIRDHOUSES
BY A.J. HAMLER
Projects range from traditional designs to a lighthouse, a cottage and a football helmet and more! Fun to build and fun to watch the birds move into their new home!

ISBN 13: 978-1-4403-0220-6
paperback • 144 pages • Z5979

POPULAR WOODWORKING MAGAZINE
Whether learning a new hobby or perfecting your craft, *Popular Woodworking Magazine* has expert information to teach the skill, not just the project. Find the latest issue on newsstands, or order online at www.popularwoodworking.com.

THE ULTIMATE WOODSHOP PROJECT COLLECTION
CD-ROM, BOOKS BY DANNY PROULX
This CD-ROM gives you all the information you need to make your shop the best it can be.

ISBN 13: 978-1-4403-0241-1
This disc includes the full book content from: *Building Woodshop Workstations, Toolboxes & Wookbenches* and *50 Jigs & Fixtures.* CD-ROM • Z6474

Visit **www.popularwoodworking.com** to see more woodworking information by the experts.

Recent Articles	Featured Product	Note from the Editor
Read the five most recent articles from Popular Woodworking Books. • Kitchen Makeovers - Pull-Out Pantry Design & Construction • Woodshop Lust Tom Rosati's Woodshop • Woodshop Lust David Thiel's Woodshop • Wood Finishing Simplified Strictly, Stickley Oak • Wood Finishing Simplified In a Pickle (Whitewash on Oak or Pine)	**Made By Hand** $21.95 *Made By Hand* takes you right to the bench and shows you how to start building furniture using hand tools. By working through the six projects in this book, you'll learn the basics of hand-tool woodworking and how to use the tools effectively and efficiently, then add joinery skills and design complexity. The accompanying DVD includes valuable insight into the tools themselves and a look at the techniques that make these tools work so well.	**Welcome to Books & More** We've got the latest reviews and free sample excerpts from our favorite woodworking books, plus news on the newest releases. Check out the savings at our **Woodworker's Book Shop,** and don't miss out on building your Wish List for the holidays. If you missed our newsletter's **"Print Is Dead"** poll results, check them here, and subscribe (below) to our newsletter to receive special sale items and book reviews not found anywhere else. – *David Baker-Thiel, Executive Editor Popular Woodworking Books*

A woodworking education can come in many forms, including books, magazines, videos and community feedback. At Popular Woodworking we've got them all. Visit our website at www.popularwoodworking.com to follow our blogs, read about the newest tools and books and join our community. We want to know what you're building.

Sign up to receive our weekly newsletter at http://popularwoodworking.com/newsletters/